A COSTLY AMERICAN HATRED

A COSTLY AMERICAN HATRED

By Joseph Rodney Dole, II

Published by
MIDNIGHT EXPRESS BOOKS

A Costly American Hatred

Published by

MIDNIGHT EXPRESS BOOKS
POBox 69
Berryville AR 72616
(870) 210-3772
MEBooks1@yahoo.com

A COSTLY AMERICAN HATRED

By Joseph Rodney Dole, II

FORWARD

At one time, lepers - people afflicted with leprosy - were segregated from society and exiled for life to leper colonies. Those types of leper colonies are mostly a thing of the past, but a new type of leper and leper colony have taken their place in America. People who commit a crime are now the new leper. The new leper colonies are prisons, which have sprung up like Starbucks across the nation. Those aren't the only new leper colonies though. There are also the colonies of "sex offenders" in free society as well.

When someone commits a crime today they are forever regarded as a "criminal" and effectively exiled from society for life. It may be a literal lifetime exile like the tens of thousands who will spend their entire remaining lives behind bars. Or it may be a figurative, but just as effective, exile in the form of complete alienation from main-stream society, like the millions with a criminal record who are forever denied the right to vote, permitted to obtain a well- paying job, or allowed to get the claws of the criminal justice system out of their flesh.

During the 1990's a new jail or prison opened up every fifteen days in America[1], laws were and continue to be passed with lightning speed sans thoughtful debate, and prison sentences were and continue to be lengthened to ridiculous lengths. We've reached the point where we now have millions of people in prison and an entire industry has sprung up to profit off of mass incarceration. Rehabilitation is out and recidivism is in, because people returning to prison, or never leaving, is what keeps the profits rolling in.

John Irwin, author of *The Warehouse Prison* is quoted in *Prison Legal News* as explaining that:

> Long sentences in warehouse-like prisons incapacitate in more ways than just keeping people off the streets. Idleness, overcrowding and despair deprive the individual of the capacity to act independently, to have adequate self-esteem, and to feel they are part of mainstream society. All of which contributes to the deepening and widening of the permanent criminal underclass in the U.S.[2]

Many people in America don't understand just how far we have ostracized the millions of people who run afoul of the law. Nor do they understand the degree to which they have been indoctrinated over the past few decades to automatically hate, like a knee-jerk response without any contemplation, anyone who has committed a crime. Nor do they understand how this hate has permitted the predicament we're in today.

It seems that every politician who runs for office will promise the public that they'll "keep criminals off the streets" or something inanely similar, and once in office they will immediately work to pass some costly and mostly unnecessary law that will prove his or her tough-on-crime credentials.

The public meanwhile, eats it all up, never thinking about the fact that the entire concept of "keeping criminals off the street" is nonsensical. How does one accomplish that? Are we to give everyone a life sentence without parole for any crime committed? Life in prison for shoplifting? It sounds ridiculous but in some states we already are.

When someone commits a crime they do just that - commit something. They do not become it. Yet American society makes that their sole defining characteristic. If someone commits a crime they become a "criminal", and in society's eyes they are always that. They are demonized, ostracized, and degraded.

Our American ethos that "everybody deserves a second chance" and the Christian concept of forgiveness are conveniently set aside in our haste to hate and alienate. We even seem to believe criminality to be some type of genetic or infectious disease, the way many of our policies punish a "criminal's" family nearly as much as it punishes the one who commits the crime.

This essay is an attempt to show just how thoroughly our hatred of those we label "criminals" has taken us, and how effectively we've ostracized millions of American citizens, often so that the rich can turn a profit.

Contents

1
ANIMALS

American society has collectively and effectively revoked "criminals'" status as humans. Why? Because the easiest way to assuage one's guilt over the mistreatment of others is to disassociate oneself from one's victims. Slavers did it with slaves ("hey they aren't the same species", then later "hey they're only 3/5 human" conveniently included in Article 1 of the U.S. Constitution); Hitler did it with Jews, Gypsies, and the mentally ill or physically deformed ("hey they're 'undesirables', they're not even part of our race - the 'master race'"); and religion is used as a dehumanizing weapon during war to disassociate from the enemy ("hey it's okay to kill them, they're infidels, heathens, etc."). Just as Native Americans were deemed "savages" to justify their maltreatment, "criminals" are deemed "evil" or "animals" in the same manner.

The easiest way to disassociate "criminals" from society is to dehumanize them to the point where people are indifferent to their plight. Tough-on-crime rhetoric and American pop culture over the past four decades have been so effective at this that society sees no problem with claiming people aren't human if they commit a crime, in order to justify treating them inhumanely. Once someone commits a crime they are no longer considered a person. Rather they are labeled with what becomes their whole identifying characteristic - "criminal", "convict", "prisoner", "offender", "thief", "murderer", etc.

The most pervasive trend is to equate them to animals. This view, that "criminals" are animals, has become so thoroughly entrenched in the American psyche that it subconsciously excuses treating people who commit crimes like animals or worse. This dehumanizing and disassociation permits things in America that are abhorred in nearly all other Western or industrialized countries - mass incarceration for victimless crimes, life imprisonment for juvenile offenders, decades of isolation in solitary confinement, and executions.

We now execute people with the same drug (pentobarbital) that has long been used to euthanize unwanted pets.[3] This is simply a progression of the long-held belief that it's okay to treat "criminals" like animals or worse. This belief has contaminated jail and prison policies all across the country.

In Louisiana, for instance, the American Civil Liberties Union (ACLU) had to write a letter to St. Tammany Parish Sheriff Jack Strain and Parish President Kevin Davis to ask that they at least treat the inmates in their jail as well as the Parish's Code requires them to treat dogs.[4] The Code requires dogs to be kept in cages no smaller than six feet by six feet. Inmates in the jail who were deemed suicidal or just being booked into the jail were being held in cells that measured just three feet by three feet - one quarter the area required for dogs (9 square feet versus 36 square feet). The cells were called "squirrel cages" for obvious reasons. We're not talking about spending a few hours in them, but rather days, weeks, and even over a month.[5]

As if cramming suicidal inmates into boxes unfit for a dog, where one must curl into a ball to sleep, weren't bad enough, inmates were then subjected to the humiliation of having to wear bright orange short shorts with the words "Hot Stuff" printed on the ass,[6] because, let's face it, what's more fun than treating suicidal men worse than animals? Dressing them up as promiscuous women or flamboyant homosexuals too, of course. This is the first time I have ever heard of using debasement and humiliation as a treatment for someone who is suicidal. Though it is neither surprising nor the worst instance of prisoner abuse I've heard of.

To justify such treatment of inmates under his "care", Sheriff Strain explained: "They performed like animals in our society and they need to be caged like animals."[7] Arbitrary statements tossed out like that are ubiquitous in American society, and are widely concurred with by the majority of the public. Proof of this can be seen in the fact that the same public officials who routinely spout them find wide public approval come election time. The fallacy or idiocy of such statements are rarely ever challenged. On the contrary, they are more often blindly repeated like a mantra. For instance, since when have animals robbed banks or committed any crime? How have these people acted like "animals"? When have you ever seen any animal forced into booty shorts because it tried to commit suicide? How does claiming that a person "acted like an animal" justify treating him inhumanely? It doesn't.

More importantly, if the objective is to convince these "animals" to cease committing crimes (i.e. stop acting like animals) then it is both absurd and unrealistic to expect people to not "act like animals" by treating them as animals or worse. If you are constantly treating people inhumanely it is ridiculous to then expect them to act humanely towards others. Sheriff Joe Arpaio of Maricopa County seemingly doesn't understand this dichotomy as, according to *The Nation,* "he cheerfully admits" to "serving prisoners food that... costs less than what he gives to his cats and dogs".[8]

Using "animals" as a synonym for people who commit a crime has so infested society that even a writer who argues against mass incarceration refers to someone being released from prison as a "free range felon,"[9] or as being "in the wild"[10] as if they are cattle or maybe a feral four-legged predator dashing towards the jungle from the prison doorstep with claws clacking on the concrete as it escapes its penitentiary cage, ready to stalk humans with its blood-thirsty fangs once again.

Stripping millions of people of their status as humans not only invites subjecting them to inhumane treatment, but equally bad, viewing

4

them as a commodity. Slaves were likewise dehumanized and commoditized. Though the institution of slavery was several degrees more nefarious than hypercriminalization and mass incarceration, the overall affect is the same - millions of human beings being expelled from the rest of American society to justify mistreating them and profiting or benefiting off of them in some manner.

You know things are bad when a United States Supreme Court Justice - Anthony Kennedy - felt it necessary to remind the nation's lawyers at a 2003 American Bar Association meeting that a "prisoner is a person. Still, he or she is part of a family of humankind."[11]

2
THE MEDIA

Our news media is a major reason why, after nearly two decades of descending crime rates, with murder rates at a 50 year low and violent crime rates overall at a 40 year low,[12] most Americans still believe that crime is getting worse. Half of the stories on any local news program are about crime, even when there is less crime to report about. The media just increasingly sensationalizes whatever crime they can find in an effort to keep viewers tuned in. As they say in the news business - bad news makes great news and good news is no news.

Also, news programs are seeing their revenues decline because with increasing competition from cable and the internet, fewer viewers are tuning in. Advertisers pay less for airtime when the number of viewers declines. Less revenue in turn makes it more likely that crime stories, which are cheap, will continue to clog the news. This creates both a misconception of rising crime and contributes to irrational fears that we aren't safe in our own neighborhoods. It also makes it more likely that voters will continue to vote for anyone who promises to pass laws that they claim will make us safe.

Why are crime stories so cheap? Because, as David Cay Johnston noted in *Prison Legal News,* "you only have to get the cops side of the story. There is no ethical duty to ask the arrested for their side of the story".[13] He further explains how "[c]heap news is a major reason that every day we [the media] are failing in our core mission of providing people with the knowledge they need for our democracy to function."[14]

Rather than asking defendants their side of the story, they are simply "perp-walked" in some striped outfit, fluorescent orange jumpsuit, or at the very least, handcuffs, each of which make quite a statement. The perp-walk makes him or her look like a "criminal" before ever having been found guilty of any crime.

Recently the French public was rightly appalled and confused over how the American media treats defendants when they saw the perp-walk and media condemnation of Dominique Strauss-Kahn (DSK) who had been charged with sexually assaulting a hotel maid. DSK, as he was acronymized by the press, was both the head of the International Monetary Fund and a French presidential hopeful.

It wasn't until after it was revealed that there was substantial evidence which severely discredited the accuser, that *Time* published a viewpoint by Adam Cohen scrutinizing the media's part in the DSK saga:

> His arrest was followed by a "perp walk", in which
> he was paraded in handcuffs before a scrum of

photographers - an American tradition that hardly seems presumptive of innocence. Then came trial by media: leaked allegations that he made passes at two concierges at the hotel before the incident with the maid, that he hurled a crude comment at a flight attendant on the plane he was removed from, that his semen was found on the maid's clothing.[15]

"Hardly... presumptive of innocence" indeed. *The Economist* likewise belatedly asked if it is "time to end the perp walk?"[16] It noted that the "practice gives the newspapers and television images for stories and lets police and prosecutors show off the big game they bagged."[17] (Again with the animal references). The article goes on to quote a number of people opposed to theses perp walks:

Nat Hentoff, a journalist and civil libertarian, says that "under such circumstances even Mother Teresa would look extremely suspicious, especially if her hands were cuffed behind her back."

Jack King, of the National Association of Criminal Defense lawyers, says perp walks "run counter... to the presumption of innocence."...Elisabeth Duigou, a former French justice minister, called the images of DSK "incredibly brutal, violent and cruel."

Jean-Pierre Chevenement, a senator condemned an "appalling global lynching". Eva Joly, a Green presidential hopeful, said that America had "a much more violent judicial system" than France.[18]

Notice that none of this made the news here before DSK's accuser's credibility was riddled with holes and the media was demonizing DSK as an elite pervert and sex offender.

After it came to light that the accuser was not credible and seemingly had a goal of getting money out of Strauss-Kahn, the criminal charges were dismissed. The American media was quick to claim this as a victory for the American justice system. What they failed to note however was that it was only because Mr. Strauss-Kahn was an immensely rich and powerful public figure that: first, there was intense scrutiny on the police and prosecutors; second, there were the resources available for the high-priced defense to investigate the accuser; and third, that the media would report on the lack of credibility of the accuser when it was discovered. Only the rich and famous receive such equal air time to put forth their defense in the press, even if it is the belated type exhibited here. In 95% of cases, the media never returns to cover the case after the arrest/perp walk.[19]

When the defendant isn't rich or famous he or she won't receive a belated retraction by the press if the accuser becomes discredited, or when the police or prosecution is shown to be wrong or unscrupulous. They are treated much worse throughout the entire process.

Recently a young Jewish boy took a wrong turn on his first solo trip walking home and was abducted and butchered. An arrest was made, and a perp walk conducted. The arrestee appeared mentally disturbed and allegedly confessed. (As will be seen later, a confession isn't always a confession). Before bail had even been set, or he had even been tried or convicted, various news reporters were saying things like "the monster who was arrested" for this crime. What happened to journalistic integrity and objectivity? What happened to innocent until proven guilty? They no longer exist. Instead our media immediately resorts to name calling and prejudgment of a man who is supposedly "innocent until proven guilty."

Even after charges are dropped the media will continue to call the exonerated names as happened when the charges were dismissed against DSK and *Newsweek* gave the following parting shot: "DSK, Enjoy your freedom, creep."[20]

Viewing crime rates objectively, one must first acknowledge that there will always be fluctuations in them and one or two percentage points either way cannot be considered significant. Also, we must acknowledge that crime is not some disease, i.e. it cannot be completely eradicated. In any other field an occurrence among an extra dozen or two people out of ten million would be considered statistically insignificant. Yet when it comes to murder it takes on biblical proportions.

In Illinois there are around 13 million people in the state, but less than 1,000 people have been killed annually over the past decade. A single disgruntled employee going postal and killing fifty people at work can therefore cause a "surge" in the murder rate of more than 5%. It doesn't mean there's a "murder epidemic" or more people committing murder. It could just mean that that was the year that some idiot snapped.

The failure of investigative reporters and the news media in general to objectively cover all sides of a crime story is seen by some as a facilitator of wrongful convictions as well. As Steve Weinberg noted in *Miller-McCune.com Magazine*, "journalists rarely conduct an independent investigation, even if red flags along the path suggest a wrongful conviction is unfolding."[21] Instead "[c]overage of criminal cases is spotty and often superficial when it occurs. Elected prosecutors tend to be treated as the last of the sacred cows, the white hats who keep the streets safe for law-abiding citizens."[22]

Yet, as we'll see when discussing the wrongfully convicted, many of these same prosecutors often withhold from the defense the only evidence available that can prove the defendant's innocence. Often they are not so much "white hats" keeping the streets safe as they are "black ski-masks" robbing innocent people of their freedom, more concerned about opportunistically obtaining a court victory to advance their careers than they are in bringing the true perpetrator to justice.

Had the media undertaken a serious investigation in many of the cases that later resulted in a wrongful conviction, instead of merely regurgitating the rhetoric spouted by the police and prosecution, the concealed evidence may have had a better chance at seeing the light of day, saving the innocent, and forcing the police to keep at it until they found the true malefactor. Instead the media immediately goes to work demonizing whoever is arrested, making it much harder to find an objective jury.

Furthermore, crime statistics never receive equal news coverage. If crime goes down, the media, if it reports on it at all, will give it all of a sentence or two, even if crime has decreased significantly. Yet if the crime rate goes up in any manner it will receive significant, and oft-times misleading coverage. You'll see reports of "crime epidemics", "murder epidemics", etc. even when crime or murder has gone down from the previous year. The news media will report things like "murder rate up 5% over the same month of last year", and then conveniently leave out the fact that that may only represent one or two more murders for that month, city, state, etc. and that for the year there was actually 15 less murders in the same area as the year before.

Here's a specific example, *The Chicago Sun Times'* "Stop The Killing Campaign", reported that during the first half of 2007 there were

13% more murders in Chicago than the first half of 2006.[23] This may seem like a lot at first glance, but it actually only amounts to 26 more murders in a city of several million people. Furthermore, the article fails to mention that it was an increase from historically low murder rates.

In 1992 Chicago had 943 murders.[24] By 2005 the number had fallen by more than half, to 447.[25] This despite steady population growth. As murder is a crime of passion more often than not, it is not possible to prevent murders from occurring completely. In a city of millions, there are always going to be murders and crime. When you've seen a steady decline in murders for over a decade, sooner or later there will be a rise.

Moreover, while the half of the year cited may have had more murders, if one considers the entire year of 2007 we see that there was actually a decrease in murders from 471 in 2006 to 443 in 2007,[26] which was the fewest murders since 1965 when there were 395 murders.[27] At that time though there were hundreds of thousands fewer residents. The second half of 2006 therefore must have had at least twice as much of a decrease in murders than the first half had an increase in order to come out with 28 fewer murders for the whole year. Yet that fact received little news coverage and what sticks in peoples' minds are news items that cause fear like a "murder epidemic". Thanks to the bombardment of fear-mongering news reports to boost ratings on TV and to sell newspapers, most people mistakenly believe that the streets of Chicago are akin to the Okay Corral or are clogged with rampant gang wars.

The news media sensationalizes every single uptick in crime, and every crime story. This makes the public feel like crime is omnipresent and getting worse. Think about all of the crime epidemics, etc. claimed by the media over the past two decades - from 1990 -2010. Today the common view is that crime is rampant. In all actuality though, the crime rate has been in a steady decline. The murder rate went from 9.8 per 100,000 in 1991 to 5.4 per 100,000 in 2008 nationwide.[28] Violent crime is now the lowest it has been in 40 years,[29] and property crime rates continue to fall even in the midst of a serious recession.[30]

This was all happening when the number of activities that were considered a crime continued to expand and rehabilitation as a goal of incarceration was largely abandoned.

Violent crime continues to decline as well. In September of 2011 it was reported (marginally) that violent crime declined 10% -12% from 2009 - 2010,[31] and Steven Pinker, a professor at Harvard, notes that, "[v]iolence has been in decline for thousands of years, and today we may be living in the most peaceable era in the existence of our species."[32] But our access to knowledge of every gruesome crime around the globe and the media's sensationalization of each one makes us believe differently.

The bias of the media is pervasive. In 2006, according to the FBI the violent crime rate overall rose by 1.9 percent. This was only one of two years that it rose in the past two decades. *The Week* described this as an "unexpected surge".[33] The rest of the media likewise hyped up the 1.9% increase as "the next crime wave,"[34] a violence plague, epidemic, etc. Yet when there's a similar decrease in violent crime like the 1.4% decline the following year (2007), it is reported as "U.S. violent crime falls slightly".[35] So if it's less than a 2% increase it's considered a "surge", "wave", "epidemic", etc., but a less than 2% decrease is simply a "slight" reduction. This is the media's idea of balanced reporting on crime.

What the media does not cover obsessively nor exaggerate like it does with most crime, is when "criminals" or prisoners are mistreated. As we will see when discussing the subject of control units and supermax prisons, the fact is that tens of thousands of American citizens in the U.S. are being held in isolation so prolonged and severe that most of our Western allies believe it to constitute torture. Yet the only time such maltreatment causes a media storm here is when it is inflicted by the U.S. upon our enemies or foreign nationals like those held in Guantánamo Bay. You would never see a media storm about the tens of thousands of U.S. citizens imprisoned in the dozens of mini-Guantánamos littered across the nation because American society cares more about its image than its second class citizens.

When asked "How well do you think the media has covered the issue of solitary confinement in prisons?", James Ridgeway and Jean Casella, the editors of *Solitary Watch,* a newsletter struggling to raise awareness on the issue answered:

Well, there has actually been some outstanding reporting on this subject. The problem we have with the media coverage is that there isn't nearly enough of it. And it doesn't get anything close to the national attention it deserves or produces the kind of outrage it should, considering the fact that it is one of the major domestic human rights issues of our day. Our impression is that the media is simply reflecting how effectively prisoners have been marginalized in our society.[36]

On a daily basis people are dying in prisons and jails due to abuse by guards and denial of medical care, yet the mainstream media almost uniformly fails to report on any of these deaths. Pick up any issue of *Prison Legal News* though and you will find stories about some of the thousands of prisoners each year who are unlawfully beaten, tortured or denied medical treatment, some to the point of disfigurement, paralysis, or even death.

It's not only our news media that works to alienate and demonize people who commit a crime and helps to make it acceptable to criminalize segments of the population that historically weren't viewed as "criminals". It is also our entertainment programs. Daytime soap operas and primetime network shows routinely feature crime playing a leading role. It seems America has an insatiable appetite for crime dramas, courtroom dramas, and the like. On primetime network channels alone we have *CSI; CSI New York; CSI Miami; Blue Bloods;*

Numbers; Criminal Minds; Bones; Rookie Blue; Law & Order; Law & Order: Specials Victims Unit; Cops; America's Most Wanted; Harry's Law; The Code; Prime Suspect; etc. Even *Desperate Housewives* is full of murder plots, burglars, hit and runs, and sex offender registries. Out of primetime you have a half dozen different court-TV shows where the judges hysterically berate people for ratings. Talk shows sensationalize the day's worst crime stories to have something to argue about. The only agreement is usually how "despicable", "evil", "monstrous", etc. the person arrested is. It is almost never debated whether or not they are actually guilty or not.

3

WHO WE LOCK UP

By incessantly equating people who commit a crime to animals and condemning them as automatically and irretrievably evil, society has been able to incarcerate millions of more people than it would have been able to otherwise. By creating an atmosphere where society is terrified of "monsters" lurking around every corner it becomes an enabler to outrageous policies. As Jason Whitlock noted in *Playboy* magazine, fear "has us... incarcerating our countrymen at an insanely vicious and destructive rate. And fear won't even let us talk about it." [37]

The rate at which we incarcerate is unparalleled anywhere else in the world. *The Economist* has called us a "nation of jailbirds,"[38] and *Foreign Policy* noted that the U.S. "locks up more of its citizens than any other nation."[39] The U.S. incarcerates 756 people per every 100,000 residents,[40] while over 75% of the rest of the countries on earth lock up less than 150 people per 100,000.[41] This adds up to 2.3million people being incarcerated in America at any given time.[42] Americans only constitute 5% of the world's people, but just as we consume 25% of the world's oil, we also house 25% of the world's prisoners.[43]

This is not something to take pride in. Americans used to look down on the Soviet Union, the "evil empire", due in part to its gulags. Now the world looks at us with those same eyes. We may claim more political freedoms than China, and call our homeland the "land of the free", but with more than three times the population, China is far from having a commensurate prison population. Instead of having three times as many people in prison, China actually has nearly a million less people in prison than we do.[44]

The reason that we incarcerate more of our citizens than any other nation in the world is manifold. One part of it is the proliferation of laws that have turned acts that were never considered crimes into crimes, and adding incarceration as a penalty for civil violations. The expansion of federal criminal laws has been particularly unreasonable. A hundred years ago the number of federal crimes was in the dozens. [45] Now they number in the thousands.[46] Don't feel bad if you don't know how many there are exactly. No one knows.[47] There are seemingly so many, and they are encoded in such a cluster-fuck throughout the federal code, that no one has been able to count them.

It's not like no one has tried. It's just that the task is too arduous - even for the same government that enforces them all. The U.S. Justice Department counted for two years and could only give a ballpark figure of around 3,000. [48] That was in the 1980's.[49] In the 1990's the American Bar Association (ABA) likewise failed to conclude with an exact number but thought 3,000 extremely low.[50] Others have estimated the number to be as high as 4,500. As quoted in *The Wall Street Journal,* the ABA found that the "amount of individual citizen behavior now potentially subject to criminal control has increased in astonishing proportions in the last few decades."[51]

The most worrisome part of all these new laws is that many of them don't require proving the person had any criminal intent. Many people are being arrested, convicted, and incarcerated (not to mention being alienated and demoted to "criminal") for acts they didn't know are illegal. I've never met anyone who has read all 27,000 pages of the federal code. Have you?

Gary Fields and John R. Emshwiller explain in a recent *Wall Street Journal* article how:

> For centuries, a bedrock principal of criminal law has held that people must know they are doing something wrong before they can be found guilty. The concept is known a mens rea, Latin for a "guilty mind".
>
> This legal protection is now being eroded as the U.S. federal criminal code dramatically swells. In recent decades, Congress has repeatedly created laws that weaken or disregard the notion of criminal intent. Today not only are there thousands more criminal laws than before, but it is easier to fall afoul of them.

As a result, what once might have been considered simply a mistake is now sometimes punishable by jail time.[52]

Even if you wouldn't consider something a mistake, you might be surprised to learn what the penalty for the crime is. The above-mentioned journalists noted that the unauthorized use of the slogan "Give a Hoot, Don't Pollute" can actually land you in prison, and relayed an example given by U.S. Supreme Court Justice Samuel Alito that killing someone's goldfish by pouring a bottle of vinegar in its bowl could be "potentially punishable by life imprisonment."[53] So now we've come to the point that a human life is of equal value to that of a gold fish.

Not only are the feds locking people up more, but they're also confiscating assets at an alarming rate (it doubled in just the five years from 2006-2011),[54] and not just from the guilty either. Police now seize money during traffic stops with no evidence whatsoever that it is connected with a crime. All they need to do is make a baseless claim that it is drug money and you'll be forced to prove otherwise in court to get it back. This is a result of the "war on drugs", and our attitude towards "criminals" - everyone is now guilty until they can prove otherwise.

The Mentally Ill

So who are all these people that we have locked away? For the most part they are neither dangerous nor need to be incarcerated. The two largest demographics of prisoners are the mentally ill and drug users, both of which would be better off with treatment for their illnesses rather than incarceration. According to the *New England Journal of Medicine* "[d]einstitutionalization of the mentally ill over the past 50 years and severe punishment for drug users starting in the 1970's have shifted the burden of care for addiction and mental illness to jails and prisons. The largest facilities housing psychiatric patients in the United States are not hospitals but jails."[55]

A significant dismantling of America's mental health complex[56] has meant that while there are still some mentally ill people being treated in mental hospitals, there are four times as many in prisons,[57] most of whom aren't being treated, but rather warehoused. The U.S. Department of Justice reported that 56% of state prisoners have a mental health problem, 43% meet the criteria for mania, 23% for major depression, and 15% for a psychotic disorder.[58]

Once in prison they are much more likely, especially without treatment, to be unable to follow strict rules and regulations than mentally healthy prisoners. This results in a higher risk of being labeled a trouble maker and placed in solitary confinement as punishment. Isolation, as Lance Tapley, author of *Texas Tough: The Rise of*

American's Prison Empire notes "is medically certified to drive humans to often-suicidal insanity".[59] He calls the more than 36,000 mentally ill in supermax isolation across America a "gulag of mass torture."[60] An inability to follow the rules also means their prison terms often get lengthened either through revocation of good time credits or by catching new criminal cases while in prison.

A large number of the mentally ill who are ensnared are our war veterans. Over half of our veterans who are incarcerated are there for drug-related crimes.[61] Due to the high rate of veterans returning from war with post traumatic stress disorder (PTSD) and traumatic brain injury (TBI), the military's long history of denial of such illnesses or injuries, and the failure to adequately treat them; veterans often turn to illegal drugs to try and self-medicate, thereby bringing them in contact with the criminal justice system.[62] So, it goes to figure that many of the more than 200,000 incarcerated veterans[63] could quite possibly have avoided incarceration with proper treatment for the injuries suffered while fighting our wars.

Drug Users

Of course our veterans aren't the only ones being locked up for using drugs. Our country's decision to flip from treating people with a drug addiction to declaring a "war" on them accounts for much of the increase in our incarceration rate.[64] The country's "War on Drugs" has simply been an irrational policy to feed an irrational growth of the prison industrial complex (PIC). In 1980 there were only 41,000 people in the entire country serving time for a drug case.[65] Today that number is a half of a million.[65]

More than half of all federal prisoners and 20% of state prisoners are incarcerated for drug crimes.[67] In an era of more and more states passing medical and recreational marijuana use laws, it is hard to justify having 50,000 -100,000 people locked up for marijuana offenses.[68] Society does so by viewing people who illegally smoke or sell marijuana as "animals", while viewing those who legally smoke or sell marijuana as patients, liberals, or entrepreneurs.

Out of all state prisoners and jail inmates, three-fourths were dependent on, or abusing, either alcohol or drugs.[69] Instead of being treated for having an addiction and seen as ill, people are instead arbitrarily written off as "criminals", as irredeemable, and thrown into jail or prison which becomes a nearly irreversible cycle. As David Simon, the creator of HBO's The Wire, remarked "we need to end our 'war on drugs'. It's a war on poor people".[70]

Minorities

More than a war on poor people though, it has been manipulated as a tool to disproportionately incarcerate minorities. As *Newsweek* noted "drug policy has become highly racialized. About 85 percent of those convicted of crack offenses in federal court are black - even though more whites use crack than blacks."[71] Senator James Webb echoed this while advocating for more rational incarceration policies, where he noted that each ethnic group uses drugs at nearly even rates.[72] Yet three-fourths of people incarcerated for drug crimes are black.[73]

Andrew Romano reported in *Newsweek* in 2011 that "[t]oday, African-Americans represent 74 percent of those sent to prison for drug possession, even though they make up only 14 percent of drug users."[74] In some cities the disparity in arrests is even more indefensible. *In These Times* magazine reported that in 2010 "Chicago police arrested 20,930 black youth 17 or younger, while arresting 936 Caucasian youth. The ratio of black to white arrests for marijuana possession was 15 to 1", and that "an African-American convicted of a low level drug crime in Cook County is eight times more likely than his white counterpart to go to prison."[75]

For the most part these are not dangerous people that we need to fear to the point of locking them away and indefinitely alienating them from society either. *Newsweek* further noted that "justice statistics for 2007 showed that nearly 60 percent of state prisoners serving time for a drug offense had no history of violence" and 80 percent of "drug arrests were for drug possession not sales."[76] Nearly half of the women entering our prisons are there for drug offenses.[77]

It's not only the "War on Drugs" that is discriminating against blacks either. The criminal justice system as a whole seemingly has segregated entrances. While the entrance for whites is akin to a steep mountain climb, where most whites really have to work hard to be ensnared, the entrance for blacks is more like a Slip-n-Slide to a trap door.

Although black men only comprise six percent of the American populace, they make up 40 percent of America's incarcerated men.[78] Black women comprise the fastest-growing segment of incarcerated Americans.[79] If you're a black American male in your mid-30's it is more likely than not that you have been in prison at some point in your life, and if you're under 35 there's an 11% chance that you're incarcerated right now.[80] Overall, black men in America possess a "one-in-three chance of being imprisoned at some point in their lives," according to *The Economist.*[81]

Lengthening Sentences

Not only do we target more people for incarceration than morally defensible, and incarcerate more of our people than is rational, but we also leave them incarcerated for a much longer time than is conscionable. U.S. Supreme Court Justice Anthony Kennedy noted both that "our punishments [are] too severe, [and] our sentences too long", and that while "[c]ourts may conclude the legislature is permitted to choose long sentences,... that does not mean long sentences are wise or just."[82] Justice Kennedy made those remarks in 2004. America was seemingly indifferent or asleep though because our laws have continued to get stricter in nearly all categories. The only bright spot has been the reduction in the disparity of sentences for possession/sale of crack cocaine compared to that of powder cocaine.[83]

Otherwise there has been an almost uniform increasing of sentence lengths for all crimes nationwide. First "politicians saw harsh sentences as one way to satisfy voters fed up with the rising crime rates of the '70's and '80's, and the violence associated with crack cocaine and other drugs", reports Carl Cannon in *Reader's Digest*.[84] Then as they saw how little downside there was to holding rigid tough-on-crime positions both parties expanded such positions to cover all crimes and criminal justice policies in general. Rehabilitation and returning people to useful citizenship became antithetical to these policies and phrases like "lock-em-up and throw away the key" became ubiquitous, applied to the smallest crimes. This has resulted in the U.S. being one of the harshest penalizers in the world, and definitely the harshest among Western industrialized countries.

Not only does the U.S. continue to execute people as both state and federal policy, while Europe and most industrialized countries have abolished the death penalty, but we also imprison people for much longer for specific crimes than they do. This has come about not because it is a more effective criminal justice policy, but rather because

America is unique in both its hysterical demonization of "criminals" and nonstop tough-on-crime rhetoric, therefore no serious thought goes into deciding what rational sentences for crimes should be. Instead, over the past four decades we have seen nearly every piece of legislation across the nation which increases prison sentences easily pass. Legislators use their vote to prove their tough-on-crime credentials, and private companies use them as a means to profit. According to *In These Times* magazine:

> In the early '90s, the ALEC's [American Legislative Exchange Council - an organization of legislators, special interest groups, and corporations] Criminal Task Force was co-chaired by Corrections Corporation of America (CCA), the country's largest private prison company. During those years, the National Rifle Association (NRA), another task force member ... initiated a campaign to introduce two pieces of ALEC - inspired legislation at the state and federal level: the so-called "truth-in-sentencing" and "three-strikes you're out" laws. ... The NRA campaign, dubbed "CrimeStrike", was seen as a reaction to the Clinton Administration's efforts to pass gun control. CrimeStrike set forth the precept that "guns don't kill people, people kill people", and declared any legislator backing gun control as being "soft on crime."...By 1996,

CrimeStrike claimed credit for passage of three strikes laws in Washington, California, Georgia, Delaware and North Carolina, as well as truth-in-sentencing laws in Arizona, Mississippi, and Virginia. Subsequently, prison populations surged.[85]

It's gotten so bad that nearly every state now has one or more of the following: "three-strikes and you're out" laws, "habitual criminal" laws, or "Truth-In-Sentencing" (TIS) laws. This means that society is now not only forcing people to spend exceedingly lengthy stays in prison, but society is also paying much more to punish a person for committing a crime. Society is failing to consider the fiscal or societal ramifications of such legislation. It's not only the three above-mentioned types of legislation that have been passed. Most crimes have had their sentencing ranges extended. Some states have gradually done most or all of the above. Illinois is a good example.

Since the 1970s Illinois has been steadily increasing the length of sentences for violent offenses. For instance, in 1978 Illinois passed Public Act 80-1099 which made all life sentences in Illinois "natural-life sentences", meaning life without the possibility of parole.[86] Prior to its implementation a person sentenced to "life" was eligible for parole in as little as 11 years. Additionally, P.A. 80-1099 provided that anyone qualifying as a "Habitual Criminal" could receive a natural-life sentence. "Habitual Criminals" are defined as those who commit a third or subsequent forcible offense.[87] The 1978 law also abolished the parole system in Illinois, making all sentences determinate instead of indeterminate. The Illinois Department of Corrections (IDOC) found that the impact of determinate sentencing on length of stay in prison was to add approximately 3.5 years to the average sentence for murder and 1.4 years to the average sentence for a Class X crime.[88] Class X is the category of crimes directly below murder, and punishable by 6-30 years unless certain other factors are present which can extend the sentence even further.

In the 1980s, Truth-In-Sentencing laws became increasingly popular in a number of states. In a study on TIS for the U.S. Department of Justice's Bureau of Justice Statistics, Paula M. Ditton and Doris James Wilson report that in 1984 the state of Washington was the first to enact a TIS,[89] and others soon followed. Ditton and Wilson describe how these laws came about:

> Sentencing reform policies have paralleled the mood of the country on crime and punishment, shifting between requiring a fixed prison time prior to release or allowing discretionary release of offenders by judges, parole boards, or corrections officials. Over the last two decades, sentencing requirements and release policies have become more restrictive, and primarily in response to widespread "get tough on crime" attitudes in the nation.[90] TIS... [were] designed to reduce the apparent

disparity between court-imposed sentences and the time offenders actually serve in prison.[91]

As has already been mentioned, Illinois switched to fixed prison terms in 1978. While many states were enacting TIS in an attempt to address the public's desire for increased punishment for violent offenders, others chose a different route to achieve the same objective-mandatory minimum sentences and increased sentencing ranges for violent crimes. Illinois initially resisted enacting TIS and instead chose the latter approach. For example in 1987, Illinois extended the sentencing range for first degree murder from 20-40 years to 20-60 years and "the extended term was lengthened from 80-100 years."[92]

By 1994, Illinois had still not enacted a TIS. That year, though, the U.S. Congress passed the Violent Crime Control and Law Enforcement Act ("the Crime Act"). According to the U.S. Dept, of Justice Fact Sheet,[93] it was "the largest crime bill in the history of the country and [provided] for 100,000 new police officers, $9.7 billion in funding for prisons and $6.1 billion in funding for prevention programs". Some of the most significant provisions were the grant programs to encourage the states to enact TIS.[94]

These monetary incentives influenced Illinois, which was in the midst of building "nine new correctional facilities between 1990 and 2000".[95] In a paper titled "The Impact of Illinois' Truth-In-Sentencing Law on Sentence Lengths, Time to Serve and Disciplinary Incidents of

Convicted Murderers and Sex Offenders", David E. Olson, Ph.D., Magnus Seng, Ph.D., Jordan Boulger, and Mellissa McClure report that "[f]ollowing the passage of the federal TIS grant program, Illinois formed a Truth-In-Sentencing Commission" which "determined the state should adopt its own version of TIS".[96]

In August of 1995, Illinois' TIS was enacted under Public Act 89-404.[97] This law required that people convicted of murder must now serve 100% of their sentence, and those convicted of other violent crimes must now serve at least 85%,[98] rather than the average of 44% that they would have served had Illinois not enacted TIS.[99]

So in addition to abolishing discretionary release (i.e. parole) and extending the sentencing ranges for numerous violent crimes, Illinois then nearly doubled, or more, the amount of time individuals would actually spend in prison serving those longer sentences. The extension of the sentencing range for murder in conjunction with TIS is a veritable one-two punch in increasing the average length of time served for murder. As the IDOC noted in its Statistical Presentation for 2004:

> The average sentence imposed for First Degree Murder continues to be relatively higher than those sentences imposed under the previous statute for Murder. This can be explained to some extent by noting that 37.4% of the First Degree Murder sentences imposed during 2004 were between 41 and 60 years,

which would have been the extended range under the previous Murder statute. In addition, a growing number of First Degree Murder Sentences are falling under the Truth-In-Sentencing statute. In 2004, 90.8% of inmates admitted to prison for First Degree Murder must serve 100% of their sentence.[100]

It was obvious that without adjustments to sentences imposed, the length of time spent incarcerated for a violent crime would increase. Many speculated, though, that the length of time spent in prison and the associated costs would not double because judges would take TIS into account before sentencing. Olson and his coauthors give the following example:

[T]he average prison sentence imposed on those convicted of murder in Illinois during 1994 (prior to TIS) was 35 years, and the offender would (without Truth-In-Sentencing) serve roughly one-half of that sentence, or 17,5 years. So, if in sentencing the average murderer the judge's intent was for them to spend 17.5 years in prison, under TIS they could impose a sentence of 20 years (with 100% of that time being served) and come close to achieving their goal of 17.5 years "behind bars".[101]

(Notice that *the mandatory minimum* number of years to be served under TIS for murder (20 years) is 12.5%, or 2 ½ years, higher than the *average* sentence handed out for murder prior to TIS).

Some states successfully adjusted after implementing TIS. For example, in Mississippi, judges, prosecutors, and defense attorneys made the adjustment to retain equivalent prison stays.[102] The IDOC was skeptical that this would be the case in Illinois. It had concerns about "the fiscal impact if the law resulted in inmates actually serving longer sentences."[103] Olson and his colleagues sought to find out if "TIS changed the sentence lengths and lengths of time to serve in prison for murderers and sex offenders, and if so, to what degree".[104] What they found was that the IDOC was right to worry, because unlike in Mississippi, in Illinois, "the length of court-imposed sentences changed very little as a result" of TIS and subsequently the time to be served "increased dramatically".[105]

The fact that sentences have not been reduced in Illinois to offset TIS is indicative of the fact that judges and prosecutors in Illinois are failing to consider the financial impact of the sentences they are seeking or imposing. After all, who cares how much anything costs, the objective of castigating "criminals" has become a sport that blinds society to all other considerations. Illinois law (730 ILCS 5/3-2-9),[106] requires that the IDOC "prepare and submit to the clerk of the circuit court a financial impact statement that includes the estimated annual and monthly cost of incarcerating an individual in a department facility".[107] After failing to comply with the statute for a few years, the IDOC released a Financial Impact Statement, based on fiscal year 2009 data, which estimated the annual cost as $24,971. Illinois law also instructs the court to "consider the financial impact of incarceration based on the financial impact statement, "as one of several factors when determining a defendant's sentence".[108]

This failure to adjust for TIS and therefore failure to take into account the financial impact of the sentences being imposed is evidence of an indifference towards one of the main goals of government, which is to carry out the functions of the state in the most economical manner, expending its resources wisely.

As has been shown, one of the deciding factors for Illinois implementing its own TIS was the federal grant program that provided monetary incentives to the states that pass laws guaranteeing that violent offenders serve at least 85% of their sentence. Katherine J. Rosich and Kamala Mallik Kane found that "among States that received Federal TIS funding, the average annual grant award of $7.9 million was relatively modest, equivalent to an average of 1 percent of the State's annual corrections expenditures".[109]

After enactment of Illinois' TIS the state applied for federal funds through the Violent Offender Incarceration and Truth-In-Sentencing (VOI/TIS) Grant Program in Fiscal Year 1996. Between 1996 and 2001 Illinois received a total of $124,765,470 from the federal government.[110] "No funds were appropriated for Fiscal Years 2002-2004".[111] Nor does it seem that they were appropriated after 2004 either.

"States could enhance their VOI funding by demonstrating that they increased punishment for violent offenders"[112] in accordance with the 1996 amendment to the Crime Act.[113] Illinois seemingly opted out, as "an Illinois official reported that changing the Illinois law to meet the 1996 federal grant requirements...would not have been cost-effective for the state".[114]

In January of 1999, Illinois' TIS "was declared unconstitutional by the Illinois Supreme Court"[115] for violating the single subject rule of the Illinois Constitution in the case of People v. Reedy.[116] Anticipating this, the Illinois legislature reenacted TIS in Public Act 90-593, which became effective on June 19,1998.[117] Therefore, all sentences handed down for crimes occurring during the three years between the initial enactment of Illinois' TIS (August 1995) and Public Act 90-593 reverted to pre-TIS calculations. Meaning that, except in rare cases where they had completed their sentence before January of 1999, these prisoners had to serve, on average, only 44% of those sentences[118] instead of the 85% or 100% they were sentenced to serve under TIS.

So Illinois was awarded over forty-three million dollars in federal funds for making violent offenders serve 85-100% of their sentences for crimes committed during fiscal years 1996-1998, even though for the most part those prisoners only had to serve, on average, 44% of their sentence, and Illinois therefore, should not have qualified for TIS grant funds until Fiscal Year 1999. Thus the state reaped the federal grant money for 1996-1998 while incurring only negligible costs for the first 3 years after initially implementing its own TIS, and overall received about $125 million for all the years combined. Even with this onetime $125 million windfall the state still comes out incurring well over twice that amount in costs every year due to implementing TIS.

It is widely accepted that it costs around three times as much to keep an elderly person incarcerated. In Tennessee the state found that while it costs $20,000 to incarcerate the average prisoner, it costs as much as $60,000 for a sick, aging inmate.[119] In Illinois the cost to incarcerate the average prisoner is nearly $25,000,[120] so it could conceivably cost $75,000 per year for a sick, aging inmate. The National Center of Institutions and Alternatives estimates incarceration costs for an elderly inmate are $69,000 per year.[121] John Mills, a researcher at the Center for Disease Control and Prevention in Atlanta, puts the number at $70,000.[122]

So simply saying that an offender who receives a 50-year prison sentence for murder will cost the state $1,239,550 ($24,971 x 50) will more than likely be an underestimation. Even if he or she is a teenager at the beginning of the sentence, some of the years spent in prison will be in the higher range discussed above. Yet just by making rudimentary calculations one can extrapolate the minimum amount that Illinois' TIS law will increase the cost to carry out one's sentence under TIS compared to if the law had not been enacted.

The one study that I found that even vaguely considered the financial impact of implementing Illinois' TIS since its passage was the 2009 report by Olson, et al., which offhandedly mentioned that:

> Among those who received a determinate sentence (i.e., excluding natural life and death sentences), TIS was associated with an average increase of 18 years of time to serve compared to pre-TIS. Using current dollar costs of incarceration in Illinois, and not including any construction costs, the average annual cost to incarcerate an adult in prison is $22,622 (Illinois Department of Corrections, 2005). Thus, the average cost of incarceration in prison <u>per murder sentence</u> pre-TIS was roughly $400,409 (annual cost of incarceration per inmate of $22,622 multiplied by the average length of time to serve 17.7 years). By comparison, the average cost of incarceration in prison per murder sentence under TIS is roughly $816,600 (annual cost per inmate multiplied by average length of time to serve of 36.1 years).[123]

So here we have a glancing examination of the costs of Illinois' TIS on a single murder sentence, which found that TIS was responsible for more than $416,000 in additional costs just for this one sentence.

The true costs though are most likely much higher. Notice that the study was done in 2009, but utilized the only annual costs of incarceration averages available from the IDOC at that time which were from four years earlier, and which are nearly 10% less than actual current costs. Also notice that the age of the offender was not taken into account and therefore the added costs when the prisoner becomes elderly and/or infirm were not considered. Here I will take a similar approach as I only seek to make a quick point about the increased cost. Keep in mind, though, that the calculations of costs will be underestimated and therefore the true costs are much higher.

Although Olson and his coauthors claim that there was a 3.9 year decrease in the length of sentence imposed for murder after Illinois' TIS was enacted,[124] I found no evidence to support that. On the contrary, the IDOC's Statistical Presentations seem to show that the lengths of sentences that were imposed for violent crimes, murder especially, either remained relatively stable or, in the case of murders, slightly increased after the enactment of TIS.

Extracting figures from the tables provided in the 2002-2004 IDOC Statistical Presentations (Table 22, p. 55 in each) we find that the average mean sentence imposed for murder in 1994 (the year before TIS was initially passed) within the 20-60 year range of the statute that wasn't extended beyond that due to falling under the various statutes which could further increase the penalty, was 35.3 years. At no point after Illinois' TIS was implemented (either time) does this number decrease. By 2004 it had actually risen to 37.2 years.[125]

So, whereas a person arrested for a murder committed in 1994 would have served, on average, 44%[126] of that 35.3 year sentence, or approximately 15.5 years, he or she would, on average, be sentenced to 37.2 years for committing that same murder in 2004, and have to serve all 37.2 years. Therefore it was actually a slight increase in the average sentence imposed and a drastic increase (21.7 years), a more than doubling, of the time actually to be served.

Even the 37.2 year number is misleading, though, because the figure for the average sentence imposed for murder given includes a number of sentences for crimes committed prior to Illinois' TIS. If one isolates the amount of time imposed on people sentenced for murder who fall solely under Illinois' TIS, it becomes clear that sentences imposed for murder in 2004 were even higher - 39.4 years.[127]

The cost to Illinois associated with incarcerating someone for 39.4 years at the 2009 IDOC estimate of $24,971 per year, without factoring in the higher age-related costs or inflation, is $983,857.40 (39.4 x $24,971) compared to only $432,897.26 if TIS had not been enacted. So you can see that, at the very least, an increase of well over a half of a million dollars in additional costs incurred by Illinois for every murder sentence imposed under TIS.

In 2004 alone, Illinois imposed 360 of these murder sentences. The total additional costs incurred by Illinois just to sentence these offenders under TIS in just that single year is nearly $200 million ($198,345,650.40 ($354,188,664.00 (TIS) minus $155,843,013.60 (pre-TIS))).

That's $75 million more than Illinois received in federal grant funds for fiscal years 1996-2004 combined. Remember, this 198 million-dollar estimate is extremely conservative and represents the additional costs incurred in just a single year for a single offense class. In the 3 years looked at (2002-2004) it cost Illinois over a half of a billion dollars extra to impose sentences for murder under TIS than if Illinois had not enacted its own TIS.[128] Furthermore, every day that goes by another person is convicted of murder and the state incurs an additional half of a million dollars in costs that it wouldn't have.

If you consider the sentences of all offenders sentenced under TIS during 2002-2004, it's more than three-quarters of a billion dollars ($791,923,373.26) in additional costs. If Illinois were to repeal TIS the state could conservatively save a quarter of a billion dollars per year. With society so rabidly hateful of "criminals" though it is highly unlikely that TIS will be repealed.

Even if you consider the $125 million dollar windfall from the federal government and disregard all costs incurred during years 1998-2001, and all age-related costs, Illinois still incurred additional net costs of a minimum of $667 million just up until 2004 and has incurred and continues to incur hundreds of millions of dollars in additional costs every year after 2004.[129] Even though the IDOC had yet to feel the full impact of these longer sentences in 2003 (due to enactment being so recent), "[b]etween fiscal years 1995 and 2003, total appropriations for IDOC increased 35 percent (as adjusted for inflation), rising from $755,369,300 to $1.2 billion."[130] There is little doubt that Illinois incurred much higher costs than it expected when it enacted its Truth-In-Sentencing Law.

Proponents of extremely lengthy sentences have convinced society that those who commit murder need to be kept in prison forever to keep society safe. In Illinois, such a sentiment ignores the goal of "corrections" espoused both in Illinois law (730 ILCS 5/1-1-2(d))[131] and the Illinois Constitution (Article 1, Section 11), which is to return the offender to "useful citizenship". Furthermore, as will be explained further on, the fact of the matter is that those who commit murder have the lowest recidivism rates out of any class of offenders.

Moreover, the wisdom of expending $75,000 per year to keep an elderly or infirm prisoner incarcerated under the guise of community safety, is virtually nonexistent. Doing so serves little purpose other than satisfying society's desire for revenge. It certainly isn't a cost- effective way to protect society. As the Pew Center on the States reports:

> [S]tatistics have long shown crime is an occupation of the young, so imprisoning offenders beyond the age at which they would have likely given up their criminal ways bring little benefit - but big expenses... The graying of the nation's prisons suggests that policy makers have not paid much heed to this well-established criminological fact. Rather many have embraced longer sentences....[132]

This has been the case in Illinois where sentences were lengthened time and time again, without any regard for costs, to the point where there are now more prisoners who will never get out of prison due to being unable to outlive their release date than there are who were sentenced to natural-life. Olsen, et al., also found that TIS actually doubled the percentage of people convicted of murder (from 15% to 30%), that won't ever be released due to having sentences that exceed their life expectancy.[133]

At some point the vast majority of these prisoners will cease to pose a threat to society. More than doubling sentences for violent crimes to keep society safe lacks evidentiary support when statistics and studies consistently conclude that the threat is minimal at most. When one considers the astronomical costs of these TIS-enhanced sentences, can anyone still, with a straight face say that those minimal benefits, if any, are worth the costs? How long will society's hatred of "criminals" preclude rational thought and outweigh all other considerations when determining sentencing policy?

Sadly, with all our vituperation against these "evil", "inhuman" "criminals", our criminal justice policies are working against society's own interests. With TIS Illinois is severely extending sentences for violent crimes, and denying the offenders most or all good time credits. Good time has always been a correctional tool to encourage good behavior and rehabilitation. Now these prisoners have less incentive to reform. Therefore they are less likely to reform and more likely to commit another crime when released. Adding to the problem is the decimation of educational, vocational, and drug programs due to the combination of budget deficits, added costs from TIS, and a public that believes that prisoners don't deserve education, etc., and people released from prison have less opportunity to reform and successfully reenter society. This not only increases recidivism but also increases the costs to society associated with those crimes that wouldn't have been committed had those prisoners been rehabilitated.

About the only thing Illinois hasn't done yet is pass an actual "three-strikes and you're out" law. Such laws can land a person in jail for life for minor crimes like petty assault or shop lifting. In 1993 the state of Washington passed the nation's first "three-strikes" law.[734] According to *The Economist,* by April of 2009 "twenty-six states plus the federal government ha[d] passed 'three strikes and you're out' laws which put offenders in prison for life."[135]

Former presidential candidate and Arkansas governor Mike Huckabee is one of the few politicians who doesn't blindly adhere to espousing tough-on-crime rhetoric and reflexively demonize "criminals". As quoted in *Reader's Digest,* he called "three strikes and you're out" "the dumbest piece of public-policy legislation in a long time."[136] He goes on to explain what few will accept: "We don't have a massive crime problem; we have a massive drug problem. And you don't treat that by locking drug addicts up. We're putting away people we're mad at, instead of people we're afraid of."[137]

California has what is generally recognized as the worst "three strikes" law in the country. There are thousands of examples one can choose from to demonstrate the injustice and irrationality of the policy. Here are just a few.

Soon after implementation of the law a California man was charged with his third felony which earned him a sentence of 25 years to life.[138] His three felonies - unarmed robbery, burglarizing an unoccupied home, and aiding female shoplifters steal sheets.[139] A homeless guy likewise received 25 years to life after being arrested for a third felony - breaking into a church kitchen where he had previously received food.[140] His two priors were purse snatching and unarmed robbery.[141] One army veteran and father of three got 50 years to life for his third felony conviction![142]

His three offenses? Petty thefts, the last one for stealing videos to support his drug habit.[143] Such life sentences for committing a property crime or other nonviolent crime are not an anomaly either. By the end of 2004 nearly a third of California's "three strikers" received their third strike for a property crime (2,344 out of 7,544).[144]

Yet another victim of California's "three strikes" law received 25 years to life for throwing a food tray at a guard while he was a prisoner at the California State Prison at Corcoran, even though the guard wasn't seriously injured.[145] Taxpayers certainly will be though. It costs $49,000 per year to house a prisoner in California.[146] Thanks in part to all of these mandatory 25 year to life sentences the state's corrections budget over the past few decades mushroomed from $300 million to $9 billion per year.[147] Just the people who receive a third strike for nonviolent offenses are costing the state a quarter of a billion dollars annually.[148]

The Wrongfully Convicted

America's love affair with incarceration and hysterical dehumanization of "criminals" has also resulted in many people being arrested, convicted, and imprisoned for crimes they didn't commit. With nearly the entire country instantly hating anyone even charged with a crime it becomes practically impossible to convince "a jury of your peers" that you are innocent. The fact is that those "peers" sitting in the jury box don't consider you their peer. Rather, to them you are someone that they have been conditioned to believe is a despicable, inhuman, evil monster, i.e. a "criminal".

While the majority of people in prison are in fact guilty of the crimes that put them there, it is unconscionable to destroy thousands of people's lives for crimes they didn't commit. If just 5% of people in prison or jail are innocent, that would mean that at any given moment there are 115,000 innocent people behind bars.

Unfortunately it has only been since DNA evidence has begun proving innocence beyond a shadow of a doubt that studies have been conducted to show how many of our long-held assumptions were wrong, and how easy it is to be found guilty of a crime you didn't commit. Only when there was irrefutable proof that innocent people were being found guilty and even condemned to death, and irrefutable proof that innocent people were falsely confessing and witnesses falsely accusing people, did serious academic studies begin to look into some of the causes and prevalence of wrongful convictions. Unfortunately the public's mentality towards people accused of a crime has not changed to reflect these findings.

There are many reasons why innocent people are arrested and convicted. The most common catalyst for false convictions are false confessions. This was how the West Memphis Three found themselves serving nearly two decades in prison for a triple murder they didn't commit. The case involved three teenagers - Damien Echols (18), Jessie Misskelley, Jr. (17), and Jason Baldwin (16).[149] Police were investigating the triple murder of three young boys. When the police questioned Misskelley, a mentally disabled teen, he falsely confessed, implicating both Echols and Baldwin, alleging that they raped the boys, and changing the time of the rape and murders numerous times from morning to night until the time fit the actual disappearance of the boys.[150] The medical examiner found no evidence of rape.[151]

Both Baldwin and Echols maintained their innocence,[152] and Misskelley recanted and refused to testify.[153] The prosecution had "no eyewitnesses, no physical evidence, and no motive to offer jurors, [so] the prosecutors decided to tell them that the teens had killed the children as part of an 'occult ritual'," according to *Newsweek*.[154] The prosecutors based their case on the fact that the teens listened to Metallica, read Stephen King novels, and Echols dabbled in Wicca.[155] All three were convicted and every appeal was shot down. Two were sentenced to life, one to death. They finally won release after national attention forced the prosecutor to offer an Alford plea in exchange for a promise not to sue.[156] The Alford plea meant immediate release.

It seems counter-intuitive that people would admit to doing something they have not done when it could mean imprisonment or even execution. Yet it is surprisingly easy to provoke a false confession and there are a variety of ways of doing so.

The most obvious is torture. One just has to watch some old episodes of the show "24" and you'll see Jack Bauer can torture a confession out of anyone. What you'll never see on "24", though, is that professional interrogators view torture as one of the least reliable means of obtaining information or a confession. The reason being is that torture prompts people to say whatever they believe will please the torturer, instead of what is actually true.

Yet that simple fact isn't enough to prevent police in America from torturing false confessions out of innocent people, charging them, and watching as juries and judges wrongly convict and imprison them. Once in a while such torture even comes to light. That was the case in Chicago. In the 1980s, Jon Burge, the commander of a unit of police detectives on the South Side used a Vietnam War-era field telephone to torture arrestees into falsely confessing.[157] Such a telephone has a hand crank which generates an electrical current which can then be applied to a person's genitals and other sensitive areas via wires attached to metal alligator clips, to create intense pain.

According to an article in *Playboy* magazine "[m]ore than 100 prisoners, including 10 men on death row, four of whom have since been pardoned, were identified as possible victims of torture committed by Burge and his subordinates. A total of 13 Burge victims have won early release, all having spent decades behind bars as the result of coerced confessions."[158] In January of 2003 Governor George Ryan cleared death row by commuting all death sentences to life, and fully pardoning four of Burge's victims. Gov. Ryan remarked "I can see how rogue cops, 20 years ago, could run wild. What I can't understand is why the courts can't find a way to act in the interest of justice".[159]

I can. It's because when someone is charged with a crime, they are automatically seen as the "scum of the earth", and a pathological liar. So while all of those defendants that were tortured by Burge accused Burge of torturing them, the public - the media, jurors, and judges - automatically dismissed the accusations as lies. This allowed Burge to continue torturing people, which meant more innocent people going to prison and even sweating it out on death row, while the people who actually committed the crimes were allowed to roam free to commit more crimes.

It wasn't until DNA evidence proved that one of those defendants, who alleged his confession was given just to stop the torture, was actually innocent that others were then taken seriously. Fortunately for Burge and his co-horts, but unfortunately (again) for their victims, the statute of limitations had run out so Burge and company were neither charged nor prosecuted for any crimes.

It doesn't always take torture to get a false confession; more often all that is needed is a little bluffing or bullying. Recently *The Economist* summarized a number of recent studies looking into the phenomenon and noted "several researchers have found it surprisingly easy to make people fess up to invented misdemeanors."[160]

A study by the John Jay College of Criminal Justice in New York found that just the shock of being accused alone was enough to prompt a quarter of participants in the study to falsely confess to causing a computer to crash by hitting a button they hadn't touched.[161] A study at Maastricht University in the Netherlands found that ten percent of participants falsely confessed to cheating even when they knew it would mean they would have to pay around $72 as a fine for cheating.[162]

As *The Economist* noted, "[t]he number of innocent confessors jumps when various interrogation techniques are added to the mix. Several experiments, for example, have focused on the use of false evidence, as when police pretend they have proof of a person's guilt in order to encourage him to confess. This is usually permitted in the United States, though banned in Britain."[163] Not only is it "usually permitted" here, it is quite common. Police routinely separate two or more subjects for interrogation and then claim they have been "ratted out" by the other(s). The objective is to get one or more of the suspects to confess or cooperate with police against the "guilty" party in revenge. Unfortunately, not only does it get people to falsely accuse others, but apparently it also gets people to falsely confess as well.

In a second computer crash test "[a]nother person in the room beside the experimenter said he saw the participant hitting the ALT key. In this case the confession rate jumped to 80% of innocent participants".[164] Maastricht University again found similar results.[165]

All of this helps to explain why, out of 271 people that the Innocence Project has helped to exonerate by using DNA evidence to prove their innocence, "around a quarter had confessed or pleaded guilty,"[166] and why in a review of various studies on wrongful convictions, each study found false confessions in anywhere from 14%-25% of cases studied.[167]

During the trial of James Degorski, who was on trial for the Brown's Chicken murders in Palatine, Illinois, Casey Haefs testified that the police bullied her into falsely implicating a former boyfriend, Todd Wakefield, in the murders.[158] Jonathan Simonek then testified that he too falsely implicated Todd Wakefield because they wouldn't let him "make a phone call or leave unless [he] told [the cops] what they wanted to hear."[169] Simonek even went on to implicate himself in the murders giving both a handwritten and videotaped statement. Yet the police don't consider either Wakefield or Simonek suspects anymore and never charged either of them.[170] Instead Degorski has been convicted based partly on his own confession which he claims was coerced and false.

Unfortunately, there are only a very small percentage of cases where DNA evidence is available to conclusively exonerate a defendant who has falsely confessed or is wrongfully convicted by other means.

So while we have now, with DNA testing, proven beyond a shadow of a doubt that people do actually confess to crimes they didn't commit, only those rare few that can prove through DNA testing that they are innocent, are likely to go free. This means that once you falsely confess and are charged, the entire theory of the American criminal justice system (which is mostly a myth anyway) has been turned on its head. It is no longer "innocent until proven guilty". Now it is guilty until you can prove your innocence. This is a nearly impossible feat without DNA evidence. A judge or jury never believes that someone will admit to something they didn't do. Especially a "criminal", who is viewed as inherently unreliable in all other instances, yet their confession is taken as gospel.

False confessions aren't the only reason why people are wrongfully convicted. The list is long. There's everything from lying witnesses to unscrupulous prosecutors, bad science, and even incompetent defense lawyers. Faulty forensics is another serious problem that results in wrongful convictions. The public has a false sense of security about the quality and accuracy of the forensics used in criminal investigations.

Recently, *Popular Mechanics* ran an article detailing the "surprisingly weak science behind courtroom forensics,"[171] noting that "forensic science was not developed by scientists. It was created by cops-often guided by little more than common sense."[172] The only two types of evidence that received high marks were the few "techniques that grow out of organic chemistry and microbiology [which] have a strong scientific foundation."[173] In other words DNA analysis and chromatography, a method for separating complex mixtures like drugs and bodily fluids, are trustworthy, most other forensic techniques are not.

While DNA has become a great investigative tool and everyone now acknowledges how accurate it is, many people convicted of a crime who have requested the DNA evidence be tested to prove their innocence are denied. Our hatred of "criminals" is so overpowering that we continually deny innocent people the only evidence available that can clear them.

The Economist observed that Texas and Illinois have "the highest number of convictions that have been overturned thanks to DNA evidence."[174] While both states have had troubling histories with their criminal justice systems, the reason that they have the highest numbers overturned may be due to something much simpler - the fact that both states permit prisoners post-conviction access to DNA testing.[175] If all states did so who knows where Illinois and Texas would rank. The fact that so many testings are resulting in over-turned convictions may be why other states are reluctant to allow people access to DNA testing. After all, who wants to admit you falsely incarcerated, or even killed someone, and then have to pay the wrongfully convicted monetary compensation?

For instance, Alaska, Massachusetts, and Oklahoma "give prisoners no statutory rights to a DNA test," while "Kentucky will only allow one if you're facing execution."[176] Innocent lifers on the other hand would be left to rot in prison until they die of old age, knowing all the while that the evidence that could free them exists but is out of reach. Other states demand a drawn-out, resource-draining court battle to get access to DNA evidence. Even then defendants are still often denied the evidence. In 2009, the United States Supreme Court ruled that prisoners have no constitutional right to DNA testing, thereby denying an Alaskan prisoner the DNA evidence to prove he was innocent.[177]

According to an article in *Popular Mechanics* magazine, of the "more than 200 people who have had their convictions overturned" by DNA evidence, in more than half "bad forensic analysis contributed to their imprisonment."[178] Brad Reagan, the article's author writes:

> America's forensic labs are overburdened, understaffed and under intense pressure from prosecutors to produce results.... Plus, several state and city forensic departments have been racked by scandals involving mishandled evidence and outright fraud. But criminal forensics has a deeper problem of basic validity. Bite marks, blood-splatter patterns, ballistics, and hair, fiber and handwriting analysis sound compelling in the courtroom, but much of the "sciences" behind forensic science rests on surprisingly shaky foundations. Many well-established forms of evidence are the product of highly subject analysis by people with minimal credentials - according to the American Society

of Crime Laboratory Directors, no advanced degree is required for a career in forensics. And even the most experienced and respected professionals can come to inaccurate conclusions, because the body of research behind the majority of the forensic sciences is incomplete, and the established methodologies are often inexact.[179]

The American public knows little of this though; instead they are under the mistaken belief that many forensic sciences like fingerprints, ballistics, and even bite mark analysis are infallible. In all actuality the science behind all of them are sketchy and have resulted in innocent people being arrested and imprisoned falsely based on this "evidence". Just ask Brandon Mayfield, a lawyer from Oregon who was arrested for the Madrid train bombings when the FBI falsely claimed his fingerprints were found on a bag of detonators.[180] Or Roy Brown who was sentenced to 25 to life and spent 15 years in prison after dentist Edward Mofson testified that the bite marks on the victim's body were Brown's.[181] DNA evidence finally cleared him of murder. The firefighter who actually committed the murder remained free until he killed himself by jumping in front of a train. His DNA was then tested and used to prove he was the killer, setting Brown free.[182]

The most often utilized evidence in courtrooms is the witness. This is one of the few that people will view with some skepticism as we all know people will lie. Unfortunately we can rarely ever be sure why people will lie. If someone has received immunity from prosecution or some other benefit from testifying, that is supposed to be made known to the judge or jury. Yet what the judge or jury won't know is what other bias the witness may hold against the defendant. For instance, does the witness harbor a secret hatred of whatever race the defendant is, or of gangs, etc. which may compel them to falsely accuse the defendant just to get them off the streets? Are they out for revenge for a previous wrong? Or are they just mistaken? Of the nearly 200 wrongly convicted who were exonerated by DNA evidence prior to 2007, "75% had been mistakenly identified by eyewitnesses" according to the Innocent Project, as reported in the magazine *The Economist*.[183]

It's not always the witness that hides things from the judge and jury either. Often it is unscrupulous prosecutors. They often fail to disclose evidence that proves the defendant is innocent or which would assist in his or her defense. One would think that a criminal defendant would have access to the same evidence as the prosecution. This is never the case though.

Here in America we leave the decision up to the prosecution as to what evidence they think the defense should know about in order to prepare and present a defense. Prosecutor's associations vociferously fight against open discovery laws. These would require the prosecution to disclose all the evidence in the files of the police or prosecution pertaining to the case. Without them, defendants are left to trust that the prosecution isn't hiding the only evidence that can free him.

As mentioned in *Miller-McCune.com Magazine, The Chicago Tribune* reported that in

> January 1999, a five-part series revealed "nearly 400 cases where prosecutors obtained homicide convictions by committing the most unforgivable kinds of deception. They had evidence that could have set defendants free. They allowed witnesses to lie. All in defiance of the law. Prosecutors swear to seek the truth but instead many pursue convictions at any cost."

> Reporters Maurice Possley and Ken Armstrong documented 381 cases, going back to 1963, in which courts reversed murder convictions because prosecutors had presented false evidence, concealed evidence that suggested innocence or both. During November 1999, Armstrong teamed with reporter Steve Mills to examine murder cases in which Illinois prosecutors, mostly in Cook County, had charged a defendant with a capital crime, and asked for the death penalty. The journalists identified 326 appellate reversals in those cases, attributed in whole or in part to prosecutorial misconduct.[184]

Ellen Reasonover, an African American woman learned just how dangerous it can be to have to trust a prosecutor's judgment about what discovery she needs to defend herself when she was a defendant charged with murder. The magazine article cited directly above noted how:

> No murder weapon had been recovered; no blood or other forensic evidence implicated the defendant. There were no eyewitnesses, no confession, no motive and no other defendants on trial, despite the state's theory that Reasonover acted with two male accomplices. All that, and an all-white jury too. The conviction rested entirely on the testimony of two jailhouse informants who said they heard Reasonover spontaneously confess to the murder almost immediately after making their acquaintance.... What the defense attorneys, the judge, the jurors and the journalists did not know at the time of trial was this: The jailhouse snitches had lied in return for favors promised by the prosecutor. The deals between the district attorney and the snitches remained undisclosed.[185]

Reasonover had to serve 16 years before she was finally freed thanks to a private investigator that started digging and came up with what the prosecutor had hidden.[186] Unfortunately, even when there is overwhelming evidence of prosecutorial misconduct, prosecutors are almost never disciplined. One study conducted by the Northern California Innocence Project found prosecutorial misconduct present in

17% of criminal cases, but found only a 0.8% disciplinary rate.[187] The study also found that from 1997-2009 there were 4,741 state bar disciplinary hearings in California, but just 10 involved prosecutors.[188]

So, why do prosecutors use false evidence or hide exonerating evidence? For a number of reasons; prejudice and deep-seated hatred of "criminals" often play a part, but just as egregious, and just as often, it is done to advance their careers. The more wins in the courtroom, the better for their career. They then get the high profile cases where they can use the publicity to gain name recognition with the public and launch their political careers. As we will see in the next section, prosecutors aren't the only people who unscrupulously victimize people in furtherance of their careers or to benefit financially.

Another common reason for people being falsely convicted is incompetent defense counsel. The majority of defendants are poor and therefore unable to afford to hire competent, caring lawyers with investigators on staff. Instead they are stuck with appointed counsel from the public defender's office. With such an enormous expansion of the criminal justice system over the past four decades, public defender offices have become completely overburdened by their ever-growing caseload and constantly shrinking budgets. According to *The Wall Street Journal*, Sacramento County laid off 50% of its public defenders,[189] and "[m]any states are seeking spending cuts on public defenders."[190]

It's not always the heavy caseloads that cause inadequate representation. Incompetent lawyers, both public defenders and hired attorneys, are often solely or partly responsible for wrongful convictions.[191] One of the most often-raised issues on appeal or collateral attack is ineffective assistance of counsel.

Many times defendants themselves will simply throw in the towel and plead guilty to crimes they didn't commit. This happens for a variety of reasons. Most people in jail are completely disillusioned with the criminal justice system, and as we've seen, for good reasons. This disillusionment makes it more likely that people will take a plea agreement rather than risk receiving a harsher sentence if they lose at trial. Prosecutors even admit "that the threat of death is used as a coercive tool to get guilty pleas for capital crimes, leading to false life-sentence convictions," according to the *New Mexico Daily Lobo*.[192]

Often people can get out of jail earlier by pleading guilty even if they're innocent because to go to trial means waiting months for trial rather than taking the State's offer of "time considered served" or other sentence that will put them on the streets faster than waiting for trial. *The Economist* reported in 2009 that "[m]ore than 90% of convictions in the United States result from [plea bargains]."[193]

So we have false confessions, faulty forensics, lying or mistaken witnesses, prosecutors hiding evidence, defense lawyers asleep at the wheel, a public automatically distrustful of anyone charged with a crime, and courts that deny defendants exonerating DNA testing, yet we still have no problem incarcerating more and more people for longer and longer periods using this system.

In his book *Stupid White Men... and Other Sorry Excuses for the State of the Nation!,* Michael Moore writes: "A shocking recent death penalty study[194] of 4,578 cases in a twenty- three year period (1973-1995) concluded that the courts found serious, reversible error in nearly 7 of every 10 capital sentence cases that were fully reviewed during that period. It also found that death sentences were being overturned in 2 out of 3 appeals. The overall prejudicial review error rate was 68 percent." Death penalty cases though, make up only a small portion of cases, and unfortunately they are the only cases that receive such intense scrutiny by the courts. Though both lifers and death row prisoners go through the same judicial system all the way up to and throughout trial, only 7% of lifers' convictions are overturned while 73% of death penalty convictions are overturned.[195] So one can assume that there are thousands of lifers and other people convicted of crimes based on false confessions, etc. who languish in prison due to courts denying them the same heightened review they would have received if sentenced to die.

The public's hatred of "criminals" is the main enabler of these false convictions. Societal disdain engenders an indifference to the fate of "criminals." Therefore it is easy to disregard the possibility that someone would falsely implicate themselves, or that the forensics we see on CSI and the forensics which is practiced in real life have little relation to one another.

Instead, we want to believe that if the police - the good guys - charge someone with a crime, then they must be guilty; that prosecutors wouldn't hide evidence or even make mistakes; but rather that "criminals" are all liars. That way we can more easily convince ourselves of our righteousness when we alienate anyone charged with a crime, torture suspects, or deny them exonerating evidence, because after all, they deserve it and aren't really human anyway.

Even if we don't care about the "criminals" or even the innocent for moral reasons, we should at least care for practical reasons. Incarcerating the wrong people allows the guilty to go free, and alienating the guilty discourages rehabilitation. Also when people are able to prove that they're innocent, society is then on the hook for paying compensation for all those years in prison.

The four men pardoned by Governor Ryan in Illinois cost Chicago taxpayers $20 million in settlement money.[196] That's in addition to the millions it cost to try the four men and litigate their appeals. According to the *chicagotribune.com,* in 2007 alone "excessive force and other misconduct payouts approved by the city Council, as well as new jury verdicts and lawsuit settlements, have tallied $25 million. Add to it the $19.8 million to settle the four torture cases and the cost to Chicago taxpayers approaches $45 million. That figure does not include legal

64

fees, such as the roughly $6 million in Burge-related court cases in recent years."[197]

This is millions of dollars that could have been paying for teachers' salaries or other desperately needed government services that are increasingly being cut nowadays. Some states are trying to weasel their way out of compensating people for wrongfully convicting and incarcerating them by adding provisions to their statutes that either cap compensation or which exclude people who falsely confess. Others like Florida are excluding anyone with a felony conviction.[198] David M. Reutter correctly points out in *Prison Legal News* that:

> Such indifference to wrongful convictions is indicative of the knee-jerk tough-on-crime mindset of politicians and other public officials, who find it hard to even consider compensating a former prisoner, regardless of the fact that he spent decades in prison for a crime he didn't commit.[199]

Juveniles

Many of the people we are demonizing and incarcerating and even wrongfully convicting unfortunately happen to be juveniles. Across the country we are locking up kids for the most ridiculous and despicable reasons. Oftentimes it's for things that most people wouldn't even consider to be a crime. Even when the reasons are legitimate the lengths of the sentences are often unconscionably long.

In an excerpt from the book *Police in the Hallways: Discipline in an Urban High School* published in *In These Times* magazine[200] Kathleen Nolan writes how:

> The nation's collective sentiments about crime and safety that have led to the culture of control at UPHS [a Bronx high school she dubs "Urban Public High School"] are pervasive. These sentiments drive national policy and shape the experiences of school children around the country, children like six-year-old Desree' Watson (who was handcuffed and arrested for throwing a tantrum in class), and the 12-year-old in Chicago who threw a hamburger at his classmate (and was arrested for "reckless conduct").

It may shock some that kids so young are being arrested but according to *Fellowship Magazine*, "[i]t is not uncommon in our country for children as young as five to be handcuffed (around their upper arms because their wrists are too small for the steel intended for adult bodies)".[201] In Rhode Island Family Court, magistrates are locking kids up for similar things - truancy, or slamming a classroom door too loudly.[202] At times, children in America are being incarcerated by judges looking to get kickbacks from the private prisons where the kids are being sent to, as we'll see further on when discussing the commoditization of prisoners. This is where all the demonization of "criminals" and zero tolerance / "tough-on-crime" rhetoric has brought us to.

It should go without saying that children don't understand right and wrong and the consequences of their actions the same way that adults do. Unfortunately, American society, exemplified by our criminal justice system, lacks the compassion to acknowledge these facts and codify them into our laws. Instead we often treat juveniles as harsh as or harsher than adults.

There are numerous studies which support what any parent will tell you (about their own kids at least) - that juveniles are less responsible than adults. Therefore, they are also less culpable than adults when they commit crimes. The main reason for this obvious fact is that their brains are not yet finished forming. In fact, studies prove that the human brain doesn't finish developing until the mid-twenties.[203] Studies unequivocally show that juveniles', and even young "adults", possess the following characteristics due to their brains not yet being fully developed:

- They are less mature;[204]

- They lack an adult's ability to assess risk [205], consider consequences [206], comprehend long-term effects [207], and make cost/benefit analyses [208];

- They have poor decision making skills [209], inadequate ability to control impulses[210], less reasoning skills [211] and immature judgment[212];

- They are unable to adequately regulate emotions and aggression [213];

- They are irresponsible, and due to the above lack of self control are prone to behave recklessly and criminally[214], and engage in risky behavior[215];

- They are more vulnerable to negative influences and more susceptible to peer pressure and coercion [216]; and

- They are thus more likely to make false confessions.[217]

Yet even with all this evidence, we as a nation, feel no qualms about sentencing a child to live their entire lives in prison for an act they performed before their brains were even physically capable of being fully culpable for their decisions. We just stopped killing kids as a punishment for crimes in 2005 [218] when the U.S. Supreme Court, acknowledging all of the above, finally abolished the death penalty for juveniles.

Even after the U.S. became the last nation on earth this year to ban mandatory life-without-parole (LWOP) for juveniles as a sentence, juveniles can still be sentenced to LWOP or life with the possibility of parole and then denied parole for the rest of their lives resulting in the same thing - "death by incarceration."

There was strong opposition to abolishing the death penalty for juveniles and there is strong support for LWOP. Many view LWOP as the perfect alternative to the death penalty for both juveniles and adults, which have contributed to the rapid expansion of LWOP. Thus many will still support denying juvenile offenders parole every time they come up for review.

When it comes to our criminal justice system, policies are too often incoherent and irrational. One of the most glaring examples of this is also one of the least pondered. It's that in a court of law we now tell juveniles that they are adults even when we know they are not. We do so without any supporting evidence, ignoring evidence to the contrary, and only do so to the juvenile's detriment. We are the only country left that will both charge children as adults and then sentence them to LWOP.[219]

When you were a child, there were probably dozens, if not hundreds of times when you wished with all your might that you could wave a magic wand and be transformed into an adult. It may have been to get out of doing homework, or to avoid having a babysitter, or maybe just because you were sick of hearing those four infuriatingly illogical words - "because I said so". There was always some privilege you were denied due to not being an adult.

As a child, you probably never thought that such a magic wand really existed though, did you? Well it does. Yet it exists for only one purpose, and it's not to grant wishes or privileges. No, its sole utility is to inflict punishment. This magic wand is used to beat children over the head, transporting them superficially into adulthood so that they can enter the adult criminal "justice" system. No, this magic wand is not a childhood fantasy. It is a societal reality. Every day children are reclassified as adults by this magical mechanism that can erase fact, logic, science, and even common sense.

Amazingly, this magical wand reappeared over 80 years after the State of Illinois originated the theory that children should not be tried as adults. As the Illinois Coalition for the Fair Sentencing of Children noted in their 2008 report, entitled "Categorically Less Culpable":

> Prior to 1899, all children in conflict with the law in the United States were treated the same as adults; there was not a court set up specifically for children. In 1899, the nation's first juvenile court was established in Illinois, and other states began to follow shortly thereafter. The juvenile justice system was founded on the idea that childhood is a distinct phase of life, that juveniles are less culpable for crimes and more amenable to rehabilitation than adults, and that rehabilitation, not punishment, is the proper way to handle deviant - even grave - behavior among youth. Eventually, the system

which began in Illinois - in which most children accused of crimes were removed from adult courtrooms, adult jails, and adult poorhouses - became a nationwide standard and an international model. In fact, Illinois pioneered one of the nation's most durable and effective legal reforms - the juvenile court.[220]

This was a phenomenal achievement of civilized society, but oh, how far we have fallen, both in Illinois and as a country. As the same report noted, "[i]n 1982 Illinois passed its first automatic transfer statute, whereby children charged with certain crimes would automatically be tried as adults, regardless of their culpability in the crime."[221] How is it that we reverted to a nineteenth century mindset? It is largely due to politics at the expense of compassion and common sense. In *Illinois Issues* magazine, Betsy Clark, the president of the Juvenile Justice Initiative, described it succinctly: "There was this political fever, and it wasn't thought to be safe to vote against law and order, to vote against supposed soft-on-crime bills. So a lot of these laws passed because there was a fear that [the lawmakers] who voted against these measures would lose their seats."[222] Of course there wouldn't have been any "political fear" had the public not been so rabidly hateful of anyone who commits a crime - even children.

Not only is Illinois now one of the most punitive states in the country when it comes to charging and sentencing juveniles, but the United States is the only country in the world (185-1) that voted against a United Nations resolution calling to abolish life without parole sentences for juveniles.[223] Why is that, you may ask? Because we are the only ones who would still sentence juveniles to LWOP.[224] In Italy the most time a juvenile can receive is 10 years, while the maximum in Germany is 24.[225] We are no longer the pioneer of humane policies for juveniles; instead, our policies are the antipathy of them. We have reverted to throwing children to the adult courts where for decades we had agreed they don't belong. Our fear of crime and our hatred of "criminals" have prompted us to dismiss all evidence and facts about their level of maturity and enact laws that are nothing more than knee-jerk reactions to horrific crimes. We do so without any analysis of whether these laws are wise, just, or even effective at anything other than revenge.

We all grew up hearing the old adage that everyone deserves a second chance. Unfortunately our society has been infected by tough-on-crime rhetoric so thoroughly that we now live by a new maxim - "lock'em up and throw away the key". That is exactly what we have done for thousands of juveniles and tens of thousands of others.

According to *The Sentencing Project*, the U.S. had 1,755 juveniles serving LWOP in 2008.[226] *Playboy* magazine puts the number at 2,387.[227] Others put the number at over 2,500.[228] Now with the U.S. Supreme Court ruling that mandatory LWOP sentences for juveniles are cruel and unusual thereby whittling away at LWOP sentences for juveniles many of the 2,000 should now get new sentences or parole hearings of some type depending on the state. Over 5,000 more are already serving life sentences with parole as a possibility.[229] However, nowadays parole boards rarely grant parole, and clemency is about as likely as the magic wand that grants privileges instead of punishments. Though these numbers are shocking, they actually understate the issue, as there are tens of thousands of others who are serving equivalent sentences that don't carry the label "life". Instead they are sentenced to 60 or 100 years for crimes they committed before they could even drive, and often before they've even started puberty. These are known as "virtual" LWOP sentences because the person is unable to outlive the sentence so it is a LWOP sentence in all but name.

It is difficult to write objectively on this subject. Not only does the act of charging a juvenile as an adult defy logic, but the advocates of harsh penalties for juvenile offenders rely on emotion and support their arguments with flawed reasoning. They use society's fear and hatred to garner support for such laws, knowing that even if they can't convince all of the public of their false claims, the majority of the public's indifference to the plight of "criminals" guarantees almost no opposition. They rely mainly on two arguments (besides the arbitrary "they deserve it" retort).

First, the tough-on-crime argument - that harsh penalties will deter others from crime. There has never been a shred of reliable, empirical evidence to support such an assertion. After all, how many kids can even tell you what the laws actually prohibit, let alone what the consequences are for breaking them? Not to mention the fact that any objective study done has shown that "criminals" of all ages almost universally believe that they will never be caught for their crimes, so the possibility of being punished, regardless of the penalty, rarely enters into the equation beforehand. So how is a harsher penalty - even LWOP - going to deter someone, who, one, isn't aware of the penalty, and two, even if he or she is aware of it, doesn't factor it into the decision as to whether or not to commit the crime?

When an advocate for harsher penalties is confronted with these facts, he or she will usually fall back on the argument that, well, it will deter those offenders from committing more crimes because they'll be imprisoned and incapable of reoffending. This ignores the great potential for rehabilitation juveniles possess. As Whitney Woodford related in *Illinois Issues*, it is rehabilitation and reform models that deter children from reoffending, not harsher penalties, such as incarceration.[230] It also ignores the fact that they can easily reoffend while in prison where crimes are still committed. Not to mention it also ignores the fact that violent offenders are the least likely to reoffend out of any offender demographic.

The second argument put forth by the "lock'em up for life" crowd is that without these laws to charge juveniles as adults, juveniles would be used as hitmen. Linda Szymanski, chief of legal research for the National Center for Juvenile Justice was paraphrased in *The Wall Street Journal* explaining this theory as follows:

74

Some criminal experts believe that because some laws are soft on children, drug dealers and gang members may be encouraged to recruit more "shorties" or youngsters who commit crimes on their behalf.[231]

Regardless of the fact that there is no research confirming this theory, there are a number of flaws in this reasoning. First and foremost is the obvious fact that the coercion itself by someone older shows that those "shorties" are less culpable than an actual adult who chooses to commit these crimes of their own free will. Second, the whole premise is irrational. If an adult gets a kid to commit a crime for him or her, he or she will be just as guilty under current law. They would simply be charged under an accountability theory (or conspiracy, or the Rico Act, etc.), and receive the same sentence as if they had actually committed the crimes themselves. From the adults perspective it actually makes less sense to have a child commit the crime due to the fact that it exposes the adult to more risk by expanding the number of people who have knowledge of the crime. If you're a "criminal", who would you trust to do the crime right and keep quiet about it, yourself or some scared kid? We should be increasing penalties for adults who use kids to commit crimes if our goal is truly to deter such a thing, rather than targeting the least culpable actors and kidding ourselves that they are adults.

A number of efforts are under way to try to bring reform to our criminal justice system for juveniles. There is one enormous pink elephant in the courtroom though that nobody seems willing to address -

it's the fact that you can't magically turn a child into an adult by decree, no matter how much you hate "criminals" and even if some politician did write it into the law.

The whole concept defies the laws of nature. Kids don't think like adults, don't act like adults, don't foresee consequences like adults, can't defend themselves in court like adults, and definitely don't receive any of the privileges of adulthood, even after the prosecutor charges them as adults. After being charged as adults they don't suddenly obtain the right to vote, drink, or obtain credit cards. Why? Because they aren't adults! So how is it that we can label them adults when all the evidence proves otherwise and we only do so to punish them more severely all the while duplicitously acknowledging that they aren't adults?

Society has for too long been unfalteringly content with charging and sentencing juveniles as adults, while well aware of the plethora of mitigating factors that argue against such a draconian practice. We have been deliberately indifferent to the fact that to do so defies both common sense and the laws of nature. We ignore that an eight-year-old is incapable of forming criminal intent. We ignore environmental factors such as lead poisoning which affects the brain and increases criminality.[232] We ignore our own state constitutions which often demand, like Illinois' does, that the goal of incarceration carries with it "the objective of restoring the offender to useful citizenship,"[233] so that we can incarcerate a 13- year-old to die in prison after serving seven or eight decades of a LWOP sentence. We ignore the fact that an officer

76

can get a child to say just about anything, even falsely confessing, if the poor kid thinks it will get him home faster, and that that same kid will be clueless throughout the entire judicial process, unable to adequately assist in his or her own defense as an adult could.

Our hatred of "criminals" causes us to ignore all of these things. It defies logic, compassion, and common sense.

These are our children, the next generation. Yet we rejoice in our tough-on-crime rhetoric and smugly repeat asinine phrases like "throw away the key" and "natural-born-killer" etc. without knowing a single additional factor about the kid or the circumstances other than the crime itself. All we need to know is the kid was charged with a crime and we automatically see him or her as born evil and irredeemable. That is the power of hate and tough-on-crime rhetoric. They make us ignore the obvious and champion the unthinkable. Mix that hate and rhetoric with a good dose of self-righteousness and we arrive at a place where we are the only country in the world that will still sentence a child to die in prison. A country that thinks it can one-up God and magically turn a child into an adult by saying it is so. A country that once led the world in human rights and juvenile justice, but which is now a pariah on both counts.

If we truly wish to be just, and rejoin the rest of humanity, we can begin by acknowledging that which is irrefutable - that children simply are not adults. Nor are they ever evil, irredeemable monsters. From there we can craft sensible policies in line with these self-evident truths. Until then we are dependent on the courts which are reluctant to intervene.

Up until 2010 we were even sentencing kids to LWOP when they hadn't even killed anyone. It took the United States Supreme Court to declare LWOP an unconstitutionally cruel and unusual punishment for juveniles who didn't commit murder, banning the sentence completely for that small segment of kids who were currently sentenced to LWOP (129[234] of the 2,500 or so).

The 2010 case was Graham v. Florida. [235] The son of crack addicts, Terrance Graham was sentenced to LWOP for armed robbery.[236] U. S. Supreme Court Justice Anthony Kennedy, writing the opinion of the court broke down just exactly what a LWOP sentence means for a juvenile:

> As for the punishment, life without parole is "the second most severe penalty permitted by law." Harmelin v. Michigan, 501 U.S. 957, 1001 (1991). [Y]et life without parole sentences share some characteristics with death sentences that are shared by no other sentences. The State does not execute the offender sentenced to life without parole, but the sentence alters the offender's life by a forfeiture that is irrevocable. It deprives the convict of the most basic liberties without giving hope of

restoration, except perhaps by executive clemency - the remote possibility of which does not mitigate the harshness of the sentence. Solem v. Helm, 463 U.S. 277, 300-01 (1983). As one court observed in overturning a life without parole sentence for a juvenile defendant, this sentence "means denial of hope; it means that good behavior and character improvement are immaterial; it means that whatever the future might hold in store for the mind and spirit of [the convict], he will remain in prison for the rest of his days." Naovarath v. State, 105 Nev. 525, 526, 776 P. 2d 944 (1989)".

Life without parole is an especially harsh punishment for a juvenile. Under this sentence a juvenile offender will on average serve more years and a greater percentage of his life in prison than an adult offender. A 16-year-old and a 75-year-old each sentenced to life without parole receive the same punishment in name only. Roper v. Simmons 543 U.S. 551, 572 (2005); cf Harmelin v. Michigan, 501 U.S. 957, 996 (1991).... This reality cannot be ignored.[237]

Unfortunately, the U. S. Supreme Court's ruling only means that they will now have parole hearings, not that they will actually ever be released. With parole nearly extinct or politically unpalatable in many states, there's a good chance that these 129 kids will still die in prison after being repeatedly, and torturously, denied parole by a society that inherently hates "criminals" and want to "keep them off the streets". Likewise for those of the remaining 2,500 who may obtain parole hearings due to the supreme courts more recent decisions.

This ruling is a small victory for juvenile lifers and inches the United States a little closer to catching up with the rest of the world in juvenile sentencing policies. Yet, while Graham v. Florida and its progeny are a good step in the right directions, we still have thousands of kids who are serving life sentences and many more serving its numerical equivalent. So it's a baby step at most.

I have to agree with Patricia Williams who wrote in *The Nation* that:

> It is manifestly barbarous that children, who by definition are immature and unformed, should be tossed away for life, with no chance for rehabilitation or recognition of the possibility of change. And it is manifestly barbarous that there is such enormous disparity in the racial composition of these particular child defendants. It is barbarous that they are ... consistently and disproportionately deemed so incorrigible as to be throwaways, forever.[238]

The same can be said though for the thousands of young "adults" whose brains had yet to finish developing when they committed their crimes who were given the equivalent of LWOP in a number of years, or a life sentence with parole being rubber-stamped "denied" by political lackeys. Americans no longer believe everyone deserves a second chance. If they do, our sentencing laws surely don't reflect it.

President George W. Bush called the U. S. the "Land of the Second Chance". This has never been more of a misstatement than it is today. There is no second chance for the nearly ten percent (or more) of prisoners in the U.S. who will never be released from prison, other than in a coffin. In 2004 the Sentencing Project reported that there were nearly 35,000 people in the U. S. serving LWOP sentences.[239] This is more than the 34,000 prisoners who were serving any type of life term (with or without parole) in 1982. That number has climbed drastically. As of 2009 it was 140,610.[240]

With lifers accumulating and overly harsh sentences still in place throughout the country, the number of people who will never be released who are currently in prison is most likely over 200,000, when you include all the "virtual" lifers and lifers arbitrarily denied parole, such as the majority of the 34,164 lifers in California alone.[241] As *The New York Times* quotes professor Joan Petersilia, an expert on parole policy, "[w]hen California courts sentence somebody to life with parole, it turns out that's not possible after all. Board of Parole hearings almost never grant releases."[242] Now compare those numbers with Europe where LWOP is banned in many countries and is rarely ever used in the others. For instance, in Spain the maximum sentence someone can receive is 40 years, while in Slovenia it is 20 years.[243]

Miscellany

Not only do the millions of people we incarcerate include too many parents, veterans, blacks, juveniles, and people who are either mentally ill or addicted to drugs; and not only do we incarcerate people for way too long; but we also increasingly incarcerate the people with the least power in society-the uneducated, the homeless, the indebted, and the immigrant.

The uneducated are exceedingly susceptible to coming into contact with the criminal justice system, and thus more susceptible to becoming incarcerated. A person's home life during childhood is highly determinative of how far along their education has progressed by the time they reach their teens and early twenties. One can hardly imagine the type of home environment that a child would have to endure to remain illiterate well into their teens or adulthood in America. Unfortunately such a thing is not uncommon in this country, and is actually even more common here than it is in many much poorer countries. So while almanacs may routinely claim that America's literacy rate is 98% or 99%, the reality is that in America as a whole 4% of the population is completely illiterate and another 21% are considered functionally illiterate.[244]

People entering prison on the other hand, have nearly five times the likelihood of being completely illiterate (19%) and are twice as likely to be functionally illiterate (40%).[245] Being functionally illiterate means, for example, that they are incapable of writing a letter to a company explaining a billing error, let alone a legal brief laying out arguments relating how they were denied a fair trial. So nearly 60% of people entering prison are either completely or functionally illiterate, which goes a long way towards explaining why over 70% of them have not completed high school.[246]

Being uneducated, especially illiterate, in America means your employment prospects are nearly non-existent, especially during tough economic times. Therefore the uneducated become more likely to find it necessary to resort to crime to provide for themselves and their families.

Homeless people are another demographic that are increasingly imprisoned in America, as vagrancy laws expand and criminalize people who are unfortunate enough not to have a home. Nearly one out of every five incarcerated mothers had been homeless the year before they were locked up[247], and altogether 13% of state prisoners and 17% of jail inmates were homeless the year prior to arrest as well.[248] Not only are we locking up hundreds of thousands of homeless people, but in some parts of the country we've even begun locking up good Samaritans who feed the homeless.[249] Of course one person's good Samaritan is another person's "food terrorist". That is what Orlando's mayor Buddy Dyer called the nearly two dozen volunteers with Food Not Bombs who were arrested for violating a city ordinance which prohibits feeding large groups of people in downtown parks, when they gave free meals to the homeless in Orlando's Lake Eola Park on June

1st, 2011.[250] See how easy it is to demonize and criminalize people. All you have to do is substitute "food terrorist" or "criminal" for charity worker or caring person, and a mayor has just justified arresting two dozen caring do-gooders. Municipalities across the country are increasingly passing similar laws which basically criminalize homelessness, helping the homeless, and poverty in general.

Although debtor's prisons were banned by states almost two centuries ago[251], people are increasingly being locked up due to an inability to pay off their debts. As will be discussed later on, people incur a plethora of fines, fees, and restitution when they come into contact with the criminal justice system. When unable to pay them on time, it more often than not means additional fines or late fees, and increasingly, reincarceration.

Courts want their money. *Newsweek* magazine reported that the American Civil Liberties Union (ACLU) obtained a memo which showed "the Michigan court's administrator is brutally clear, reminding judges of 'tough economic times' and urging a 'culture shift' toward pay-or-prison collection tactics".[252]

Not only are the courts incarcerating people for failure to pay criminal justice debts, but they're also acting as enforcers for the business community. *The Wall Street Journal* reported that lenders are exploiting "the court system to obtain the arrest of its customers," according to Sue Hofer, a spokeswoman for the Illinois Department of

Financial and Professional Regulation.[253] *Prison Legal News* likewise reports that "[o]ver a third of states allow people to be locked up for failing to pay their debts", and the "use of arrest warrants to jail people who have defaulted on debts is increasing."[254] Collection agencies can therefore buy up debt and let the courts do their job for them by just requesting civil arrest warrants.

Additionally thousands of parents are being jailed each year for failing to pay child support. Bexar County in Texas locked up over a thousand parents for that reason in 2009 alone.[255]

Since "debtor's prisons" are supposedly outlawed, courts instead claim that people aren't being locked up for not having money to pay their debts, but rather because they are in contempt of court... for not having money to pay their debts as ordered by the court.[256]

So if you're a parent paying child support with no savings you better pray you don't lose your job or you might end up like Randy Miller. A 39-year-old military veteran, he lost his job with AT&T in 2009, and without any income, could no longer pay the $452 monthly child support payments. His savings dwindled to 30 cents and his house went into foreclosure.[257] By November of 2010 he had racked up $4,000 in unpaid child support payments and was jailed for four months.[258]

As will be seen later, when a parent becomes incarcerated the child becomes a victim. Furthermore, it makes little sense to incarcerate someone for months due to failure to pay child support. The other parent obviously won't get paid anything if the parent who is unable to pay is in jail where they are unable to earn an income or even look for employment.

Society is paying an unconscionable sum of money to incarcerate people that don't need or deserve to be incarcerated. Yet we continue to do so because we have been indoctrinated with a "lock'em up" mentality. Derogatory monikers can be arbitrarily placed on anyone now. Therefore Mr. Miller isn't a loving father who fell on hard times, but rather a "deadbeat dad", so America says "lock'em up!" It doesn't matter that locking him up cost taxpayers thousands of dollars, negatively affected his family, and failed to accomplish anything positive. Who cares, lock-em up!

Immigrants

Increasingly illegal immigrants are also being arrested. Not because they present any threat but rather because those who profit or make a living off of keeping prison and jail bunks full are inflaming racist, anti-immigrant passions and getting laws passed to criminalize immigrants. They are the most recent segment of our society to be criminalized, viewed as worthless from a human perspective, and therefore easily transformed into a commodity by others. Around 400,000 people are held in state, local, and private prisons and jails each year as part of America's immigration detention system.[259] As more and more states pass anti-immigrant laws at the behest of those who benefit from criminalizing people who for decades have worked the jobs Americans shun, this number is sure to rise.

Immigrants are collectively demonized in order to facilitate their increased incarceration. Politicians' antagonistic hyperbole about immigrants being a criminal menace is all self-serving rhetoric based almost entirely on misrepresentation of the facts.

As Alexander Cockburn noted in *The Nation* magazine:

> Nothing more easily elicits roars of assent across a good slice of the political spectrum than the hoarse alarums that wave after wave of brown-skinned illegals flood across the border, plunging neighborhoods and whole cities into an inferno of crime, overwhelming cops and prosecutors, clogging the justice system, cramming the prisons.[260]

He goes on to explain how both political parties distort the facts, inflaming the public's fears, even though, due to the undercounting of the Hispanic population, "[a]lmost beyond the shadow of a doubt, white crime rates nationwide are significantly higher that Hispanic ones."[261] Rather "[i]t's all nonsense. There's no crime wave swollen by brown gangbangers to city- destroying proportions."[262]

So, why are we bombarded with this disinformation? Because the fear-mongering of politicians kills three birds with one stone. First, it gives the politician additional proof of his or her tough-on-crime credentials. Second, it pleases the private prison lobbyists who designed and push the anti-immigrant legislation which fills the private prisons, generating revenue for them from the government. Third, it panders to the unemployed during tough economic times by falsely claiming that kicking illegal immigrants out of the country (after imprisoning them) will open up jobs for them.

Fear sells, so the media jumps at the chance to report on the "crime epidemic", even when crime rates are falling. Police supply the media and politicians with ample "evidence" of Latino gang problems because, as *The Nation* notes, "the feds dole out hundreds of millions each year for gang prevention. Pay a city to find a gang problem and the city will oblige".[263] This also engenders public support for policies that cost taxpayers money while giving them little benefit other than a false sense of security.

The simple fact that there are currently more illegal immigrants in the U.S. than at any other time, and that we have a crime rate that hasn't been this low since 1965 should dispel the myth that they are a criminal hoard threatening our safety. Yet it doesn't. Hatred and fear trump common sense every time.

Claiming that illegal immigrants are stealing jobs from Americans takes on an especially hysterical tone during a recession with nearly double-digit unemployment. These claims are likewise disingenuous.

Illegal immigrants are not taking American's jobs. Even during the worst recession since the Great Depression Americans refuse to work the jobs that immigrants are willing to work. Time and again when farmers find themselves unable to find immigrants to work the fields they are left with no alternative but to watch their crops rot in the fields. The reason being that Americans refuse to do such back-breaking work for such low pay. That's why when states like Georgia pass anti-immigrant laws that chase immigrants out of the state there isn't a sudden rush by Americans to fill those jobs. Instead there's a bunch of farmers with insufficient labor to work their fields.[264]

Instead of protecting American jobs this legislation actually threatens our agricultural industry and may force us to outsource our food production, according to *The Wall Street Journal*.[265] Georgia was 11,000 laborers short after passing HB 87 - its anti-immigrant law.[266] Alabaman farmers and contractors felt the impact well before their bill even gained passage. *The Wall Street Journal* reported that Alabama's "state agriculture commission says squash, tomatoes and other produce are rotting in their fields,"[267] because immigrants and their legal resident or American family members started fleeing the state in June of 2011 in anticipation of the enactment of HB 56 in September.

HB 56 "criminalizes many aspects of illegal immigrants' lives, including being in the state as well as seeking employment there ."[268] It also makes it illegal for American citizens to give them rides, shelter, rent to them, and knowingly hiring them.[269] The experience of Hal Hayes, a peach farmer with a jam and basket-weaving factory is telling. The "handful of Americans who showed up to apply for jobs demanded [to be paid] off the books so that they can continue to collect unemployment benefits ."[270] With insufficient labor to continue operations profitably, let alone expand as he had planned, he said he would be laying everyone off and filing for unemployment himself because "the state put me out of business ."[271]

So if all these jobs that immigrants work are undesirable by Americans and those businesses are not only against these laws, but are living proof that these laws are not good for the economy, then why do we keep passing them and turning immigrants into "criminals"?

It's because other businesses make money off of immigrants joining the ranks of "criminals". According to a May 2011 news release by Detention Watch Network: "For years, private prison firms have played a critical role in shaping public policy around immigration detention, pursuing the bottom line at the expense of basic civil rights and tax payer dollars."[272] One just needs to look at what's known locally as "Prisonville" in Raymondville, Texas. It's a compound of what Matt Taibbi describes in *Rolling Stone* magazine as "a freaky-looking phalanx of gleaming-white, windowless, modular tent-like domes that, much in the spirit of our cheerfully bloodsucking modern American society, simultaneously recalls both Auschwitz and Space Mountain."[273] Prisonville is four private facilities that are run by CCA, Corplan, and others to hold immigrant detainees.[274]

In These Times magazine has likewise reported on this phenomenon. In the article "Corporate Con Game: How the private prison industry helped shape Arizona's anti-immigrant law,"[275] they traced the numerous private prison corporations, lobbying firms, and politicians who conspired to pass Senate Bill 1070 to "increase the numbers of undocumented residents who are arrested and jailed."[276]

The main conduit for Arizona's SB 1070 was the American Legislative Exchange Council (ALEC),[277] of which Geo Group and Corrections Corporation of America (CCA), two of the world's largest prison companies are members of.[278] ALEC, you'll recall was instrumental in the expansion of both "Truth-In-Sentencing" laws and "Three Strikes and You're Out" laws,[279] both of which greatly contributed to expanding the prison populations benefiting private prison corporations greatly.[280]

In another *In These Times* article, this one about divesting from private prison corporations, Joel Handley tells how:

> CCA, the private prison industry's largest company
> which has contracts with Immigration and Customs
> Enforcement (ICE) and the U.S. Marshal Service, is also

the nation's largest detainer of undocumented immigrants .... Detainment is a lucrative trade. Prisons can earn $90 - $200 per inmate, per night, which translates into nearly $5 billion in revenues each year. The industry has lobbied diligently to secure profits, supporting and even writing laws to increase prison sentences and populations, especially among undocumented immigrants. Between 2003 and 2010, private prison companies spent more than $20 million lobbying legislators and the Department of Homeland Security .... Arizona state senator Russell Pearce, the purported writer of SB1070....met with CCA representatives at an American Legislative Exchange Council (ALEC) conference in 2009, where together they reportedly drafted the legislation. When Pearce introduced the bill in January 2010, 36 senators signed on as co-sponsors. Over the next six months, 30 of them received donations from CCA, GEO or MTC .... Since SB1070 was signed into law in April 2010, five other states - Utah, Indiana, Georgia, Alabama and South Carolina - have passed similar or near-identical legislation. On May 13 [2011], Georgia governor, Nathan Deal, who has received thousands of dollars worth of campaign contributions from CCA, signed his state's version of the bill, HB87, into law.[281]

So now we begin to see how we truly came to be the top incarcerator in the world. Whereas we used to have less than 200,000 people in both state and federal prisons in 1970,[282] we now have twice that number locked up each year just for immigration,[283] and seven times that number in prison now. The Pew Charitable Trusts remarked in a 2006 report that, "[a]fter a 700-percent increase in the U. S. Prison population between 1970 and 2005, you'd think the nation would finally have run out of lawbreakers to put behind bars."[284]

Yet we don't. Instead we just criminalize ever-larger segments of the population and keep extending sentences, because too many powerful people have a vested interest in expanding the prison population; and society's hatred for "criminals" enables people to be commoditized for the benefit of those few at the expense of the many - tax payers and "criminals" both.

4

HUMAN COMMODITY

Immigrants aren't the only ones to be viewed as a commodity via criminalization. It's all "criminals". Anyone who commits a crime is not only forever labeled a "criminal", but is also now viewed as a commodity by a multitude of people. For the past couple of decades it has been a free for all on how many ways society can exploit prisoners now that they've been entirely marginalized from society.

Not only are there thousands of companies that benefit from keeping people incarcerated, but all of their employees, stockholders, and the hundreds of thousands of prison guards, administrative staff, etc. all have a vested interest in maintaining and/or increasing the incarceration rate. Their job security depends on it. So even when the crime rate goes down, as it has for decades, they will continue to push for laws that increase prison populations. Furthermore, others view "criminals" as a captive work force, captive consumers, or chattel, as will be seen in the following pages.

The livelihoods of literally thousands of businesses and millions of people are now dependent on keeping millions of people incarcerated, and in order for those various businesses to expand their markets they must continually convince Americans to lock up even more people. Prisoners and anyone that can be criminalized have therefore become both an economic and political commodity at the mercy of both the Prison Industrial Complex (PIC) and society's hatred. The latter allows politicians to mislead voters into believing the most tenuous justifications for mass incarceration. They do so via "tough-on-crime" rhetoric and other fallacies similar to those used to criminalize immigrants. The end result of which is both a waste of tax payer money and the passage of harmful and counterproductive legislation.

The PIC, according to Lorenzo Jones, the executive director of the Connecticut-based A Better Way Foundation, "comprises construction companies, private corrections companies, prison labor companies, surveillance technology companies, lobbyists and interest groups, and more".[285] He notes that "nearly every major U.S. industry needs the PIC. From beef production in Texas to social services in Connecticut, from prisoner-made furniture sold to Ivy League universities to stuffing envelopes for media outlets."[286]

One twenty-five year veteran of Pennsylvania's death row and a published author, Mumia Abu-Jamal, explains in *WIN Magazine* how "along with the immense and unprecedented explosion in business for corporations trading behind bars. Prisons today ... are captive markets where billions are made by merchants."[287] Dial sold more than $100,000 in just one year in New York jails, while VitaPro Foods reaped $34 million by unloading its soybean meat-substitutes to Texas prisons.[288] Mr. Abu-Jamal's article crops a page from a pamphlet written by prison activists Linda Evans and Eve Goldberg which notes how:

> The prison industrial complex is an interweaving of private business and government interests. Its two-fold purpose is profit and social control. Its public rationale is the fight against crime.

> Not so long ago, communism was "the enemy" and communists were demonized as a way of justifying gargantuan military expenditures. Now, fear of crime and the demonization of criminals serve a similar ideological purpose: to justify the use of tax dollars for the repression and incarceration of a growing percentage of our population .... Most of the "criminals" we lock up are poor people who commit nonviolent crimes out of economic need. Violence occurs in less than 14 percent of all reported crime, and injuries occur in just 3 percent.[289]

Yet we, as a country, have been so thoroughly indoctrinated by decades of tough-on-crime rhetoric that whenever the words "criminal" or "prisoner" appear we have an almost Pavlovian response equating both with "murderer", "rapist", etc. We never think "cousin Jessica" or the thirteen year old sentenced to LWOP because a 30-year-old man convinced him to act as a lookout. It is because we have been trained not to think of "criminals" as members of society. By thinking of them as all being "animals" we facilitate the imprisonment of more people with less justification.

Two types of businesses are especially scurrilous - correctional healthcare companies and private prison corporations.

The for-profit prison healthcare business is "a billion dollar industry."[290] The industry is infested by dozens of companies that make profits off of routinely denying prison and jail inmate's adequate medical, dental, and mental health services, while simultaneously and disingenuously claiming otherwise. The predictable result is that prisoners are suffering, being paralyzed, and even dying on a regular basis in order to maximize the profits of these corporations.

Recently a merger occurred between American Service Group, Inc. (ASG), which is the owner of both Prison Health Services (PHS) and Correctional Health Services, LLC (CHS), and Valitas Health Services, Inc. (VHS), which was the parent company of Correctional Medical Services, Inc. (CMS), to become the largest private correctional health care company in the nation, if not the world.[291] The combined company serves over 400 correctional facilities nationwide and has more than 11,000 employees,[292] all of whom, along with the shareholders, have a vested interest in maximizing profits at the expense of inmates' health.

Prior to the merger, VHS had made a 2010 profit of $9.3 million dollars.[293] The chairman and CEO, Dick Miles, predicted that "a lot of states are going to be considering outsourcing correctional healthcare to companies like ours...".[294] What he failed to mention though, was what *Prison Legal News* has long reported, that these companies have a long history of being the cause of harm instead of health to inmates, especially PHS. As David Reutter, a journalist who reports regularly on prison issues, noted: "Numerous lawsuits filed against PHS demonstrate that ASG's profits have resulted from understaffing and denying prisoners adequate treatment for even serious medical needs. To gain contracts, PHS tends to bid low and then reduce its costs to ensure the company makes money".[295]

Numerous examples stand out as particularly heinous, and show how indifferent these companies are to the health of the inmates they are contracted to treat. Ashley Ellis was sentenced in Vermont to serve 30 days in state prison for "careless and negligent operation of a motor vehicle."[296] She had gotten into a car accident. She wasn't speeding or under the influence of any drugs or alcohol, but the man she hit, who was riding a motorcycle, was seriously injured as a result. The guilt over that fact spurred Ms. Ellis to become a licensed nurse's aide in the two years prior to her sentencing.[297] Ms. Ellis also suffered from anorexia-bulimia nervosa and "required regular potassium supplements to keep her heart from shutting down," according to *In These Times* magazine.[298]

PHS was the healthcare provider at the prison. Her doctor, several days prior to her arrival, faxed in her medical file which notified PHS staff that she required potassium.[299] Instead of serving 30 days though she didn't make it past the weekend. She was basically executed by neglect. Arriving on Friday, she was dead by Sunday morning due to being denied potassium.[300] PHS did not stock it in preparation for her arrival and staff at the prison had nicknamed her "Potassium Girl", because she was "begging so often and fervently" [301] for the drug that could have saved her life.

PHS indifferently claimed that Ms. Ellis "received care that met applicable standards."[302] Seth Lipschultz, the Vermont Defender's Office supervising attorney is blunt when explaining how lawsuits don't deter these companies as it's just part of their business model: "It's in their interest to provide inadequate care and take lumps when sued ... The fewer services they provide, the more money they make."[303]

One of those services used to be having an inmate advocate. Inmates, the majority of whom have little education and few family members or anyone else in free society both willing and able to advocate for them, are at an incredible disadvantage when it comes to trying to obtain adequate care. Likewise, the odds of an inmate being able to successfully sue for an unconstitutional denial of care are stacked against them. The position of inmate advocate is not to help sue, but to at least visit the prison and field grievances. According to *In These Times,* when PHS received their contract with Vermont this position was cut, just one of numerous cost-saving changes PHS was allowed to make. Another was to cut 20 nursing shifts.[304]

Lorene Gendron, an inmate advocate for PHS for two years, is quoted in the article as remembering: "I would say, 'Why can't you just give the patient the med they need?' And PHS would say, 'It's too expensive, or not on our formulary.' It was hard to see something so simple to do for someone and not be able to get it done. There was so much pressure not to prescribe." Ashley Ellis died for want of a $4 bottle of potassium pills. That $4 was just a drop in the bucket of neglect that allowed PHS to reap $160 million in just that quarter when Ashley died.[305]

Ashley isn't the only inmate who has died due to the negligent "care" provided by PHS. According to *The Root*, "one inmate, struggling with Parkinson's disease, died after a jail medical director cut off just a few of his 32 pills."[306] Nor is PHS the only private health care provider who has been the cause of inmates dying due to providing inadequate medical care. The sad thing is that it's only when a pretty girl like Ashley dies, or when someone like Brett Allen Fields successfully sues PHS, that anyone hears about how these companies are profiting off of refusing to treat inmates.

Mr. Fields won a $1.2 million lawsuit after PHS failed to accurately diagnose and treat his spinal epidural abscess while in the Lee County Jail in Florida. The end result, according to *Prison Legal News* was that

"Fields spent the next eight months in a wheelchair, a year with a walker and now walks with a spastic gait. He cannot feel the ground and requires braces for his ankles. To urinate he has to sit so he doesn't lose control of other bodily functions, and he suffers sexual dysfunction and excruciating pain."[307] He was in jail on a misdemeanor.[308]

Just as dangerous as the private companies that provide an inmate's healthcare are the private prison companies that are housing an increasing number of people in their prisons and jails. These corporations have the same mind-set as the correctional medical companies - profit over people. Therefore, any way that they can save money furthers the objective, whether it's by providing inadequate meals, underpaid and undertrained staff, or overcrowding their facilities. Each are seen as positive business practices because they each keep costs low and profits high.

As already mentioned they have an economic interest in incarcerating as many people as possible, regardless of whether they need to be incarcerated to keep society safe. Therefore, they will go to extraordinary lengths to grow their business. As Stephen Nathan, editor of the Prison Privatization Report International who is quoted in *The Economist*, puts its "Capitalism 101...[y]ou've got to expand your markets - you've got to fill your beds."[309]

In order to fill those beds, laws have to be enacted which either lengthen prison sentences for existing crimes, or criminalize activity that was previously legal or not punishable by incarceration. We've already seen how Corrections Corporation of America (CCA) and Geo Group, Inc. played a large role in numerous laws which extend sentences and criminalize immigrants. They have perfected the art of getting politicians to do their bidding.

Increasing prison populations in order to increase the profits of private prisons is no secret either. In 2008 *The Wall Street Journal* ran an article titled "Larger Inmate Population Is Boon to Private Prisons."[310] Three years later, in the depths of the greatest recession since the Great Depression and with crime rates at 45-year lows, the paper ran a second article titled "Prison Companies Are A Conviction Buy."[311] Wall Street isn't worried about lower crime rates because they understand that CCA, GEO and others can create their own "criminals" to fill however many beds they operate.

In the first article, Stephanie Chen noted that the "Federal Bureau of Prisons and several state governments have sent thousands of inmates in recent months to prisons and detention centers run by Corrections Corporation of America, Geo Group Inc. and other private operators, as a crackdown on illegal immigration, a lengthening of mandatory sentences for certain crimes and other factors have overcrowded many government facilities."[312] That was in 2008, when the crime rate had been in a steady decline for almost two decades and the number of illegal immigrants crossing the border had been greatly curtailed due to a weak economy, hundreds of miles of fences and thousands of additional National Guard soldiers patrolling the border. Yet three years later Leam Denning still considered the stocks of both CCA and GEO as a good buy because the U.S. prison population would increase by an additional 160,000 people by 2020.[313] He asked readers to "imagine a real-estate business where your tenant finds it hard to move and you provide the barest of amenities. No this isn't the world of the New York apartment landlord. It's the private prison business."[314]

That first article noted just how bare the amenities can get and just how far these corporations will go to increase profits:

> The American Civil Liberties Union has filed lawsuits involving several prison companies over the past decade alleging poor treatment of inmates. Last year [2007], the organization and other parties filed a lawsuit against Corrections Corp. and the Department of Homeland Security's Immigration and Customs Enforcement arm in federal court in San Diego, alleging that the company was operating an overcrowded, unsafe immigrant-detention center in [Los Angeles].... The suit also alleged that detainees had little access to mental health care.[315]

Jody Kent of the ACLU's National Prison Project is quoted as saying that the ACLU has "serious concerns about the for-profit prison companies because they are notorious for cutting essential costs that need to be provided to maintain a safe and constitutional environment for prisoners ."[316]

It's astonishing how easily these corporations have been able to play the American public. They lobby politicians to write laws playing on people's irrational fears (which they inflame), about non-existent crime-waves and urban myths about illegal, job-stealing immigrant hoards. These laws in turn pack the prisons with people who don't need to be there, increasing the amount of tax payer money devoted to prisons. Now, though, not only are we paying for over incarceration, but taxes are also being allocated to ensure a profit for private prison companies. This means the government has less money (unless it raises taxes) to spend on other essential services like teacher, fire-fighter, and police salaries. Which not only means less jobs available, but children being denied a decent education, and less cops on the street which prevent crime, and fewer firefighters to save people and property from fires.

When profit, rather than keeping society safe, is the true objective of incarcerating people, greed perverts the correctional system until it makes everyone less safe. This is what happened to Pennsylvania when a couple judges decided to get in on the profits.

Two Pennsylvania judges, Mark Ciavarella and Michael Conahan, were basically selling kids to private juvenile detention facilities. They were receiving kickbacks for sentencing thousands of kids to serve time in the facilities. In all, the two received about $2.8 million according to *The Wall Street Journal.*[317] Adam Graycar of the Rutger's Institute on Corruption Studies provided a breakdown of the scheme to *The Economist* which summarized it as follows:

> First the judges received monetary awards for sanctioning the building of a new private-sector prison in their area. Second, they were paid for closing a county-funded prison nearby. And, then, of course, they offered up the "juvenile delinquents" for the benefit of the owners of the new jail.[318]

So who were these "juvenile delinquents"? They included a 15-year-old who spent three months incarcerated after being denied a lawyer, on charges of constructing a phony MySpace page to make fun of her high school principal, and a 14-year-old girl who was sentenced to 9 months incarceration for slapping a friend.[319]

Though former Judge Ciavarella still sees nothing wrong in what he was doing, thankfully the federal judge that heard his case disagreed and found him guilty, sentencing him to 28 years in prison.[320] Thanks to his buddies in the private prison industry he will have to serve all 28 years,[321] since federal laws abolished parole. His partner in crime, former Judge Conahan pled guilty to racketeering conspiracy for his part in what has been called the "kids for cash" scandal and received a 17½ year federal sentence.[322]

106

Many politicians are just as crooked as the two judges named above, even if they aren't in fact breaking any laws. Not only are they unscrupulously reaping the donations to their political campaigns paid by these private prison companies, lobbyists, and other businesses who depend on mass incarceration, but they are likewise using prisoners as both a political and economic commodity.

When submitting and voting on these bills, which as we've seen are often written by the lobbyists or corporations themselves, these politicians are fully aware of the fact that these bills will take taxpayer money from the government to fatten the pockets of the bills' advocates and are not actually in the public's interest. Likewise they are also fully aware that that is where those campaign donations come from. So they are basically passing legislation in exchange for funds for their reelection campaigns.

This isn't the only way politicians use "criminals" to get reelected either. As the editors of *Solitary Watch* note, "for at least the last 30 years, politicians from both parties have been cynically exploiting public fears about crime to win elections...."[323] These constant fear-mongering, scare tactics in campaign ads are a major factor in why the public holds such irrational fears of non-existent "crime waves" and "super-predators." All of which culminates in an electorate incapable of making rational decisions about criminal justice policies, which in turn has America spending an increasingly disproportionate amount of our tax dollars on policies that are either unnecessary or ineffectual, if not downright counterproductive.

Even the rare politicians, who aren't actively profiting off of incarceration or perpetuating American's hatred of "criminals" by using tough-on-crime rhetoric to increase campaign donations and voter turnout, are too scared to speak out. As Andrew Romano noted in *Newsweek,* "politicians have developed an allergy to any reform that could get them tagged as 'soft on crime'. They're afraid of becoming Michael Dukakis."[324] When a politician does try to take on criminal justice reform, like Senator Jim Webb did, he "got a lot of advice not to talk about it."[325] It's interesting to note that Senator Webb is not running for reelection, and five years later he's still struggling just to get a bill passed that would simply establish a bipartisan panel to study the problems and make recommendations.

Elected officials in some districts are benefiting from prisoners in another way as well. Prisoners are counted by the Federal Census Bureau as residents of the prison towns where they are housed rather than in the towns where their homes were.[326] As most prisons are located in rural towns with small native populations, adding the prison population to the rural districts artificially inflates those populations. This leads to "prison-based gerrymandering - the cynical practice of drawing legislative districts with populations inflated by inmates who do not have the right to vote," according to an editorial in *The New York Times* .[327] The added bodies gives these districts increased political power and unfairly take that power away from the districts where the prisoners came from and where they'll most likely go home to and use that districts resources.[328] New York State Senator Eric Schneiderman explained that these "disenfranchised people become an undeserved source of political power for legislators who benefit from locking up more people for longer sentences."[329]

So you have numerous politicians viewing "criminals" as either an economic or political commodity, or both. They're scaring the public into voting for them by exaggerating the crime problem and promising to pass further "tough-on-crime" legislation, when really they are intent on passing the legislation against the public's interest, to increase incarceration rates to either benefit financially via campaign donations (and at the behest of the PIC) or benefit politically by obtaining undeserved political power.

Politicians and judges aren't the only government officials lacking scruples who often view prisoners as a commodity to be exploited for personal gain. Many prison administrators get rich off of kickbacks from corporations as well, all to the detriment of the prisoners in their "care". For example, the ex-director of the Illinois Department of Corrections (IDOC), Donald N. Snyder, Jr. pled guilty to accepting $50,000 in "cash kickbacks from lobbyists for vendors who held multi-million-dollar state contracts," according the *The Chicago Tribune*.[330]

Snyder accepted $30,000 from Larry Sims who worked as a lobbyist for Wexford Health Sources, and $20,000 from John J. Robinson who was a lobbyist for Addus Healthcare.[331] Between 2003 and 2007 Addus Healthcare "received more than $250 million from [Illinois] to provide healthcare to inmates."[332] Wexford Health Sources is another company that is contracted by Illinois to provide medical care to inmates in numerous state prisons - most notably the infamous supermax prison in Tamms, where a number of inmates filed lawsuits against Wexford alleging inadequate care and deliberate indifference to their medical needs. United States Attorney Patrick Fitzgerald remarked that Snyder "was forbidden from receiving cash kickbacks from anyone, much less from lobbyists representing companies doing millions of dollars in business with [the prisons]."[333]

There are also the hundreds of thousands of prison guards who view prisoners as a commodity. Prison guards have a vested interest in keeping the incarceration rate stable or growing regardless of the crime rate, because if we lock up less people we will need fewer guards to watch them. Ergo a prison guard's job security and livelihood are now dependent on continued mass incarceration.

Although this applies to guards at both private and public prisons, it is the unionized guards at the latter that benefit more from mass incarceration, and consistently push for tougher criminal laws. This creates a strange dichotomy. For the most part private prison companies are their allies, but now they are also fighting against private prisons.

Private prisons, on average, pay little more than minimum wage in order to keep down costs and increase profits. To hold down wages they also fight against their employees joining unions. Unions see private prisons as a threat to their jobs because cash-strapped states are increasingly contracting with private prisons either because politicians are beholden to the private prison companies or they are under the mistaken belief that it will save the state money.

The American Federation of State, County, and Municipal Employees (AFSCME), a union that represents thousands of prison guards put together a paper in 2011 entitled "Making a Killing: How Prison Corporations Are Profiting From Campaign Contributions and Putting Taxpayers at Risk. An in-depth look at the private prison industry: violence, escapes, cash flow and some politicians' plans to make our communities less safe and more prone to violent crime."[334] Here are a few choice excerpts:

> Every year, America's largest private prison companies - The Geo Group, Inc., Corrections Corporation of America (CCA), and the Management & Training Corporation (MTC) - pour hundreds of thousands of dollars into the campaigns of governors, state legislators, and judges in the hopes of advancing their political agenda-establishing more private prisons and reducing the number of public ones. Despite significantly higher rates of inmate-on-guard assault,

violence, and escapes in broad day light in private prisons than in public,[1] these companies' strategy of pay-to-play has proven successful. A state think tank in Ohio recently documents a <u>48 percent increase</u> in private prison inmates between the year 2000 and 2009 - leading almost 8 percent of incarcerated Americans to be housed in private prisons by the end of the decade.[2]

However, in February 2010, the Florida-based Private Corrections Working Group issued a press release stating that CCA had lost contracts for 7,594 prison beds in the previous 16 months, and could lose 3,186 by the end of the year.[3] As it became clear that some states were canceling prison contracts out of budget and safety concerns, the private prison industry became more aggressive in seeking ways to fill beds (the measure by which private prison companies gauge their profitability). A prime example of this surfaced in late 2010 when National Public Radio exposed the role of the private prison industry in crafting and passing SB1070-Arizona's controversial immigration- enforce- ment law.[4]

The Republican sweep of the mid-term elections in 2010 provided the private prison industry with new friends on the state level in Washington. The upshot is a broad network of powerful private prison companies and pro-privatization legislation and budget initiatives linked by thousands of dollars in political donations to the party in power. This year, the industry is betting on these newly-elected allies to deliver the contracts they were losing under former state leadership.

...

Dispelling the myth: What do states get when they embrace incarceration for profits, besides thousands of dollars in contributions to local campaigns and elected officials? The answer is far from what companies like The Geo Group, CCA, and MTC would have the public believe.

"Work force instability at private prisons has resulted in riots, rapes, assaults and escapes." - Report, American Civil Liberties Union[14]

In order to maintain a profitable industry, private prisons cut corners with indisputably devastating results. Private prisons routinely experience more inmate escapes and higher rates of violence due to chronically lax security and poorly trained, minimally paid staff. "The Bureau of Justice Assistance reported that private prisons experienced 49% more assaults on staff and 65%

more inmate-to-inmate assaults than public prisons."[15] The most egregious incidences of violence and disruption at private prisons demonstrate what happens when America's prisons are run to make a profit.

...

"As prison quality greatly suffers, there is little evidence that these private prisons save governments money."   - Report, In the Public Interest.[20]

Conclusion: After 25 years in business, the private prison model remains a hazard for local communities. Private prisons see higher levels of violence, rape, escapes, recidivism and inmate and staff deaths than public prisons do, yet the for-profit industry continues to thrive in almost every region of the country. In the interest of public safety and crime-reduction, it is imperative that states abandon for-profit prison companies and rely on public prisons to house the country's inmates.

1) http://www.acluohio.org/issues/CriminalJustice/PrisonsForProfit201104.pdf

2) http://www.policymattersohio.org/pdf/CellsForSale2011.pdf

3) http://www.prisonlegalnews.org/CsCjx2k5d5534w1stvd penghwvf))/5098displayListServ.aspx

4) http://www.npr.org/templates/story/story.php?storyId=1 30833741

...

14) http://www.acluohio.org/issues/CriminalJustice/PrisonsF orProfit201104.pdf

15) http://www.grassrootsleadership.org/Texas%20resources /CPJ%20Second%20Edition.pdf

...

20) http://inthepublicinterest.org/sites/default/files/Private% 20Prisons%20BackgrounderO.pdf [335]

While AFSCME is accurate in all that it pointed out about private prisons above, what they conveniently fail to mention is that AFSCME and the other unions that represent prison guards have been riding the GEO/CCA/MTC gravy train all the way to the bank for years. It's only now, when governments are in fiscal dire straits and are starting to give their prisoners to private rather than public prisons, and their private counterparts have successfully kept out the unions, that the unions now cry foul over the politics and prison conditions.

As has already been seen, the same tactics that GEO and CCA employed (through ALEC) to get anti-immigration legislation passed, were the same tactics that GEO and CCA employed (again through ALEC) to get both "Three Strikes" and "Truth-In-Sentencing" legislation passed. All of which was legislation ardently supported by the unions because more prisoners serving longer sentences means the more guards that are needed. Not to mention the accompanying increase in political power prison guards' unions gained.

Take California's prison guard union for example. The California Correctional Peace Officers Association (CCPOA) has become the "most powerful union in the state."[336] *The Economist* called Don Novey, the president of the CCPOA from 1982-2002, "the most important man in California politics that no one ever heard of."[337] By the time he left, CCPOA guards "earned around $70,000 a year and more than $100,000 with overtime," and received better pensions than teachers and nurses.[338] The CCPOA has blocked nearly all attempts to reform the California prison system in the face of harsh scrutiny and rulings by the courts.

In the 20 years of Don Novey's reign, the state built 21 new prisons, while the CCPOA sponsored or supported tough-on-crime laws including "three strikes" legislation, "that helped to fill those prisons to twice their capacity at times."[339] United States Supreme Court Justice Anthony Kennedy called the notion that the CCPOA sponsored California's "Three Strikes" law "sick".[340] Just as the private prison corporations have a financial interest in keeping people in prison, so too do prison guards unions. So for the unions to cry foul when they start getting beaten at their own game is prevarication at its finest.

The CCPOA has obstructed the release of prisoners for years, to the point where in May of 2011 the U. S. Supreme Court had to order the state to reduce the prison population by 33,630 prisoners within two years,[341] because the prisons were so overcrowded and prisoners received such poor medical care that it was resulting in preventable deaths on a weekly basis. Governors for the past two decades have been powerless when it comes to battling the CCPOA. Jason Whitlock explained in *Playboy* magazine in 2008 that although Governor Schwarzeneggar "would like to release 20,000 of the 180,000 prisoners [,i]t's unlikely he'll be able to do so, because his power-like that of the two governors who preceded him - pales in comparison with the [CCPOA, who] ... have no interest in fewer bodies to supervise."[342] He was right. Schwarzeneggar backed down. Hence the necessity of the U. S. Supreme Court's ruling.

Mr. Whitlock goes on to break down how the prison guards who need no higher education past the six-week training have a starting pay and benefits that "dwarf those of the 300,000 member California Teachers Association."[343] Some guards working overtime even pull in more than the governor's $212,000 salary.[344] Indifferent to what the waste of limited government resources does, the CCPOA rode the "three strikes" law and other tough-on-crime measures all the way to both the bank and the pinnacle of political power, and drove the state of California into the ground. While the state's corrections budget escalated from $300 million to $9 billion,[345] the educational system has been in free fall seeing thousands of teachers laid off and university tuition rates quadruple.

Calling the CCPOA's political clout "preposterous", Mr. Whitlock explains how:

> Under the direction of former Folsom prison guard Don Novey, CCPOA hired a public-relations firm in the 1980's and laid the groundwork for its use by spending millions on political candidates. Every California governor since Wilson has been in the thrall of the labor union. Sehwarzeneggar's early attempt to break the union's hold on the governor's office and reform the prison system failed.

> Rod Hickman, the black prison czar Schwarzeneggar appointed, had a two-year tenure as a reformer before he succumbed to CCPOA intimidation and stepped down as secretary of the Department of Corrections. Hickman's failure was a painful reminder of the CCPOA's formidable political strength, a shrine of power fortified in the late 1990's when the union sabotaged the reelection bid of a district attorney who dared to convene

a grand jury to examine allegations that Corcoran State Prison guards viciously pounded 36 inmates.

"CCPOA runs the prison system," explains Wanda Briscoe, the former chief of education and inmate programs for the California Department of Corrections. "Based on the fact that there is strength in numbers and money, I would think the system works very well for them. They are hiring more prison guards. I see employment opportunities every month. They want more custody, more guards. It is the most powerful union I have seen in my lifetime."

The union is so powerful, it got former governor Gray Davis to hand over raises when nearly everything else in the budget is being slashed.[347]

Think about it. Even in the face of fiscal disaster the citizens and government of California still won't overturn the "three-strikes" law due to the mix of constant hatred of "criminals", the fear-mongering employed against the public, and the political clout and campaign contributions used by the guards union which act as dog chokers strangling its politicians. So now you've got the state sentencing people to 25 years to life for stealing videos. This amounts to public extortion and a colossal waste of taxpayer money.

According to *The Economist,* "California spends $49,000 a year on each prisoner."[348] The majority of that cost goes to the salaries of staff, the majority of whom are unionized prison guards. So if, by some miracle, the videotape thief was actually paroled after 25 years - something that is almost unheard of - then the state just spent $1,225,000 to punish a man for shop-lifting a few hundred bucks worth of videos. The majority of that money was a direct transfer of funds from taxpayers, who have been irrationally terrified into acquiescence by tough-on-crime rhetoric, to the guards who not only worked to get the "three-strikes" law passed but also use their political power to punish politicians who try to challenge the status quo or to punish prosecutors who investigate criminal acts committed by guards. If that isn't a racket I don't know what is.

It's depressingly laughable that the unions will now claim that the private prison companies are unscrupulous for their political maneuverings and poor treatment of prisoners. The unions don't support any prisoner rights, and definitely don't have any problem with locking up more people for increasingly pettier offenses - unless its union members being locked up for abusing prisoners. Nor do they have a problem with anti-immigration legislation which contributes to their job security. What they have a problem with is this: if private prisons take over they'll lose their outrageously high pay, perks, and political power.

For society it matters little who runs the prisons. Once the notion that prisoners are people was replaced with prisoners are a commodity, where the major actors all have a financial interest in keeping as many people incarcerated as possible, the criminal justice system ceased being a legitimate arm of the state. Instead it is an arm of destruction, destroying people's lives and the well-being of society as a whole, just to enrich the few.

I used to roll my eyes when I would hear prisoners or others equate the prison system to a modern-day slave plantation. I thought such a comparison the result of both ignorance and exaggeration bordering on idiocy. Now though, I am beginning to understand that it was I who was ignorant. Many may have been ill-informed as to the specifics, as most people are who repeat sound bites that convey a feeling but relay few facts, but the sentiment that being a prisoner is akin to being a modern-day slave is proven out more and more each day.

As we have already seen, prisoners, like slaves, are no longer viewed as fully human, and have been reduced to little more than a commodity. It's not even unconstitutional to force prisoners into slavery, as the U. S. never actually abolished slavery.

Most people are unaware of that fact. Abolish means to do away with completely. The 13th Amendment to the U. S. Constitution didn't abolish slavery though, it only restricted it to our "criminals". Don't believe me? Read it for yourself: "Neither slavery nor involuntary servitude, <u>except as punishment for crime</u> whereof the party shall have been duly convicted, shall exist within the United States, or any place subject to their jurisdiction."[349] So basically we could criminalize any act and turn anyone who commits that "crime" into a slave as punishment.

Recently the Ninth Circuit Court of Appeals in California ruled unanimously that: "Prisoners do not have a legal entitlement to payment for their work."[350] A lawyer who also happened to be a prisoner had argued that the 19¢ per hour he was paid to water the gardens for the Federal Bureau of Prisons violated a United Nations standard requiring fair wages for inmates. The court disagreed saying that the standard isn't a treaty and therefore not binding on the U. S. The court referenced the 13th Amendment to support its ruling that inmates don't have to be paid anything.[351]

In most cases prisoners are paid pennies per hour, if they receive a wage for their work at all. Those who do receive a higher wage see most of it taken by the prison administration, government, or victims' right groups, through statutes passed as tough-on-crime measures to further punish "criminals". Even those who don't work are, as we have seen, earning money for others just by serving their sentences, such as the $90-$200 per day that their warm bodies generate for private prison companies.[352] So whether prisoners work or not they are often generating revenue for someone who is exploiting their captivity.

Writing in *WIN Magazine,* Lorenzo Jones claims that the Prison Industrial Complex "exists because the United States has a market for prisoners. Like slaves, those prisoners enable the PIC to produce what other businesses need for a lower price".[353] He has a point. Factory workers' unions a few decades ago were greatly opposed to prison industrial jobs for the same reason that they are now opposed to offshoring jobs to China - because they can't compete with what they consider the slave wages that are paid to both U. S. prisoners and the Chinese. Also just as call centers have outsourced their labor to India where people will work for pennies, New York State's Department of Motor Vehicles has prisoners working its call center for as little as 46 cents an hour, saving the state millions of dollars.[354]

Playboy magazine noted that prisoners' "dirt-cheap labor is in high demand throughout California. In some industries they're more valuable and coveted than illegal immigrants."[355] (Speaking, of course, of the illegal immigrant workers in the free community, not the ones transformed into "criminal" prisoners).

The Illinois Correctional Industries "employed" (some might say enslaved) about 1,000 inmates in 2008.[356] While it generated nearly $45 million in revenues, the inmate workers were paid just 35¢ to $1.20 per hour.[357] Inmates make garments, furniture, eye glasses, and even train service dogs.[358] The Federal Prison Industries "employed" "about 22,000 inmate workers in 2008".[359] Federal inmate workers do some jobs not found or permitted anywhere else in the United States, like disposing of computers that contain lead, mercury, and other hazardous materials.[360] Dell Computers cancelled its contract with Federal Prison Industries "days after the national media reported on an environmental group's charge that the prison operation was a 'poor example of worker health and safety'," according to *Fortune* magazine in 2003.[361] *Fortune* said around 10,000 prisoners are employed by some 250 private companies,[362] and "computer recycling is difficult, labor - intensive work - exactly the type now being exported to China and other bastions of cheap labor."[363]

So now we see that prisoners have not only been dehumanized, but effectively commoditized, either economically, politically, or both. In some cases they are viewed as little more than chattel. All of this is only possible because of societal indoctrinization that "criminals" are evil and irredeemable.

5
FAMILY

Those who commit a crime aren't the only ones to feel society's wrath. The stigma and exploitation also extend to their families. Family members feel a shame and humiliation that often leads to a breakdown in interfamilial relations. As Jason Whitlock writes in *Playboy,* a prisoner "does not suffer the anguish of internment alone. Every person who loves him suffers too and is afflicted with the cancers of hostility and bitterness".[364]

Many times the person sent to jail or prison is the sole provider for the family, pushing the family into poverty and onto welfare. Even when they aren't the sole provider it can still create serious financial hardships on that person's family. When they are a partial provider it takes income away from the family and can cause serious expenses for the family such as the cost of hiring a lawyer. If they were paying child support this will obviously be interrupted. Even if they provided nothing to the family, someone who was at least financially self-sufficient now becomes a financial burden on the family.

Society's hatred and demonization of "criminals", prisoners in particular, has made exploitation of their family members acceptable as well. The fact that the majority of prisoners and their families come from the poorest neighborhoods doesn't stop state governments and corporations from imposing what could be called "genetic criminality taxes" on prisoners' families. A "genetic criminality tax" basically extorts a prisoner's family member because they're related to a "criminal". The leverage they use is contact. Basically if you want any contact with your loved one in prison you have to pay some outrageous fee.

Prisoners basically have three means of maintaining contact with family members - letters (and sometimes emails), phone calls, and visits. With prison jobs scarce, and wages for the few that are available at or near slave wages, prisoners are more often than not dependent on their family to support them financially.

Unless they are one of the few given access to emails, prisoners must have paper, envelopes, and postage if they want to correspond with their loved ones. Few prisons still allow prisoners to have any of these items mailed in to them by their family. Instead they ban this and force prisoners to purchase each, as well as other necessities like hygiene items, clothes, and snacks, from a commissary or canteen.

In order to do so a prisoner must have the money to purchase these items. Most prisons don't permit prisoners to receive money on visits or through any other means than by having it sent in and credited to their inmate trust fund account. Some prisons still permit money orders to be sent in the mail which will only cost the loved one the buck or two to purchase the money orders. Increasingly though, prisoners' families must use Western Union or JPay, both of which charge exorbitant fees to wire money. These types of companies also have agreements with many state correctional departments that add an additional fee that is kicked back to the state or correctional agency. So, in Illinois, for instance, if you want to wire you're loved one $20.00 you will have to pay JPay either $4.95 via online or $5.95 by phone using a credit card.[365] Either way the IDOC will receive a kickback. Or you can send a money order or cashier's check via snail mail, but this is much more risky, as the mail is often delayed for weeks or lost altogether.

Many states also take a portion of any money a prisoner receives to pay for things like costs of incarceration or restitution. Therefore the prisoner's family is being forced to pay back society for their loved ones crime or punishment. In some states these deductions can be 50% or higher.

When the prisoner does get whatever is left into their account and is able to purchase items from the prison canteen or commissary, they are usually forced to pay exorbitant prices for low quality products. Many of the products sold are designed to fail soon after purchase in order to insure repeat purchases. Commissary companies obtain exclusive contracts with states' correctional departments for each prison and thus a monopoly over captive consumers.

As if this weren't bad enough many states' correctional departments will then go one step further and place additional surcharges on the items to raise more revenue, increasing the purchase price and decreasing the purchasing power of the prisoner's money. Even worse is when state correctional departments, such as the IDOC, violate their own state statute and exceed the surcharge allowed and force prisoners to pay unlawful surcharges as well.[366]

When a prisoner does finally obtain the paper, envelopes, and postage to write home, many prisons stamp the outside of the letter with a large stamp that reads "Correspondence from a Prisoner" in red ink which embarrasses the prisoner's family. Often it's enough to cause family members to break off contact completely or ask the prisoner not to write because they don't want the neighbors or postman to see it.

The most commonly used means of maintaining contact with ones' family while in prison is the telephone. Especially considering the high rate of illiteracy among prisoners. Unfortunately family members are routinely extorted as a prerequisite to having this option of communication available. Or as the *examiner.com* called it - "a scam" where family members are basically told: "Give me your money and you can talk to your kid."[367] Actually it's more accurate to say "accede to our outrageously exorbitant prices or you can't talk to your kid." *Examiner.com's* corrections policy examiner Michail Hamden breaks down the scam as follows:

Correctional agencies request bids for prison phone services. They are not looking for the least expensive bid or the best possible service. Instead, they choose between offers of payment from the telephone companies. These payments, known in the industry as "commissions", are promised in exchange for the exclusive right to provide telephone services. Monopolies often engage in abusive practices, and that is the case here. Rates are as much as 5 times higher than the cost of a payphone call outside prison, and the cost of the exploitation is borne by families that are among the least able to afford it.[368]

Prison Legal News calls these "commissions" by a more accurate name - kickbacks.[369] In a report released in April of 2011 Prison Legal News found that 42 states accept kickbacks from prison phone companies, and that they "average 42% of gross revenue."[370] Nationwide in 2007- 2008 alone prisoner's families shelled out $152 million just to cover the kickbacks alone. A few states, acknowledging how cold-hearted these kickbacks are, decided to ban them or at least adopt lower kickbacks. When New York and California banned them, the prison phone rates declined 69% and 61% respectively.[371] When Montana agreed to lower kickbacks, rates dropped by 64.5%.[372]

The price of a fifteen-minute, interstate collect call from state prisons can therefore vary widely depending on whether the state the

129

prison is in accepts kickbacks, and how greedy the correctional agency and telephone company are. For instance, calls from Missouri state prisons will only cost $2.50,[373] because Missouri doesn't accept kickbacks.[374] While if the call comes from Washington, the kickback king, it will cost $17.41.[375]

As *Prison Legal News'* editor Paul Wright noted, "This is gross profiteering at its worst. State officials are lining their pockets to the tune of tens of millions of dollars, by fleecing prisoners' families with exorbitant rates. Why? Simply because they can."[376] We already know why they can. It's because America's hatred of "criminals" is so single-minded that there is a disconnect from reality. Society can no longer even view a prisoner's family members as innocent. Now they must be punished too. So they become victims to be exploited by the PIC as well.

In 2009 Texas became the last state to allow prisoners to make telephone calls. The state, victim's rights groups, and Embarq, the company contracted to run the phone and email systems, were all disappointed because they were only able to collect $15 million from overcharging prisoners' families 44 cents per page for an email and charging prisoners nearly $6 for an out-of-state phone call - an amount more than half of prisoners don't even possess.[377] They're now reviewing ways to increase profits (i.e. how to further exploit both prisoners and their families).

In Washington, before a prisoner can even say "hello" to his or her family they're already charged nearly five dollars as a connection fee.[378] The kickbacks paid to correctional agencies, while on average represent 42% of revenue generated,[379] can be as high as 65% in some states.[380] As if the kickbacks weren't enough of a kick in the face, *examiner.com* details what else is in store for the prisoner's family members:

> The prison pay-phone companies have developed unethical practices that include: "service/set up" fees (charged to customers setting up a required pre-paid account for the first time); "recharge fees" (billed when a customer reopens an account); "process fees" - imposed either by a service provider or a third party business - for processing a customer's payment; the confiscation of sums remaining in an account after a specified period of inactivity (3-6 months); and bogus security measures like "3-way call detection" which can be used to improperly but purposely disconnect calls to increase per-call costs and overall revenue.[381]

This last one is especially sinister. In Florida, the Public Utilities Staff found that it was deliberately and illegally used to bilk consumers out of $6.3 million.

Society's hatred for prisoners has allowed all of these deductions, fees, surcharges, etc. to be imposed on the money sent to and spent by prisoners, and money spent by prisoners' families to maintain contact with their loved ones, because nobody cares if prisoners are treated arbitrarily. This unnecessarily increases the financial burden on the prisoners' families unjustly, which also contributes to the already present animosity they feel due to their loved one not being there and can cause permanent damage to familial relationships. This has adverse consequences for the rest of society as well because, other than education, nothing contributes to lower recidivism rates more than strong family support.[382]

Often what's more expensive for the family than phone calls and stationery for correspondence, are the visits to the prison. Prisons are usually located great distances away from cities where the majority of people live. This means that, more often than not, a visit costs hundreds or even thousands of dollars. In-state visits often mean driving over 200 miles round trip, often necessitating not only a tank of gas, but also a stay in a motel. Even worse is if your loved one is in a Federal prison. They could be anywhere in the federal prison system. One family spent nearly $4,000 just to visit their loved one due to the cost of airline tickets, lodging, food, and other expenses.[383] In 2011, Arizona prisons began charging people a $25 background check fee to visit their friends and family in state prisons regardless of the fact that background checks don't cost the Arizona Department of Corrections any money to obtain.[384]

The most vulnerable and most severely affected family members are the children of prisoners. Societal disdain for prisoners results in most prisoners' children either being lied to about where their parent(s) is/are or themselves lying about the reason behind the parent's absence.

There are numerous reasons why children sometimes aren't told that their parent is in prison. Sometimes it is to save the child from having to explain their parent's absence to friends and others. Sometimes it's to prevent the parent from being diminished in the eyes of the child. Sometimes it's the parent's or family's discomfort with the task of explaining to the child why the parent is in prison. All of these though, find their root in the shame associated with being a prisoner or having a prisoner in the family. Whatever the reason, the result is usually the same - no visits or physical contact between parent and child, and often feelings of betrayal when the child eventually learns that they have been lied to by the family for months or years on end.

On the other hand, when children are told it allows for a closer relationship between parent and child, but the societal stigma of a person being in prison causes deep embarrassment for the child. The shame of having a parent in prison or jail often results in the child fabricating stories about the parent's absence -for instance, he/she is in the military at war, dead, etc. Such fictions are getting harder to get away with though when every prisoner is easily located on the correctional department's website, even if the person escaped becoming fodder for the local media before and during trial.

More rare is when a child is told the truth about the parent and in turn tells the truth to their friends and others. When that's the case, they themselves become vulnerable to the ridicule and alienation that kids are so readily willing to dish out. Kids mimic the rest of society's feelings towards "criminals" and thus it can affect the social standing or relationships of the prisoner's child.

In any of these scenarios the child suffers in one form or more. The number of children experiencing these situations is not insignificant. Just as the U.S. incarcerates a higher percentage of its population than any other country, one can assume a higher percentage of America's children have a parent locked up. All told 2.7 million children have a parent in either prison or jail.[385] More than 10% of African-American children have at least one parent who is incarcerated,[386] and over half of all state and federal prisoners report having kids who are minors.[387] Three-fourths of all women in prison have children under the age of 18.[388]

Even when a child is aware of their parent's incarceration, the locations of prisons make seeing them problematic. Fathers are, on average, located 100 miles from their children.[389] Since there are fewer women's prisons mothers are even further - 160 miles on average.[390] Distance, added to concealment of the fact that the parent is incarcerated results in more than half of incarcerated parents never having a visit with their child,[391] and only about 20% visit as often as once per month.[392]

Besides the absence of face to face contact between children and their incarcerated parents, the absence of the parent from the home can completely uproot the child and alter their life's course by affecting their behavior. The Osborne Institute found that having a parent incarcerated can result in behavioral problems like truancy, drug abuse, and early pregnancy.[393] Not having a father in the home for whatever reason means kids are five times more likely to suffer from poverty; become involved in drugs and alcohol; drop out of school; suffer emotional and health problems; get involved in crime; get pregnant; or become a teen father.[394]

These "prison orphans" are also either "six times more likely than their peers to end up in prison themselves", according the *The Economist*[395], or are "seven times more likely to be incarcerated if a parent has been in prison", according to Debbie Denning the Illinois Department of Corrections acting chief of programs and support services.[395] So not only are prisons failing to rehabilitate prisoners and prevent recidivism, but mass incarceration is also contributing to the next generation of prisoners and obviously failing to "scare straight" the children of prisoners. Another scary statistic relative to future criminal activity is the fact that 23% of kids with a father locked up are expelled or suspended from school compared to 4% of kids overall.[397] Less education is an indicator of higher likelihood of both criminality and future imprisonment.

While losing a father to prison is horrific, it more often than not means the child remaining with the mother. Overall about 80% of children live with the other parent when one is incarcerated. About 20% end up living with grandparents or other relatives, and 2% end up in foster home or other public institution.[398] Kids with a mother incarcerated are four times more likely to end up living with grandparents than kids who have a father incarcerated (53% v. 13%); and five times more likely to live with other relatives (26% v. 5%), or in foster care (10% v. 2%).[399] Altogether, mothers reported that 89% of the time their children were living somewhere other than with the father.[400] Incarcerating so many parents also means that more than 50,000 kids are pushed into the foster care system, costing taxpayers a billion dollars annually. [401]

6

JAILS and PRISONS

Prisoners feel society's hatred magnified at every turn in prison, and as we'll see later, equally so once released. Rachel Kamel and Bonnie Kerness of the American Friends Service Committee in Philadelphia note "U. S. prisons seem increasingly bent on denying and destroying the dignity and the very humanity of all who fall within their grasp."[402] This helps explain why, as Senator Jim Webb says: "Once a kid is incarcerated, that's it for him."[403] When a man or woman goes through years or decades of being degraded, hated, dehumanized, and told that they are unwanted by society, is it any wonder that they become dejected and no longer see re-entering society as a possibility?

As we've already seen, prisoners are despised across the country. This visceral hatred contributes to not only the exploitation of prisoners (and their families), but also the maltreatment of prisoners in a number of ways. Whether it's Sheriff Joe Arpaio in Arizona who gets his kicks by dressing male inmates in pink underwear to humiliate them,[404] or women inmates in Chicago being forced to give birth while in handcuffs and shackles,[405] it is perpetrated by people who believe the public supports what they are doing.

Joe Arpaio's approval ratings are always high, and of his harsh treatment of prisoners he'll tell you, "[v]oters like it everywhere. I'm on thousands of talk shows. I never get a negative."[406] One governor, William Weld from Massachusetts said prison life should be "akin to a walk through hell."[407] And so it has been for far too many in America.

Rehabilitation is largely a thing of the past in U.S. prisons. Instead the aim is merely to punish and warehouse society's undesirables. In the book *American Furies* Sasha Abramsky detailed how rehabilitation fell out of favor, and the crucial role that Robert Martinson and the media played.[408] Reviewing the book for *The Nation* Daniel Lazare summed it up as follows:

> Berkeley - educated sociologist... Robert Martinson, who, after several years investigating programs offered at the time by the New York State prison system summed up his findings in a sensational 1974 article titled "What Works?" His answer: nothing.... his conclusions, published in the neoconservative journal Public Interest, were grossly one-sided....
>
> In short order, Martinson's article became the bible of the vengeance - and - punishment set, which seized on it as proof that rehabilitation was a lost cause and that the only purpose of prison was to penalize wrongdoers. Once this ideological impediment was removed, the

criminal-justice system slid downhill with remarkable speed. If punishment was good, then more punishment was better....[409]

Amazing how much a single article can do, eh? Yet when a conscience- stricken Martinson published a mea culpa in the Hofstra Law Review five years later ("contrary to my previous position, some treatment programs do have an appreciable effect on recidivism"), the media yawned. No big shots interviewed him on TV, and no politicians called to solicit his views. No one wanted to hear that rehabilitation programs work, only that they don't. Beset by personal troubles, professional setbacks and perhaps the realization of how grievously he had allowed himself to be misused, Martinson committed suicide by throwing himself out of a ninth-floor Manhattan apartment in 1980.[410]

In a country where three-quarters of the population claims to be Christian, it is telling how easily we have abandoned the goal of rehabilitation and will offer no forgiveness to "criminals" by assisting and welcoming them back into society. Of course, there are some that believe that while counterintuitive, it is our Christian heritage that has allowed us to dehumanize people who commit a crime. Director of the Prison Studies Project at Harvard University, Kaia Stern writes in *Fellowship Magazine* that:

Our prison system is rife with theological hypocrisy. The refusal to allow people who have committed crimes the opportunity to hope and work for genuine transformation is to deny them the very possibility for redemption that is so exalted in traditional Christian theology.

Yet our current policies, influenced by religious values, suggest that people who commit crimes are beyond forgiveness, beyond reformation, and may even be evil. As if theology itself is imprisoned, our crisis reveals profound alienation at every level - alienation from ourselves (which often creates pathways of crime), alienation from community, (evidenced in the unprecedented "re-entry" crisis), and spiritual alienation in which traditional theology is at odds with itself.

We ourselves, are captive to a spirit of punishment embedded in religious ideology....Our zeal to punish is part of a legacy - a religious ideology that assumes violence is redemptive and posits the one who has transgressed, as one exiled from God and therefore not fully human or eligible for the rights we automatically grant those we do count human.[411]

Anne-Marie Cusac, author of the book *Cruel and Unusual* also believes that our "culture of punishment" has grown from Christian roots. [412]

Whether our love affair with retribution and dehumanization is due to religious ideology or indoctrination by political rhetoric ("tough-on-crime"), or a combination of a variety of factors, one thing is certain - as a society we now see "criminals" as inhuman, or even "evil", and undeserving of forgiveness and redemption, and incapable of rehabilitation. Therefore we believe it a waste of money, resources, and effort to rehabilitate the "animals".

All of this, of course, ignores the fact that people do change, aren't born evil, and can become productive, law-abiding citizens; and if they aren't rehabilitated the majority will in fact commit another crime or crimes which will cost society more money in the long run. More importantly, more people will end up being victimized - murdered, robbed, etc. To save society money and heartache four types of rehabilitation programs are effective but are decreasingly offered to prisoners - drug treatment programs, educational courses, vocational courses, and counseling.

As already stated, we now lock up hundreds of thousands of drug addicts and mentally ill people each year instead of treating their addictions or illnesses. Once in prison few of these people have access to any drug treatment programs or mental health treatment. What they do have access to is drugs. Guards smuggle in drugs to nearly every prison and jail in the country as a way to supplement their income, get sexual favors, or due to fear of or manipulation by prisoners.

Inmates also smuggle in and/or sell drugs in prison to either support their own addictions or to earn an income because there are so few opportunities, if any, to do so legally in prison. Mentally ill prisoners without legitimate treatment for their illness find escape or relief in illegal drugs. For whatever reason, all these people who remain addicted, or pick up addictions, while in prison will also be addicts on the day they are released. This increases their likelihood of recidivating for the obvious reason that drug addicts have a hard time keeping stable employment and resort to crime to support their addiction. Not to mention "ex-cons" have an incredibly difficult time convincing anyone to hire them.

There is universal agreement in the correctional industry and academia that the most effective way to reduce recidivism is through education and/or vocational training. Dozens, perhaps hundreds, of studies have shown how effective education can be in getting people to quit a life of crime. A college education has been the most successful. In Maryland they looked at the recidivism rates of the over 19,000 prisoners released from general population and found that nearly half (46%) returned to prison within three years, but out of the 120 who left prison after having received a college degree while inside, not a single one returned.[413] James Gilligan, a psychiatrist and former director of mental health in Massachusetts' prison system, found similar results when looking at the issue there. He reported that "[w]hile several programs had worked, the most successful of all, and the only one that had been 100 percent effective in preventing recidivism, was the program that allowed inmates to receive a college degree while in prison. Several hundred prisoners in Massachusetts had completed at least a bachelor's degree while in prison over a 25-year period, and not one had been returned to prison for a new crime."[414]

Yet in a frenzy of tough-on-crime rhetoric in 1994 the federal government, at the insistence of a public which felt prisoners don't deserve an education, stripped Pell Grant eligibility for all prisoners, decimating prison college programs across the country. According to a policy brief by The Education from the Inside Out Coalition:

> The 1994 elimination of eligibility for Pell Grants for the incarcerated was a severe blow to post-secondary correctional education programs. Without funding, community colleges, colleges and universities withdrew from the correctional education market. According to a 1997 study, within three years of the ban's enactment, the number of prison higher education programs dropped from 350 to 8 nationally. In 2004, a nationwide survey of prison systems found that postsecondary correctional education was available only to about five percent of the over-all prison population.[415]

So the only proven method of preventing "criminals" from returning to crime that had near-perfect results was largely abandoned. It seems as a society we're not as worried about people continuing a life of crime as we claim. Or at least not as much as we enjoy punishing people. We seemingly want them to continue. Then we take an inordinate amount of joy in self-righteously hating "criminals," and conniving to pass harsher sentencing laws, conjuring up new ways to punish and alienate them.

It's not just college programs going the way of the dodo either, rather all educational and vocational programs are being cut. All of these programs reduce recidivism, so without them more people will commit crimes when released from prison than would have. According to *The Wall Street Journal* "only 6% of prisoners were enrolled in vocational or academic postsecondary programs during the 2009-2010 school year. Of those who were enrolled, 86% were serving time in 13 states, suggesting other states provide little access to inmate education."[416] This is unfortunate as according to the Federal Bureau of Prisons, recidivism rates among federal prisoners who participated in vocational and apprentice training were 33% lower.[417]

One state that still offers a few college and vocational courses is Illinois. For how long though is unknown, as they are disappearing at an alarming rate. In April of 2010, the John Howard Association (JHA) of Illinois released a report about their findings after conducting a "Monitoring Tour of Menard Correctional Center"[418], which happens to be the title of the report. Written by Robert Manor, the JHA found:

"[a]lmost no educational programs for inmates"; simply that "[m]aximum security inmates at Menard are warehoused"; and that, although "[p]rison management says it would like to offer programs,... [the] state's financial crisis prevents them from doing so." It further noted that "Menard's maximum security inmates are not alone in having virtually no access to programs. The same situation holds true at Pontiac, Stateville, and Tamms correctional centers."

As the "Executive Summary" of another JHA report written by Mr. Manor, entitled "Cuts in Prison Education Put Illinois at Risk" (2010),[419] states "[f]or much of the past decade, Illinois has allowed its prison vocational and academic programs to wither away", and now the pace of "the diminishment of Illinois college-based prison education programs" is accelerating. The full report found an almost 30% reduction between 2002 and 2009 alone, and that there are now less than 100 vocational programs left in all of Illinois' prisons. It also found no benefit in cutting these programs because, although they cost the state $9.8 million per year, they actually save the state $10.4 million per year.[420]

The fact that educational and vocational programs are diminishing in Illinois and that this poses a threat to society shouldn't be a surprise. As far back as a decade ago the papers were reporting on it. On Dec. 12, 2001 Susan Dodge wrote an article for *The Chicago Sun-Times* titled "Budget Ax Hits Prison Education". [421] She reported that "[g]raduates of Roosevelt University's program in the [Illinois] Department of

Corrections have a 4.6 percent recidivism rate, compared with the state's overall recidivism rate of 46 percent." Five years later AFSCME, the union to which Illinois prison guards belong to, surprisingly released a report titled "Failing Grade: The Decline In Educational Opportunities For Illinois Inmates,"[422] as part of their "Campaign For Responsible Priorities." It cited similar benefits in the "life skills reentry educational programs". Participants not only had a markedly lower recidivism rate (14% compared to 52%), but 65% also found gainful employment upon release.

None of this helped to stop the withering of these programs. In the face of the tsunami of prisoners coming into the IDOC, the JHA found in 2011 that even though appropriations had increased to the IDOC more than 60% since 1995 alone, "there are still not enough resources to staff educational and vocational programs that help inmates get jobs and stay out of prison."[423]

So we know education has proven to be the best tool for returning people to useful citizenship, and we know educational programs actually save more money than they cost. We also know that the Illinois government claims that returning people to useful citizenship is one of Illinois' overriding objectives in incarcerating people. The state constitution is unequivocal: "all penalties shall be determined both according to the seriousness of the offense and with the objective of restoring the offender to useful citizenship."[424] The Illinois Code of Corrections is equally clear: "The purposes of this Code of Corrections are to: (a) prescribe sanctions proportionate to the seriousness of the offenses and permit the recognition of differences in rehabilitation possibilities among individual offenders;... and (d) restore offenders to useful citizenship."[425] Yet Illinoisans actively deny the needed funds to achieve this goal, shutting down programs, even in the face of proof that doing so will make society less safe and deny the state greater savings in the long run. All seemingly to satisfy their hatred of "criminals" and illogically ensuring that most of them remain "criminals" by returning to society to commit other crimes.

Most states are the same way. Take Alabama as another example. The Alabama State Board of Education found that "[c]orrectional education appears to be the number one factor in reducing recidivism rates nationwide."[426] *Prison Connections* reported in 1997 that in "Alabama the general prison population recidivism rate in any given 12 month period averages 35% as compared to 1% for inmates who completed post secondary degrees in prison."[427] Yet when the rare warden focuses on rehabilitation to help inmates re-enter society (and thereby prevent crime) "[s]ome Alabamians complained that taxpayers' money should not be wasted on educating criminals", according to *The Economist.*[428]

American society clearly could not care less that most inmates are either completely or functionally illiterate,[429] thus have few opportunities for employment upon release, and therefore must resort to crime to survive. Of course, keeping inmates illiterate also cuts down on the number of letters home and increases the need to use the phone where their families can be extorted with unconscionable phone rates. Not to mention, keeping them illiterate and recidivating keeps the beds filled, thereby providing profits to the private prison companies and job security for correctional employees.

7

PLRA

With society so anti-prisoner, prisons have very little public oversight to protect the rights of prisoners and ensure that they aren't abused by their keepers. As we'll see below, prisoners have few ways to peacefully protest ill treatment. Prison administrators specifically design rules to prevent peaceful protest. The only avenue for relief for prisoners used to be the courts, but Congress has legislated away most prisoners' access to the courts with the Prison Litigation Reform Act (PLRA).

The Center for Constitutional Rights and The National Lawyers Guild correctly note that the PLRA is "an anti-prisoners statute which became law in 1996, [and] has made it much harder for prisoners to gain relief in federal courts."[430] The PLRA:

1 "[L]imits the 'injunctive relief ...that is available in prison cases."[431]

2 Prohibits prisoners from bringing suit unless the prisoner has first exhausted all remedies available to him in the prison system.[432] This has prompted prisons to enact

Byzantine grievance procedures and short filing deadlines to make it all but impossible for prisoners (who are more often than not functionally illiterate) to be able to timely and correctly exhaust their institutional remedies in order to sue in court to protect his or her rights.

3   Prohibits any prisoner from suing for "mental or emotional injury suffered while in custody without a prior showing of physical injury."[433] This means that no matter if the guards isolate you naked for days, don't let you sleep, and lie to you telling you your family all died in a plane crash, you can't sue because you weren't physically hurt (even though this violates numerous international treaties).

4   "[L]imits the court's ability to make the prison officials [that prisoners] sue pay for 'attorneys fees' if" the prisoner wins the case.[434] As Rhonda Brownstein notes in the preface to the book *Protecting Your Health & Safety: A Litigation Guide For Inmates,* by reducing "the amount of attorney's fees that can be collected in successful cases, many private attorneys are no longer able or willing to file prison cases. As a result many prisoners have had to litigate their claims without the benefit of counsel. The results have been far too

predictable. When powerless people confront a mammoth system without the tools necessary to protect their interests, they usually fail to obtain relief. Statistics show that the majority of pro se prisoner petitions are dismissed, usually on procedural grounds. Given the widespread problems in facilities and penal systems all over the country, the dismissal of so many pro se cases reflects the fact that most prisoners cannot protect their rights without legal assistance."[435]

5   "[A]llows for courts to dismiss a prisoner's case very soon after filing if the judge decides the case is 'frivolous', 'malicious', does not state a claim, or seeks damages from a defendant with immunity... without requiring the defendant to reply to [the] complaint."[436] Therefore prisoners who have trouble expressing themselves, articulating which of their rights were violated, etc. may have their suit dismissed even though they had meritorious claims.

6   It requires all prisoners, even those who are indigent, to pay the $450.00 filing fee, and if the prisoner has three suits dismissed as "frivolous", etc. they must pay the fee up front in order to file the suit unless his or her life is in danger.[437]

Many prisoners, when they feel they can't find any recourse in the legal system for the injustices perpetrated against them feel that their only recourse is to resort to violence. Though the government may have saved money by unjustly keeping the prisoner from obtaining monetary relief for the violation of his or her rights in the courts, the tax-payers will see a far greater expense when that inmate assaults the staff member who violated their rights. Not only will the lockdown of the prison and investigation cost money, so will compensating the victim, prosecuting the prisoner, and paying for his or her additional incarceration. Furthermore, when guards no longer have to worry about being taken to court for abusing prisoners it gives them free reign and engenders a cycle of violence and retaliation.

Society will then shake its collective head at the "evil" "criminals" that just refuse to act civilized. It will never consider that the prisoner may have acted out of frustration over having his or her rights repeatedly violated and being constantly degraded and victimized. That's because society doesn't allow for the fact that prisoners can be victims too.

Most "criminals"/prisoners have also been victims of crimes (a quarter of all women prisoners were sexually abused[438]), not to mention victims of the abuse they take from police and prison guards. Yet no victims' rights groups or victims' rights laws ever recognize them as victims. (As we've already seen, if you've ever committed a crime you are disqualified from Florida's wrongful conviction compensation statute). This is just one more way society marginalizes "criminals". Studies show that the overwhelming majority of prisoners have been the victims of violence, yet you'll never see state victims compensation funds spent on, or victim's rights group fight for, treatment for prisoners.

When courts won't ensure the fair treatment of prisoners it also encourages prison administrators to cut costs in drastic ways that are indifferent to the consequences for inmates. Add this to the fact that legislatures fail to allocate sufficient funds to pay for the expense of mass incarceration after decades of tough-on-crime sentencing laws and it leads to poor living conditions and overcrowding, which contributes to an agitated prison population, which in turn leads to increased staff assaults, inmate-on-inmate assaults, or general rioting.

That was the case in August of 2009 when Chino Prison in California, which was holding twice the 3,000 prisoners it was built to house, "exploded in violence that took close to twelve hours to contain, leaving 250 prisoners injured, seven housing units damaged, and a prison dormitory burned down", according to *The Progressive.*[439] "Officials estimate repairs will run as high as $6 million", the article states, and "the root causes are inhumane prison conditions and inadequate resources."[440] *The Economist* the same week noted that the "riot...was not the first and won't be the last in California's dreadful prison system", and that Chino had the "same degree of overcrowding that plagues California's 33 prisons as a whole."[441]

Almost two years later the U. S. Supreme Court finally stepped in to address the state's overcrowded and inhumane prison system. A step that is incredibly rare after the passage of the PLRA. On May 23, 2011 the court ordered the state to reduce overcrowding which is partly responsible for the fact "that preventable suicide and medical neglect 'needlessly' cause the death of at least one inmate a week in California's prisons", reported *The Wall Street Journal*.[442]

Censorship

Prisoners are censored in numerous ways. What they write, say, read, watch, and even what style of haircut they can sport, all must make it past the monitors. Every letter going in or coming out of prison that isn't legal mail or privileged - i. e. going to a lawyer, legislator, etc. - is read by prison mailroom and gang intel staff.

All movies shown must pass monitors, which in some prisons amounts to the morality police because it is often a chaplain. Some states prohibit inmates from receiving anything downloaded off the internet, and some prohibit inmates from posting anything online. South Carolina is even trying to criminalize prisoners setting up an account on Facebook, which recently declared it will no longer allow prisoners to have an account anyway.[443] Indiana's Department of Corrections has banned inmates from placing any ads for pen-pals,[444] joining Florida and other states. Also prisoners in 48 out of 50 states are politically censored by being denied the right to vote. Most prisons also ban posting or passing petitions and assembling in groups as well.

Some of the most outrageous censorship though, comes in the form of banning books from entering prison. While there are legitimate penological purposes for banning books on how to escape, commit crimes, make weapons, etc., many of the bans are just illogical and done for punitive reasons.

Numerous literary classics have been banned from prisons. Virginia has banned, among others, *Ulysses* by James Joyce, *Lady Chatterley's Lover* by D. H. Lawrence, *Wars of the World* by Niall Ferguson, and even *The Autobiography of Malcolm X*.[445] Adam Serwer notes on *prospect.org* that Virginia also banned erotic fiction "under a seemingly arbitrary rule that nevertheless allows the inmates to possess nude photographs - - as long as they are of people of the opposite sex."[446] Banning pictures of the same sex in prison seems particularly pointless when one considers the fact that inmates are forced to shower with large groups of naked people of the same sex. The Virginia Department of Corrections (VDOC) banned an article written by Mr. Serwer because the accompanying picture showed a gang tattoo on one of the men.[447] Are they really trying to say that if inmates see this picture it would constitute a threat to security? If so then what about the thousands of prisoners walking around the VDOC with gang tattoos that prisoners see on a daily basis?

In Texas, prison administrator's barred *Texas Tough,* a book written by Professor Robert Perkins. Their reason - because he included a short passage about a girl's childhood molestation, in a section "about how a huge portion of prisoners were abused themselves." [448] Texas has a history of banning books that deal with the prison environment, and not just those written by prisoners, but also if written by guards or wardens. I guess Texas prisoners are allowed to live prison life, but not read about it. They're also not allowed to see drawings of a woman's breast, even if they are the ones who drew it. According to www.statesman.com the Texas Department of Criminal Justice banned *Prison Coffee Table Book Project* because it included "a drawing of a naked breast."[450] All the artwork included in it was created by prisoners.

By far the most devious censorship comes in the form of prisons banning publications that teach prisoners how to protect their rights. This is a constant problem for the publishers of *Prison Legal News* which reports on prison issues and related litigation nationwide, and is also "a nonprofit organization which advocates for prisoner rights."[451] *Prison Legal News* has challenged censorship of its publications in more than 21 states.[452] As Mr. Serwer noted though, this is rare, as most publishers couldn't care less about prisoners not being able to receive their publications.[453]

One other publication that VDOC banned and was challenged by its publishers was the book *Jailhouse Lawyer's Handbook; How to Bring a Federal Lawsuit to Challenge Violations of Your Rights in Prison.*

According to the Associated Press in 2010, "officials claimed the book was a danger to prison security or 'good order'."[454] As one of its authors, Rachel Meeropol, is quoted as saying; "If it is dangerous to educate people about the Constitution, there are a lot of law schools who are going to be in trouble."[455] I guess the prison administrators see things differently. They seem to view the issue much like slavemaster's views on educating slaves - that it should be prohibited completely if not punishable by death.

In a rare victory for prisoners, the publishers of the *Jailhouse Lawyer's Handbook* - the Center for Constitutional Rights and the National Lawyers Guild - sued the VDOC "and won a settlement requiring a number of things, such as making sure the *Handbook* was in the law library of every prison in Virginia."[456] The vast majority of the time though, when the publications sent to prisoners are arbitrarily banned, the prisoner lacks the legal knowledge (or even literacy) to successfully challenge the ban or to navigate the legal maze of the court system to sue. Instead the prisoner recognizes the injustice, and becomes angry at the administration for the obvious violation of his or her constitutional rights. Moreover, when they can't challenge it in the courts, they also feel frustration over their lack of education or inability to do anything about this injustice. Some will resort to violence and all who can't challenge it will take yet another blow to their self-esteem.

Food

Violating inmates' few remaining rights isn't the only contributor to violence in prison that can be attributed to prison staff or administration. There are many things that prisons can do to reduce violence, which if aren't done, contribute to violence. One of the easiest, but rarely ever done, is to feed prisoners a truly nutritious and well-balanced diet. While the courts routinely rule that any prison diet is constitutionally adequate as long as the caloric and nutrient make up is sufficient to survive on, rarely is the food being served truly nutritious or well-balanced, and rarer still is it ever appetizing.

Sheriff Joe Arpaio has no shame in telling people that the food he serves to his prisoners costs less than what he feeds his cats and dogs.[457] This helps to explain in part why even a federal district judge found Arpaio "inflicted 'needless suffering' on prisoners through inadequate medical care, unhealthful food, and unsanitary living conditions", according to the magazine *The Week*.[458]

One of the five core demands of the 7,000 California prisoners who went on a hunger strike for nearly a month in 2011 was for adequate and nutritious food. [459] This has been a problem for decades. According to *The Chicago Tribune*, over 2,000 inmates in Cook County Jail protested by refusing to eat lunch to protest a lack of variety in lunch meals.[460] Some of the country's worst prison riots were over food. [461] Few prisons or jails spend more than a dollar per meal to feed prisoners.[462] Most meals consist of "meat substitutes", an overabundant percentage of soy, and hardly any fresh fruit. Instead the fruit that is served is usually kiddy portions of canned fruits full of preservatives. In some state prisons the old saying "three hots and a cot" is a quaint notion that no longer applies because prisoners only receive two meals a day now - brunch and dinner.

Many jails and prisons contract out the service of feeding their prisoners. These along with private prisons have a profit motive in skimping on meals. It becomes an unending journey to increase profits at the expense of prisoners' physical and mental health. Prisons that run their own kitchens take a similar journey. Each budget crisis they find ways to purchase food for less money, which means they constantly purchase lower quality food, because when the budget crisis is over the prisons never get additional funds to return to the previous quality of foods. Instead policy makers see no reason why the state shouldn't continue saving money by serving the poorer quality fair. Neither journey ends until prisoners revolt. This usually doesn't occur until after they've been served, often barely edible, rotten, nutrient deprived, gristle-littered, tasteless food for years on end until they finally snap. A lot of the meat and other staples are of such poor quality that they could not be sold anywhere else in the country but to prisons and jails.

There is no question that poor food in prison increases violence, or as *The Chicago Tribune* noted, that there is "a common understanding among corrections officials that good food creates good inmates."[463]

Scientific experiments over the past decade or so have proven this understanding. One study in England of 231 inmates found that those who received daily vitamins, minerals, and essential fatty acids like Omega 3s committed 37% fewer violent offenses than inmates who received placebos. [464]

Unfortunately, knowing this rarely translates into a policy of feeding prisoners nutritious meals. Instead meals are poor to save money or increase profit, and violence in prisons is unnecessarily higher than it otherwise would be.

In some prisons inmates can't even get a hold of safe drinking water. In 2005 it was discovered that the water had "up to twice the federally permitted standard for arsenic levels" at California's Kern Valley Prison in Delano.[465] *Prison Legal News* reported that "[a]ccording to the U. S. Environmental Protection Agency long-term exposure to arsenic can cause 'cancer of the bladder, lungs, skin, kidneys, nasal passages, liver, and prostate'."[466] Yet over five years later they still had not bothered to install an Arsenic Treatment System and didn't anticipate doing so until August 2012.[467] What clearer evidence does one need about society's attitude toward prisoners than forcing them to drink poisonous water for as long as seven years?

Excessive Force

Often just as violent as the prisoners, or even more so at times, are the guards and other staff. With prisoners completely dehumanized in the eyes of society, many people who work in prisons and jails in America both feel no sympathy for prisoners and no remorse for abusing them. They feel society's hatred of prisoners gives them carte blanche to physically harm them. Thus prisoners are arbitrarily maced, tazed, and beaten on a daily basis in one prison or another.

According to *The Week*, Sheriff Arpaio was threatened with a lawsuit by the U. S. Justice Department because his corrections officers "used excessive force on inmates, including hog-tying and pepper-spraying," and the county faced nearly 3,000 lawsuits from just 2003-2007 alone, costing the county $30 million in settlements. [468] One inmate, Scott Norberg, was shocked with a stun gun and strapped into a restraining chair with a towel stuffed in his mouth. He died of asphyxiation.[469]

The Chicago Sun-Times reported that in 2008 the U. S. Attorney's office concluded a 17- month civil review of the Cook County Jail that found "[u]nnecessary deaths and amputations, grossly inadequate medical care and routine inmate beatings."[470] Citing the report, the newspaper further noted that:

In one case, an inmate left untreated for a gunshot wound developed sepsis and died. One man's leg was amputated after complaints about pains in his bandaged leg went ignored. Guards allegedly beat another man, kicking out his dentures and sending him to the hospital on a respirator.... The report found a culture among guards that fostered beatings to the point of hospitalization when inmates talked back or rebuffed orders. [471]

In June of 2004, Human Rights Watch wrote an article in *Peacework Magazine* that noted:

The sadistic abuse and sexual humiliation by American soldiers at Abu Ghraib prison has shocked most Americans - but not those of us familiar with U.S. jails and prisons. In American prisons today, wanton staff brutality and degrading treatment of inmates occurs across the country with distressing frequency.

We know that two of the soldiers charged with abuse at Abu Ghraib were prison guards in the United States....

A federal judge in 1999 concluded that Texas prisons were pervaded by a "culture of sadistic and malicious violence." In 1995, a federal judge found a stunning pattern of staff assaults, abusive use of electronic stun devices, guns, beatings, and brutality at Pelican Bay Prison in California, and concluded the violence "appears to be openly acknowledged, tolerated and sometimes expressly approved" by high-ranking corrections officials.

In recent years, U.S. prison inmates have been beaten with fists and batons, stomped on, kicked, shot, stunned with electronic devices, doused with chemical sprays, choked, and slammed face first onto concrete floors by the officers whose job it is to guard them. Inmates have ended up with broken jaws, smashed ribs, perforated eardrums, missing teeth, burn scars - not to mention psychological scars and emotional pain. Some have died.

Both men and women prisoners - but especially women - face staff rape and sexual abuse.[472]

The rape and sexual assault of male prisoners by guards is not as unheard of as most people would think. Contrary to the public's image of prisoners as all "tough guys" and killers, it does happen with some frequency. For example, in 2011, the *Pittsburgh Post-Gazette* reported that Harry Nicoletti, the eighth guard to be suspended in five months at the State Correctional Institute at Pittsburgh, "was arrested on charges that he assaulted - both sexually and physically - more than 20 inmates."[473] A 10-year veteran of the prison, Nicoletti was "charged with 92 counts of institutional sexual assault, official oppression, terroristic threats and simple assault."[474] He and seven other guards were sued in federal court for allegedly having a "common plan and conspiracy to sexually abuse, physically abuse and mentally abuse inmates who were homosexual," transgender or convicted of sex crimes.[475]

Assaults on prisoners by staff occurs in both private and public jails and prisons, juvenile and adult facilities, male and female institutions. In 2010,18 Hawaiian prisoners who were serving time in a private prison in Arizona sued the operator CCA and state officials alleging that CCA staff, the warden among them, had beaten, kicked, and threatened them according to an article in the August 2011 issue of *Prison Legal News* (PLN).[476] Flipping through the same issue you'll find other instances of prisoner abuse as you will in every issue. Such as the article where you learn that sometimes guards are so blatant that they'll beat up a prisoner right in front of an ACLU monitor, as happened to James Parker who received "stitches to his face, injured ribs, and a swollen cheek and eye" while putting up no resistance to the sheriff's deputies assaulting him at the Twin Towers Correctional Facility in California, all while Esther Lim of the ACLU watched stunned.[477]

"We believe Mr. Parker's beating is not an isolated incident," said Hector Villagra, executive director of the ACLU/SC. "Rather, it highlights the rampant violence that continues to plague the county's jails and demands court intervention to protect detainees from brutal attacks and retaliation. That the ACLU/SC monitor witnessed a brutal attack in plain sight is alarming and can only lead us to conclude detainees are subject to even greater cruelty when no one is looking."[478]

With the PLRA helping to hide prison conditions and abuse from public view, and keeping most complaints from getting a hearing in federal court there aren't too many people looking either.

Medical Care

When prisoners are assaulted, as usual they rarely ever receive a high standard of medical care, if any at all. As already discussed, private companies contracted to provide medical care have a profit motive in denying prisoners adequate medical care, which leads to unnecessary suffering and/or death. State governments likewise have a motive in denying adequate medical care. Politicians know both that voters aren't keen to pay for the healthcare of prisoners (even if they do zealously support mass incarceration) and that this is an easy expense to cut or underfund. Politicians know that there will be little discontent, if not outright public support, even if voters do learn that prisoners are being harmed or dying from lack of medical care.

The same August 2011 issue of PLN tells how one "court noted that the Dallas County Jail had a prisoner MRSA infection rate of close to 20% in 2003" and that a "MRSA outbreak had been ongoing for at least three years."[479] The article noted how the court failed to mention inmate Mark Duvall's "allegation that after Dallas County had signed a jail medical care contract with the University of Texas Medical Branch - Galveston for a flat rate of $5.49 per prisoner per day in January of 2003, prisoners were routinely denied medical treatment, which was known to the county."[480]

It isn't just one jail in Texas that's dangerous to prisoners' health either. Citing the Texas attorney general's office, PLN reported in May of 2011 that:

> 282 prisoners died due to medical causes in county jails run by the state's 254 sheriffs' departments between January 2005 and September 2009. That represents an average of around 63 jail prisoner deaths related to illnesses each year - about the same number who die annually in Texas' state prison system. The difference is that the prison system holds about twice as many prisoners as the state's county jails.[481]

Also Texas prisons themselves provide inadequate medical care. So we can see that the needless one death per week from inadequate medical and mental health care found in California's prisons are just the tip of the iceberg when talking about unnecessary prisoner deaths in America. It is common not only for medical providers to deliberately deny treatment to increase profit or save taxpayer money, but it's also common for staff to view all prisoners as liars (or enjoy seeing prisoners suffer), and refuse to let them see the doctor or be slow to grant access. Again, PLN's August 2011 issue gives a perfect example:

> Shawn Desmond Woodward, 33, was being held at the Washington County Jail on a probation violation when he became sick on the evening of September 24, 2008. He then began to complain of chest pains.

> "Before he was able to make it into his cell, he actually collapsed," said attorney Samuel J. Briskman, who represented Woodward's estate. Other prisoners helped Woodward to his bed. For the next 30 minutes they beat on the walls to gain the attention of the only guard on duty, Elton Sullivan.

> Sullivan contacted dispatch, who relayed Woodward's condition to Chief Deputy Terry Beasley. According to the complaint, Beasley instructed Sullivan to give Woodward aspirin. Prisoners at the jail made two other fruitless efforts to obtain help for Woodward; however, an ambulance was not called and he died.

... An expert was prepared to testify that had jail officials acted quickly, there was a 90 percent chance that Woodward would have survived.[482]

The case never went to trial though because a settlement was reached beforehand in the amount of $450,000.[483]

Dental care in the nation's jails and prisons is likewise inadequate if not non-existent. Often if it is available at all it is downright medieval. *The Chicago Sun-Times* reported that the Cook County Jail had only a single dentist to serve nearly 10,000 inmates there, and "he only deals in extractions. Twenty-five percent of [which] resulted in infection."[484]

With more and more immigrants being arrested, more are also dying while in custody. Evidencing how little respect there is for both immigrants and prisoners, the deaths often aren't even reported. As *The Wall Street Journal* reported in 2009 "[t]en previously unreported cases [were] discovered bringing the total to 104 since October 2003."[485] Eight of the unreported deaths "occurred at facilities operated by the Federal Bureau of Prisons, including four at the U. S. Medical Center for Federal Prisoners in Springfield, [Missouri]".[486] The other two died at a prison in Eloy, Arizona run by Corrections Corporation of America.[487]

Pocket Picking

Not only are prisoners abused physically and mentally, but as we've seen, they are also exploited economically. It isn't just the slave wages paid for the few jobs that are available in prisons either. They're increasingly having their pockets picked. Prison administrators, governments, and society in general, are constantly coming up with new ways to get money out of prisoners. With prisoners being the poorest demographic in the country, this not only garners very little money, but is exceptionally mean-spirited. It's like snatching the change cup from a legless homeless man and running.

Prisoners are being taxed, fined, and outright robbed at every turn even though the vast majority have no income and little money. For instance, half of the inmates in Texas' prison system have less than five dollars in their prison trust accounts,[488] and in the U. S. in general prior to going to prison 80% of people convicted of a felony had incomes below the poverty line.[489]

These facts don't stop states from constantly trying to recover the costs of incarceration from prisoners.[490] Governments are taking kickbacks from a whole range of companies that are charging indefensibly exorbitant prices for commissary items - items that are often purchased to supplement the inadequate food and hygiene items grudgingly provided by the state. In Illinois, the IDOC also adds a 25% surcharge allowed by state law.[491] This wasn't enough to satisfy the

169

IDOC though so they also exceeded what the law allows by another 9% to rake in millions of dollars per year from the nearly 50,000 inmates in Illinois. [492] Although prisoners may not have much money, an extra dollar or two from each of their pockets every week or two adds up. Of course that dollar or two means a lot to a prisoner. It may mean the difference between being able to purchase deodorant or writing home to the kids.

When prisoners do try to support themselves or their family by making and selling artwork or handicrafts, or by writing for publication, or even when they just inherit money from a relative; the government will often rush in to seize the money. In Illinois, as in many states, state law allows for each of these occurrences.[493] Another common practice is to permit prisoners to purchase products in one prison, but when the prisoner transfers to another prison many of the items are deemed contraband at the new prison so the prisoner is forced to then purchase a new TV, typewriter, etc. at the next prison, just different models. This ensures increased sales, meaning increased revenue and profit for the companies, and increased surcharges for the government.

Sometimes the IDOC is so nefarious that it will actually encourage prisoners to work and save money for when they're released, only to then try and take it all from them in one lump sum. That is what happened to Kensley Hawkins. Serving a 60 year sentence, he worked for close to three decades making furniture for about $2 per day, and was able to save nearly $11,000.[494] The state had already deducted 3%

of his wages to pay towards his costs of incarceration as part of the program designed to reduce recidivism by giving prisoners job skills and a way to save for release to make re-entry into society easier. Goals rarely sought by today's criminal justice system.

Three percent seemingly wasn't enough. The state wanted more. So it sued Mr. Hawkins for it all. Ironically if Mr. Hawkins had spent it all on porn and junk food that would have been okay. Since he saved it though - one of the objectives of the program - he was sued instead. Not only did the state want the $11,000, but it also wanted the entire $455,203.14 that it claimed it spent to incarcerate him for all those years.[495] The state wanted him leaving prison with a debt of nearly a half of a million dollars on his back.

An appellate court ruled that the state had every right to seize Mr. Hawkins savings.[496] Luckily a law firm represented him pro bono and appealed all the way to the Illinois Supreme court which ruled he had a right to keep the money.[497] It shows though, the lengths the state will go to to exploit and impoverish prisoners at every turn.

8

SUPERMAXES

By far the worst prison environments in the U.S. are found in control units and supermax prisons. Think Guantánamo Bay, but often even worse. Amazingly the level of outrage expressed over mistreating American citizens in U.S. prisons has been miniscule compared to society's uproar over how foreigners were treated in Guantánamo Bay. A public that would normally punish any politician who suggests closing any prison had no qualms about electing a president who promised to close Guantánamo Bay. This disconnect is curious. Do we really hate our own citizens who commit a crime more than we hate people who want to wipe America off the map? It seems we do.

As *Solitary Watch* noted "[m]illions of Americans have been haunted by the spectre of Guantánamo Bay and Abu Ghraib where isolation and deprivation have been raised to the level of torture. Yet every day, here in the United States, tens of thousands of prisoners languish" in similar environments.[498] President Obama claimed "we don't torture", yet according to *The Capital City Courier;* the "prototype for the sealed off and fortress-like Camps 5 and 6 at Guantánamo Bay" was "the prison at Florence - along with dozens of similar super high security facilities in the U.S."[499] The authors noted that "there are dozens, and perhaps as many as a hundred Guantánamo Bays right here in the United States".[500]

Writing in the *Smithsonian,* Joseph Lelyveld recounted how when he visited Guantánamo in 2002:

> Many of the guards had worked as correctional officers in their civilian lives. When I asked to meet some of them I was introduced to two women normally employed in state prisons in Georgia. The harsh conditions in which the supposed terrorists were held, they told me, were a little harder than normal "segregation" for troublesome prisoners in the Georgia system, but not nearly so hard as Georgia-style "isolation". I took this to be expert testimony.[501]

Supermax prisons and control units in the United States go by many different names and acronyms often in an attempt to conceal their true nature. Here are just some of them: "SHU" for secure housing unit; "SMU" for special management unit; supermax units; adjustment centers; administrative segregation; and many others like ADX, the more infamous of the Federal Bureau of Prisons' (BOP) facilities. It stands for Administrative Maximum facility (ADX) and is located in Florence, Colorado. They all employ the same strategy of long-term isolation which most industrialized countries view as both barbaric and a form of torture.

Sometimes the name will be changed to disingenuously proclaim the prison or unit is no longer a supermax. The supermax prison in Tamms, Illinois for instance, was originally named Tamms Supermax Correctional Center. Illinois law even calls it a supermax.[502] To this day it is located at 8500 Supermax Road in Tamms, Illinois. The town used to have a sign that read "Welcome to Tamms, Home of the Supermax." Less than a decade after opening in 1997 though, the Illinois Department of Corrections (IDOC) claimed it was no longer a supermax prison even though neither the security classification nor any of the policies or conditions changed. It rechristened it a "closed maximum security prison", or "C-MAX". I guess they felt this sounded less harsh than supermax. *Illinois Issues* magazine seemingly took this farcical renaming hook, line and sinker, as they began to parenthesize "supermax" as if those who call it a supermax are being exaggerative.[503] Instead thcy referred to Tamms as "the states strongest maximum security prison" and other euphemisms.[504]

As Bonnie Kerness noted in *WIN Magazine* "one of the first control units was established in the late 1960s."[505] It was in San Quentin Prison's 0 Wing.[506] It is commonly misreported that the first such unit was at the Marion Federal Penitentiary in Illinois in 1972.[507] In large part this is due to how little known by the public these units often are. Marion established their "infamous H Unit, made up of cruel boxcar cells,"[508] after a guard was killed that year.[509] Numerous other states such as New Jersey and Massachusetts also established similar control units in existing prisons around the same time.[510]

The BOP built the first prison dedicated solely to being a completely controlled environment when it built the ADX in Florence.[511] During the 1980s and 1990s many states imitated the BOP. These higher security level facilities garnered them the moniker of supermax. By 1997 all but five states in the union, along with the BOP and the District of Columbia, operated control units, supermax prisons, or both.[512]

Over the past few decades as supermax prison and control units opened for business coast to coast as if parts of a franchise, and tough-on-crime legislation peppered states' criminal codes increasing incarceration rates nationwide, the number of people held in Guantánamo-like conditions or worse, grew rapidly. The number held in isolation though, didn't simply grow commensurate to the prison population as a whole. Rather it expanded at a much faster rate.

Just as it is difficult to identify all the different control units and supermaxes around the country (which governments work so hard to keep out of view of the public), so too is it difficult to get concrete numbers on how many people are in those isolation chambers on any given day or year. In 2002 Human Rights Watch calculated the number at over 20,000, or nearly 2% of the prison population.[513] The American Friends Service Committee (AFSC) in 2009 estimated it was as high as

2.5 percent.[514] In 2010, the Coalition for Prisoners' Rights, citing a study by The Commission on Safety and Abuse in America's Prisons, reported that the "number of prisoners in solitary confinement grew 40% from 1995 to 2000 - when there were 80,870 such segregated prisoners" while the prison population as a whole grew by 28%.[515] Yet a few months earlier the same coalition reported that on "any given day, as many as 100,000 people are living in solitary confinement in U.S. prisons."[516] The 20,000 number given is almost definitely too low as California alone had over 14,000 in solitary confinement by 2008.[517] Suffice it to say though, tens of thousands of Americans are being held in isolation cells similar to the Guantánamo cells holding the few hundred enemy combatants that caused such an uproar.

Correctional departments claim that these control units and supermaxes are vital to keeping prison staff and inmates safe and are the only available option to control prisoners who are uncontrollable. The reality is often much more sinister. Instead of these cells being used to house dangerously violent inmates, or as prison staff and the media love to term them, the "worst of the worst", more often than not they are used to house the mentally ill, prisoner activists, jailhouse lawyers, or anyone the prison administration just doesn't like.

Rachel Kamel and Bonnie Kerness at AFSC note that "once supermaxes are built, such institutions acquire their own momentum. Correctional authorities must fill them to justify the cost of their operation, leading to arbitrary decisions about which prisoners are sent to supermax prisons and why".[518] Furthermore, while prison administrators often claim these supermaxes and control units reduce violence in the prison system,[519] there is no conclusive evidence that this is in fact true.[520]

According to the California Department of Corrections and Rehabilitation (CDCR), the only prisoners it sends to the SHUs are those who have attacked a guard or another inmate, are caught selling drugs, caught with weapons, or are validated gang members.[521] Concerning the latter category, an inmate's validation, according to the AFSC, "comes about at the discretion of the prison staff."[522] As we'll see later, validation is often arbitrary or racist. Also just because someone is a gang member doesn't mean that they are breaking any rules. The AFSC also found that, although the CDCR administration denies it, jailhouse lawyers are also frequently sent to the SHUs, and these latter two groups of prisoners, "who have not actually done anything are the ones who serve the longest time in these units."[523] Gloria Romero, a California state senator, noted at a Select Senate Committee hearing in 2003 that a "validated gang member could conceivably spend the rest of his life in SHU."[524]

Using control units and supermaxes to bury inmates who challenge unconstitutional prison conditions is a common practice in the U.S. Prisoner activists and jailhouse lawyers are especially hated by prison guards and administrators. They find it particularly galling when prisoners fail to fit the mold of dumb brute and are intelligent enough to challenge being treated like animals or worse. So prisoners are often sent there "for filing grievances, lawsuits, or for otherwise opposing prison injustices."[525] *The Capital City Courier* noted in 2009 that many Tamms:

> prisoners and their attorneys suspect that the real reasons for their transfer to Tamms was that they were "jailhouse lawyers", or because they refused to act as snitches. (Indeed, the IDOC Webpage on Tamms Correctional Center flatly states that the unit houses "some of the most litigious inmates in the department's custody").[526]

WIN Magazine reported that isolation has been used as a means to punish jailhouse lawyers since the 1960s.[527] Prison officials have a love/hate relationship with snitches. They love snitches who snitch on prisoners; hate snitches who snitch on prison staff. The editors of *Solitary Watch* tell how:

> There's no doubt that solitary confinement is routinely used to punish prison whistle-blowers and to suppress nonviolent dissent and free expression in prison.... In Massachusetts, an inmate named Timothy Muise was sent to solitary after he tried to expose a sex-for-snitching ring run by guards at his prison; they said his offense was "engaging in or inciting a group demonstration".[528]

During his short time as director of the IDOC, Michael P. Randle repeatedly claimed that the supermax in Tamms was reserved for the "worst of the worst".[529] *The Belleville News-Democrat* found that more than half of Tamms' residents hadn't committed any crimes while in prison, "and that others were seriously mentally ill and did not receive treatment."[530]

With the previously-mentioned dismantling of mental health facilities nationwide and the resulting flood of mentally ill people filling the nation's prisons, they are increasingly finding themselves disproportionately occupying isolation cells. Bonnie Kerness summed up the problem as follows:

> Currently, people who are mentally ill, learning disabled, or illiterate constitute a large percentage of the prison population. Whether the origins of their problems are neurological, socioeconomic, or both, these populations often experience the greatest difficulties following prison rules, controlling their anger, or handling the prison environment. As a result, they are the most likely to be written up for disciplinary infractions and transferred to a control unit or supermax facility.[531]

It's not always that they are especially dangerous either. Often it's just wardens trying to get rid of an inmate who they consider a headache. Professor Mark J. Heyrman, a specialist in issues concerning the mentally ill likens it to a game. "If you are familiar with the card game Hearts, you get to pass the three cards that you don't want to the left, so what often happens in prison systems, the moment we create a supermax prison is every warden passes the three or the 10 or the 15 prisoners that are the most trouble. These are people who are difficult to manage. Unfortunately, it's often people who have untreated, and I want to underline that word, untreated mental illnesses that can't follow the rules".[532]

Getting under the skin of staff members also makes them vulnerable to being arbitrarily labeled as gang members. Gang members, or members of a "Security Threat Group" or STG, are extremely vulnerable to being isolated in control units or supermax prisons. They often don't need to have violated any rules. Just being a gang or STG member is sufficient. Actually being an ex-gang member, associate, or even a minority is often enough to get one validated as a current member of an STG. Just having a gang tattoo is enough to validate someone so most retired gang members remain validated. If the ex-gang member took the drastic measure of burning or cutting the tattoo off, he or she could then be subjected to discipline for "altering their appearance" which is against most prisons' rules.

Laura Magnani of the AFSC in Oakland, notes that the "use of the 'gang' label by prison authorities is fraught with racial stereotyping and political repression. What is sometimes labeled a gang could be a group of activist prisoners who are organizing on their own behalf."[533] Prison administrators also have a financial incentive to label people as members of an STG. The AFSC in Philadelphia reported in 2003 that:

> government policies, including financial incentives, have encouraged the proliferation of control units in their latest incarnation as "security threat group management units". Currently, the inclusion of such units is mandated by federal standards that govern how subsidies are awarded for state prison construction.

In the contemporary prison environment, use of the "gang" label by prison authorities is fraught with racial profiling, racial harassment, and other forms of abuse. The very definition of what constitutes a "gang" merits questioning. In a 1997 survey issued by the U. S. Department of Justice, for example, the Minnesota Department of Corrections was cited as listing "Native Americans" as a "gang"; both Minnesota and Oregon defined all Asians as "gang" members.

AFSC criminal justice staff in Massachusetts likewise note that prison authorities there consider use of Puerto Rican cultural symbols to be evidence of gang membership, with the result that an overwhelming majority of the state's Puerto Rican prisoners have been labeled as gang members. One prisoner who was tattooed with the logo of a reggae band was classified as a "gang of one" and confined in isolation for ten months.

Massachusetts prisoners have been transferred to the "gang block" - with control unit conditions, including permanent lockdown - simply because police have identified them as "associating" with gang members, regardless of their behavior inside the prison.[534]

Victor C. Rodriguez, a prisoner in California wrote that "[a]t anytime, officers search cells and are instructed to confiscate our art, Nahuatl studies, and any Nahuatl literature. The reason we're told: "gang related". This is nothing but cultural deprivation, as well as racial discrimination".[535] Nahuatl is both a language and a group of Native Americans so large that it includes the Aztec.

The military adopted these same tactics in regard to running Guantánamo Bay. As long as they labeled someone a "terrorist" or "the worst of the worst", they would have less to worry about outside scrutiny. Just as American society for the most part will cease to care about the fate of someone labeled a "gangbanger", so too do they cease to care about the fate of a "terrorist". In fact, the two are beginning to become synonymous, with "gang members" routinely referred to as "domestic terrorists".

Joseph Lelyveld explains the folly of taking the government's word on who is a "terrorist", and the deviousness and premeditation associated with such tactics. He rhetorically asks:

> who but a certified bleeding heart could call into question the guidelines for treatment of "terrorists" classed by a Pentagon spokesman as "the worst of the worst"? Years later, we'd be told there was no hard evidence linking at least one-fifth and possibly many more - of the Guantánamo detainees to terrorist movements. This belated coming to grips with the facts of each case could have been written off as carelessness were it not for the foresight displayed by members of Congress who legislated a provision barring lawsuits by Guantánamo detainees on any grounds. Suspicion alone, it seemed was enough to keep them in the category of "the worst" if not "worst of the worst."[536]

We would also learn that some of these "worst of the worst" "terrorists" were nothing but prepubescent kids not even old enough to drive had they been American. Some we locked up there because China labeled them "terrorists". Yet after September 11, 2001 society's hatred of "terrorists" grew by such bounds that all "Arabs" became suspect and any false accusation was sufficient justification to validate them as a "terrorist". Similarly, anyone in prison can be validated as a member of an STG with nothing more than a false accusation, and rarely will that person be able to get that label removed. He or she will then be forced to endure the added stigma and discrimination that accompany such a label. Often this will include control unit or supermax confinement.

History is full of examples where people who were considered second-class citizens were arbitrarily discriminated against and demonized. From "witches" at the hands of religious zealots, to "undesirables" at the hands of Nazis, society has long justified uncivil policies towards certain categories of people. Most people today would not believe that committees like the House Un-American Activities Committee (H.U.A.C.) could exist in our now more enlightened times. Unfortunately that's far from the truth. Nowadays though, it is just kept out of the public's eye and used as a prison administration policy.

H.U.A.C. is now acknowledged as being nothing more than a political witch-hunt. It was begun to investigate Nazi propaganda and German involvement in the Ku Klux Klan in 1938, but over its almost 40 year history it came to be a tool used by government officials to blacklist anyone from artists to politicians. Its methods were arbitrary and its stigma, once associated with you, was impossible to get out from under.

In his book, *The Warren Court and Pursuit of Justice,* Morton J. Horowitz describes H.U.A.C. as follows:

> H.U.A.C.'s most important function was to hold
> hearings at which those who were willing to recant their

Communist-sympathizing past were required to engage in public repentance....Sincere repentance was largely determined by witnesses' willingness to "name names" of those who had participated with them in a suspect organization. For those whose consciences would not permit them to involve others, a very different ritual evolved. These unwilling witnesses typically pleaded the Fifth Amendment, claiming that their refusal to testify was based on the concern that they might incriminate themselves by offering testimony that could subsequently be used against them in a criminal trial. Senator McCarthy regularly denounced these witnesses as "Fifth Amendment Communists", and many of them were fired from their jobs after invoking their constitutional rights. Those witnesses who stood on their consciences by refusing to name names were portrayed as completely uncooperative and contemptuous of congress....In fact, while these witnesses might have been willing to testify about their own past activities, any cooperation might trap them into having to answer every question, which would inevitably involve others.[537]

The similarities between H.U.A.C. and the Illinois Department of Corrections' STG renunciation policy at Tamms leaves little question as to where the designers of the latter got their idea from.

STG labeling is the latest fad in prison control tactics. Today, after decades of demonizing criminals (and years of fear-mongering about terrorism), gangs or STGs have become an easy target for attack, and renunciation has become an all-encompassing, extralegal tool for prison administrators. Label someone a gang member and society will immediately agree that isolation is justified. Prison administrators now have carte blanche to carry out any scheme they would like. This creates an environment where anyone who is so much as a nuisance is labeled as a gang/STG member so that administrators can have a free hand to isolate, censor, and retaliate against them. As we'll see later, this also often converts into carte blanche to banish people from paroling back to their own neighborhoods.

Just as H.U.A.C. members used that process to harass individuals whose political opinions offended them, thus ruining their careers, so too did prison administrators falsely label prisoners who become a nuisance to them, thereby ruining their chances of transferring out of Tamms Supermax Prison, being granted parole, being denied job assignments, etc. Unfortunately a prisoner who files a lawsuit to protect his constitutional rights is often considered a nuisance by prison administrators, as is anyone who has a staff assault, often resulting in a STG label.

Once a person is labeled as a STG member it is virtually impossible to get rid of that label. Renunciation hearings are arbitrary and mainly used as an intelligence gathering system for Internal Affairs. If a prisoner refuses to inform on other inmates' activities his renunciation will not be accepted. Also, just going to the hearing can often put his life in danger with his former gang members, if he was truly a member of a STG.

Many individuals in Illinois prisons who would like to renounce their gang affiliation at present, do not do so mainly because the mismanagement of the policy and hearings has created the belief that there is little chance of a successful result (especially those who are falsely labeled), and that those who have been approved have implicated others in crimes. This leads to the perception that little would be gained while simultaneously putting yourself at risk of being targeted for retaliation by both the administration (for not telling them what they want to hear) and by the gang (because you're now labeled as a snitch).

Renunciation should be concerned only with the individual seeking to renounce. Instead the majority of the hearing consists of questions regarding others, and if an individual doesn't give them the information requested, they are said to be insincere and their renunciation is not accepted. Also, it is not what an individual knows or relates, but rather what the committee believes he should know, and what or who the committee chooses to believe. Thus, if one individual gives false information and the committee believes it, it can have a devastating trickledown effect where anyone else who fails to confirm this false information, or contradicts it during their own renunciation hearing, is denied as not being sincere.

Another major concern and impediment to successful renunciation is that of self-incrimination. Individuals are asked about numerous prior incidents. These renunciation proceedings are taped and preserved. If an individual pleads the Fifth his renunciation is not accepted as sincere. If he does answer he may have that evidence used against him later in a court of law.

So at present, both the process of labeling gang members and the administration of the renunciation programs are fraught with errors, mishandling, and abuse. Non-gang members and former gang members are frequently being falsely labeled as active gang members. Gang members who genuinely try to renounce are being told that their renunciation was not accepted. The unsaid reason being either: 1) they refused to implicate other gang members in crimes or gang activity; 2) the administration chose to believe another inmate's testimony and any inconsistency or contradiction is taken as proof of their insincerity whether true or not; 3) out of retaliation by prison officials for prior staff assaults, filing civil lawsuits, or advocating for prison reform; or 4) even as a way to deny transfer out of Administrative Detention, thereby keeping both the inmate isolated, and the AD population at a sufficient level.

If H.U.A.C. is now recognized as nothing but an arbitrary political witch-hunt then why isn't the almost identical renunciation process?

Trying to challenge ones placement in control units or supermaxes is therefore extremely difficult. Just as the "gang" label can be arbitrary, inaccurate, and sufficient to justify placement, so too can other reasons for placement. Sometimes the reasons are even kept secret by prison administrators allowing the prisoner no realistic opportunity to marshall a defense to placement. Alan Mills, a lawyer at Uptown People's Law Center in Chicago, who represented prisoners at Tamms made what *The Capitol City Courier* called the "inevitable comparison":

> This is like Guantánamo Bay. If there are people at Guantánamo who are terrorists, let's have a hearing and present the evidence and punish them. If not, they shouldn't be held there. Similarly if there are men at Tamms who can't be controlled in the State's thousand plus segregation cells, then the Department should be required to present evidence proving the danger.[538]

The same article noted that the Illinois Department of Corrections claims that "they have valid reasons for every transfer," but for "security reasons" won't tell anyone what those reasons are.[539]

At most supermax prisons and control units across the country, the length of time that inmates must remain in them is indefinite. On occasion the public and legislature have been lied to about this very fact in order to obtain funds for, or approval to, build or open them. Once again Tamms is one of the most glaring examples.

The Illinois legislature and public were told that Tamms would house inmates for only a year as a sort of shock treatment. Therefore it was built with that objective in mind, meaning no exercise equipment, phones, educational programs, etc. Within a few years after opening its steel, perforated cell doors to inmates, this claim was shown to be nothing but misinformation employed to secure approval and funding to build Tamms. Attorney Jean Maclean Snyder informed the Illinois House Prison Management and Reform Legislation Committee in 2001 that "[w]hen Tamms opened in March 1998, the word was that prisoners would have to serve a year there. After that, if they behaved they could be transferred out. But it's been three years now, and only a handful of prisoners have graduated from Tamms. Every month that passes with nobody moving out makes it harder to understand the rationale for this prison."[540]

Eight years later www.justseeds.org reported in 2009 that Tamms "was designed to be a short-term shock-treatment, but one-third of prisoners have been held indefinitely since the prison opened over ten years ago."[541] Then-director Michael Randle that year acknowledged that the average stay in Tamms was about five years.[542] Many inmates are sent to Tamms because they have the "potential" to commit acts of violence, not because they have done so. How they determine who has potential to do so is unstated.[543]

Even when a prisoner does commit an act of violence to justify placement, the length of placement in a supermax or control unit can

191

become needlessly extensive and good behavior will rarely get them released from isolation. More often than not they'll remain there until their out dates, a court orders their release to general population, or he or she dies. Those unfortunate enough to be serving life sentences may live the majority of their lives there. Thomas Silverstein has been in solitary confinement for nearly three decades. He began his isolation in Marion in 1983 after he killed a guard and is currently in the Federal ADX in Colorado. At 59 years old he has had an immaculate disciplinary record for over twenty years.[544]

Some prisoners have served even longer. Two of the most famous are Herman Wallace and Albert Woodfox who have been in solitary confinement for nearly four decades in the Louisiana State Penitentiary at Angola.[545] *Solitary Watch Newsletter* reported that both men were charged with killing a prison guard but maintain their innocence, and "that they were targeted for the crime because of their membership in a chapter of the Black Panthers....Both men are now in their 60s, but the warden maintains they must be kept in isolation because they are 'still trying to practice Black Pantherism' and he does not want to 'have the blacks chasing after them'".[546]

So just what are conditions like in these control units and supermaxes? Although they vary from one to the next, nearly all have the following in common. Obviously the prisoner is isolated in a one man cell, and even exercise is solitary.[547] All communication with the outside world like mail, telephone calls and visits from family and (maybe) friends is severely curtailed.[548] Reading material is even more censored than in general population.

There is usually little public oversight of these units or prisons because they are "carefully hidden from public view, intentionally located in isolated...rural areas."[549] The courts have described the conditions at times as "ghastly", "sordid and horrible", "depressing in the extreme", and more recently constituting an "atypical and significant hardship" compared to ordinary prison life.[550]

The AFSC of Oakland noted how prisoners are confined alone in:

> cells [that] contain only the most basic of accommodations...bed, a toilet and sink, and possibly another protruding slab for a desk...Most cells have no windows...Prisoners eat alone in their cells... "shakedowns" are common, and prisoners are routinely strip searched before leaving their cells.[551]

In his memoir *In the Place Of Justice,* Wilbert Rideau describes the "bone-cold loneliness" of solitary confinement in Angola where he was on death row:

> Removed from family or anything resembling a friend, and just being there with no purpose or meaning to my life, cramped in a cage smaller than an American bathroom. The lonesomeness was only increased by the

constant cacophony of men in adjacent cells hurling shouted insults, curses, and arguments - not to mention the occasional urine or feces concoction.[554]

The AFSC notes that many of these prisons or units are creating "their own innovations in controlling and dehumanizing prisoners," such as the control unit in Corcoran where "armed guards patrol the Plexiglass ceilings over the cells, and peer in at the prisoners through Plexiglas cell walls.[553]

Human contact is either totally non-existent or nearly so, and can last for decades. At Tamms there was no exception to the rule about no-contact visits. Even when prisoners were escorted by guards, the guards wore rubber surgical gloves. Attorney Jean Snyder told an Illinois House Committee how:

> One little girl who was dying of cancer told the Make A Wish Foundation that she wanted to visit her father at Tamms and hug him one last time. The Foundation wished that she would pick a trip to Disney World - but she didn't. So the Foundation paid for the girl's visit to Tamms, where the girl saw her father through a glass booth and could not hug or kiss him.[544]

One of the limited privileges that most prisoners in isolation retain is the opportunity to go to "yard". The reason being is that prisoners have a right to exercise, which is protected by the 8th Amendment to the U.S.

Constitution. Unfortunately "yard" is usually a misnomer. The "yards" found in control units and supermaxes are almost universally less square footage than a semitrailer and made out of either thick gauge wire mesh walls and ceiling, or are simply a large cement tomb with twenty-foot high walls and chainlike fence roofing to allow in light. There are usually no weights or sports equipment so the only exercise one gets is calisthenics. These "yards" are commonly referred to as "dog runs".

They always have cameras for constant surveillance, but inmates almost never have access to water or a toilet, and yard time is routinely cancelled for the most arbitrary reasons - too hot, too cold, ice on the ground, snow on the ground, camera not functioning, it's thundering, lightening, raining too hard, etc.

Some Tamms inmates feared the "yard". During summer the yard walls and floor were graffitied with bird feces. Those aren't the only feces that found their way onto the yard either. Inmates, especially elderly ones, feared being stranded on the "yard" and losing control of their bladder or bowels. Other inmates felt a flood of emotions when they learned that someone had defecated on the "yard". They're angry at staff for ignoring the inmate's pleas to be let in to use the bathroom; and angry over the fact that they now can't go to yard unless they're willing to share a confined space with another man's feces - the thought of which alone engenders disgust. On the other end of the emotional spectrum though, inmates felt sympathy for the often elderly gentleman who was both incontinent, embarrassed, and reduced to begging kids a third or a half his age to be let in to use the washroom. There was also the possibility that he would be written a disciplinary ticket or even placed on what's known as "Mealloaf".

Just as control units are used to punish jailhouse lawyers and prison activists, they are also used to try to silence them by not only severely limiting contact with the outside world and censoring most communication, but also by punishing prisoners for peacefully protesting the inhumane conditions in them. Inmates who go on hunger strikes in protest often find themselves in the most nonsensical chain of events. At Tamms for instance, when an inmate declared a hunger strike, staff immediately shook down his cell and removed all commissary or other food items, to make sure he was actually starving himself. What's more is they also took all of his toothpaste because staff claimed people can survive off of eating toothpaste. Such a claim is curious seeing as how nearly all packages of toothpaste bear a warning label that reads something like: "If more than used for brushing is accidentally swallowed, seek professional help or contact a Poison Control Center immediately". One wonders how one can survive by consuming poison.

If the prisoner lasted 10 days without eating though he would then be forcibly removed from his cell, taken to the health care unit, and have a rubber hose forced up his nose and down this throat so that staff could force feed him. This was all written policy and procedure at Tamms - first insure that he can't eat, and then forcibly feed him. It used to be that prison officials needed a court order to be able to force feed someone. On January 2, 2005 though, all that changed. Illinois enacted a law that became effective that day, which was called the "Hunger Strike Statute". Tamms inmates were informed of it on January 12, 2005 in Warden's Bulletin 05-06, which read "a law has been enacted regarding hunger strikes which allows us to force feed inmates without a court order."[555]

The unwritten policy and procedures at Tamms when an inmate went on hunger strike entailed cutting off his communication with the outside world to prevent him from publicizing his hunger strike and thereby bringing attention to the heinous conditions or unjust treatment he was experiencing. Often he'd find that his mail had been "lost" or delayed until after his hunger strike had ended. All of this was designed to deprive him of one of the only peaceful means a prisoner has to protest the inhumane treatment he is subjected to. Similar tactics are used in prisons around the country.

Take California for example, for the first three weeks of July 2011, over seven thousand inmates protested about conditions in California's prison system, including decades-long confinement in SHUs. According to *Prison Health News,* "[h]unger strikers said that medications they had previously received were being denied as punishment",[556] and the *Los Angeles Time* was being denied access to interview those participating in the hunger strike.[557]

Speaking of hunger; one common punishment employed in supermax prisons and control units is to feed inmates the above-mentioned Meatloaf - an entire meal ground up and baked into a hard loaf. Prisoners can rarely stomach it so they eat nothing instead. This punishment can last for days, weeks, or even longer. At Tamms the list of reasons for being placed on Mealloaf was exhaustive as Warden's Bulletin No. 99-88 made clear:

> Inmates who display inappropriate behavior such as throwing food items or utensils, containers, trays, failure to return or properly dispose of uneaten food, drink items, serving utensils, containers or trays, obstruction or prevention of the closure of the food passage, spitting, throwing, making weapons, or improper disposal of human waste discharge or fluids MAY be placed on controlled feeding status (Meal Loaf).[558]

Not only are inmates alone and forced to endure all of the previously mentioned conditions in these prisons or units, but there is also little intellectual stimulation other than self-education. Unfortunately this is not possible for the large percentage of inmates who are illiterate, have learning disabilities like dyslexia, or lack resources to obtain the necessary materials. The AFSC's Bonnie Kerness writes that access to educational or therapeutic programs like drug courses, AA groups, or counseling is non-existent.[559] While not a hundred percent accurate, it is nearly so. Tamms for instance, didn't even permit prisoners to take the GED test for the first dozen years it was open.

There are also different levels of conditions inside supermax prisons and control units. So although the conditions explained above are found in most of them, in certain units or wings of supermaxes it can be much, much worse. For instance, no clothes, mattress, or property for days or weeks at a time; daily cell extractions; etc. Supermax prisons and control units have been called the "prisons within the prisons", but in "elevated security wings" in supermax prisons the conditions are even worse and this is where many of the severely mentally ill wind up. There walls are frequently smeared with feces and blood and certain cells are reserved as suicide watch cells. These are the prisons within the prisons within the prisons.

Not only are control units and supermaxes being used to warehouse the mentally ill, but they are also driving sane people crazy and the mentally ill crazier. One of the foremost experts on the mental health effects induced by long-term solitary confinement is Dr. Terry A. Kupers, a clinical psychiatrist at the Wright Institute at Berkeley.[560] Dr. Kupers has testified across the country in numerous trials and interviewed hundreds of prisoners,[561] and calls these types of environments "cold storage" where prisoners are subjected to "psychological torture".[562] Writing about prisoners in solitary confinement in Maine for *The Bangor Daily News*, Dr. Kupers along with David Moltz, explain how:

It is stunning how pervasive a known set of serious symptoms in this population are, including massive free-floating anxiety, incessant cleaning or pacing in the cell, paranoid ideas, sleep disturbances, problems concentrating and remembering.... The isolation and idleness that cause psychiatric symptoms in relatively healthy prisoners cause psychotic breakdowns, severe affective disorders and suicide crises in prisoners with histories of serious mental illness.[563]

The AFSC quoted a Human Rights Watch briefing paper from 2000 to note that "[p]risoners subjected to prolonged isolation may experience depression, despair, anxiety, rage, claustrophobia, hallucinations, problems with impulse control, and an impaired ability to think, concentrate, or remember.[564] As the editors of *Solitary Watch* note:

If it weren't already obvious enough, research conducted over the last 30 years confirms solitary confinement has an extremely damaging effect on mental health. One study found that a single week in solitary produced a change in EEG activity related to stress and anxiety. There's evidence that long-term isolation profoundly alters the brain chemistry, and that longer stretches in solitary produce psychopathologies at a considerably higher rate than other forms of confinement.[565]

It's not just bleeding heart liberals either who will acknowledge that mental anguish can amount to torture once they have first-hand knowledge. Senator John McCain, a Republican who was a prisoner of war during the Vietnam War, said that the isolation and accompanying mental torment was worse than the physical torture he endured.[566]

One inmate who was a victim of police lieutenant Jon Burge's torture found himself in Tamms supermax and described his nine years there as follows:

> Tamms is a hell-hole. It is not a place for humans. Tamms was made to break you mentally, physically, and spiritually, in every detail of its operation.[567]

Another factor that almost certainly adds to mental deterioration is the use of torture devises such as five-point restraints, restraint hoods, restraint belts, restraint beds, stun grenades, stun guns, stun belts, tethers, chemical agents, and waist chains which seem to be used almost exclusively and regularly in control units and supermax prisons.[568]

Cell extractions are also common. This is "where prisoners are confronted with from four to six riot-clad officers, batons drawn, descending upon the prisoner, often hog tying him/her, and removing him/her from the cell."[569] This usually occurs after the prisoner has already been maced.

At its worst, all of these mental ailments culminate in the prisoner becoming a "cutter" or suicidal. "Cutter" is the name prisoners give to those who cut or mutilate themselves. In Tamms some inmates bit or cut off whole chunks of flesh. At least one inmate had, after numerous nearly successful attempts to completely cut off his penis and testicles, finally removed a testicle. Numerous inmates there required trips to an outside hospital after swallowing fingernail clippers or inserting ink pens or tooth brushes into their urethra.

Nicholas Lampert noted on www.justseeds.org that "[s]uicide attempts, self-mutilation, and other psychotic symptoms are common at Tamms, and are an expected consequence of long-term isolation, which can induce or worsen mental illness."[570] As noted though, this is not simply a Tamms phenomenon. *Solitary Watch* reports that "studies have found that two-thirds of all prison suicides take place in solitary confinement."[571] With as little as 2 percent, and at most 10 percent, of the prison population in solitary confinement, it's telling that 67 percent of suicides happen in control units and supermaxes. For instance, in 2006 sixty-nine percent of suicides in California prisons were in solitary confinement cells,[572] and in 2007 seventy percent were.[573]

There have even been prisoners who were facing a lifetime of solitary confinement that have asked judges for a death sentence instead.[574] This is a sort of twisted version of the old "death by cop" where someone who can't bring themselves to commit suicide tries to force the police to kill them instead. Here though its "death by judge". Conditions that push people to desire death in order to escape them are the epitome of inhumane.

Unfortunately, while the mental health effects are well known, there has been little research done on the physical effects caused by long-term confinement in control units and supermaxes. There can be little doubt though, that such conditions do result in adverse physical effects on prisoners. Both stress and anxiety are known to cause problems with the health of one's heart, and as *Solitary Watch* reports:

> evidence from recent court cases suggests a relationship to things like extreme insomnia, joint pain, hypertension and even damage to the eyesight - which make sense when you are talking about not being able to walk or look more than ten feet in any direction for years or decades on end. We will clearly see more evidence of health damage as more and more prisoners grow old in long-term solitary confinement.[575]

These conditions and the resulting mental health implications are why in 2010 the European Court of Human Rights granted a stay of extradition to the United States to four terrorism suspects,[576] who were claiming that the conditions in the ADX, where they were likely to be sent were inhumane.[577] The court feared that such conditions amount to "torture or... inhuman or degrading treatment.[578] As *WIN Magazine* noted, "[i]solation units, supermax prisons, sensory deprivation, brutality toward prisoners, and the use of devices of torture are all violations of human rights and of fundamental human decency."[579]

Solitary Watch noted that Europe has largely abandoned isolation in prisons because it's "widely viewed as a form of cruel, inhuman and degrading treatment, in violation of international human rights conventions."[580] It isn't only our allies in Europe who views things this way. The United Nations has repeatedly cited the U.S. for violating treaties that prohibit such treatment of prisoners. Jody L. Sundt, an assistant professor in Portland State University's Division of Criminology and Criminal Justice explains that "[s]ome might say it isn't torture because no bones are broken, but it causes pain and suffering",[581] all the same.

According to the AFSC[582] there are three United Nations treaties that apply to prison conditions, all of which the U.S. is in violation of:

- The International Covenant on Civil and Political Rights (ICCPR);

- The International Convention on the Elimination of All Forms of Racial Discrimination (ICERD); and

- The Convention Against Torture and Other Cruel, Inhuman, or Degrading Treatment or Punishment.

Bonnie Kerness of AFSC - Newark made the following remarks at Emory University in February of 2008 which were reproduced a few months later by AFSC - Oakland in their report *Buried Alive:*

The conditions and practices that the imprisoned testify to are in violation of the Universal Declaration of Human Rights, the United Nations Convention Against Torture, and the United Nations Convention on the Elimination of All Forms of Racial Discrimination. U. S. prison practices also violate dozens of other international treaties and fit the United Nation's definition of genocide.

Article 1 of the UN Convention Against Torture prohibits policies and practices that "constitute cruel, inhuman or degrading punishment". The history of international attention to these issues is compelling. In 1995, the UN Human Rights Committee stated that conditions in certain U.S. maximum security prisons were incompatible with international standards. In 1996, the UN Special Rapporteur on Torture reported on cruel, inhuman and degrading treatment in U.S. supermax prisons. In 1998, the Special Rapporteur on Violence

Against Women took testimony in California on the ill treatment of women in U.S. prisons. In 2000, the United Nations Committee on Torture roundly condemned the U.S. for its treatment of prisoners, citing supermax prisons and the use of torture devices, as well as the practice of jailing youth with adults. The use of stun belts and restraint chairs were also cited as violating the UN Convention Against Torture. In May of 2006, the same committee concluded that the U.S. should "review the regimen imposed on detainees in supermaximum prisons, in particular, the practice of prolonged isolation".

In 1998 and again in 2005, the AFSC contributed to the World Organization Against Torture and Prison Reform International's Shadow Reports on the Status of Compliance by the U.S. Government with the International Convention Against Torture. We found that the U.S. was not meeting its obligations under that treaty. Given what has happened at Abu Ghraib and Guantánamo Bay and given that the entire Executive Branch of the U.S. government seems to sanction torture, it becomes imperative that we as advocates give more long-term attention to what is happening to people in U.S. prisons.[583]

So altogether the UN, the AFSC, Human Rights Watch, Amnesty International, and many others who have reviewed our control units and supermax prisons have concluded that they amount to modern day torture chambers. These organizations and a handful of others are bucking society's animosity of prisoners to challenge conditions in these units and prisons. The AFSC's "STOPMAX Campaign" has been struggling to gain momentum. Launched in May of 2008 it calls for ending isolation in U.S. prisons. The AFSC found that the story of prisoner abuse in supermaxes "is not a story that the public seems to want to hear."[584]

One campaign that has found limited success in bringing scrutiny on a supermax and accomplishing a few reforms, and then closure, has been that of Tamms Year Ten, a coalition of prison reform organizations, activists, artists, and the family members and friends of prisoners at Tamms. As the name suggests, it was established in 2008 after Tamms had been opened for a decade.

They lobbied legislators and the governor of Illinois, held coordinated prayer vigils across the state, and even picketed *The Chicago Tribune's* editorial board when they disagreed with an editorial on Tamms.

The most successful action was their tactical media campaign. By teaming with artists, Tamms Year Ten tagged up Chicago with six-foot by nine-foot mud stencils of a map of Illinois with a star where Tamms is located and bold letters reading "End Torture In Illinois." [585] Jesse Graves, a Milwaukee artist, designed the stencils and thirty volunteers[586] roamed Chicago plastering walls, sidewalks, underpasses, and even tourist attractions like Navy Pier and the Chicago Zoo, as well as the Logan Square Skate Park and numerous art institutes and museums.[587]

This grassroots collaboration got many to take notice, most importantly the press. Numerous newspapers, magazines, and websites reported on it. Nicholas Lampert from Justseeds Radical Artists posted that the "action was designed to draw attention to the supermax prison in Illinois", because, as Laurie Jo Reynolds noted "[m]any people don't realize that our supermax is more isolating than Guantánamo Bay, where identical treatment has been judged by Attorney General Eric Holder to be too isolating for prisoner safety".[588]

Ms. Reynolds reported that "people were surprised to see the word torture being used in connection with the state of Illinois".[589] Such surprise shows how forgetful or clueless people can be about what occurs in our criminal justice system. After all, this was at a time when Jon Burge was still making headlines in Chicago for the scandal concerning the torture of dozens of innocent people.

All of the work by Tamms Year Ten and the dozens of lawsuits filed by inmates at Tamms and a few dedicated civil rights lawyers first helped to at least make the conditions at Tamms a little less harsh.

Prisoners at Tamms gained the opportunity to make phone calls, and take the GED test.[590] More importantly, it helped convince the governor to shut down Tamms in January of 2013.

With increasing activity by anti-supermax activists and heightened scrutiny by the international community, combined with the high cost and counter productiveness of these control units and supermaxes, a few other states are starting to abandon them as well. Just as Guantánamo is supposedly going to close, a few states are closing their Guantánamos too. www.justseeds.org noted in 2009 that "[n]ationally supermaxes are on the decline with some closing or converting to regular maximum security prisons due to the unwanted consequences of long-term isolation as well as the high cost of supermax prisons".[591] By spring of 2011, Colorado, New Mexico, Maine and others saw legislation introduced to limit solitary confinement.[592] Laurie Jo Reynolds, the head of Tamms Year Ten, and Stephen Eisenman wrote in 2009 in *The Capital City Courier* that "in several states, including Ohio, Missouri, Maryland, and Virginia, as a result of lawsuits, budget shortfalls, and a recognition of both the inefficiency and cruelty of the supermax model", states have "shuttered or changed [them] to less isolating institutions."[593] Mississippi reduced their isolated population from more than 1,000 to about 150, and in 2010 Texas reduced its isolated population by more than 700 people according to the Coalition for Prisoners' Rights.[594]

Unfortunately, they also noted that Colorado, "with deep budget cuts to education and social services, ... opened up 300 additional solitary confinement cells." [595] So it's not all good news and nor is reform fast-paced. Prison guards unions, prison administrators, victims' rights groups, and prosecutor organizations all fight to keep them open. As do both the towns where the supermaxes are built and the legislators of those districts. With a public that is for the most part indifferent to the ill treatment of the "worst of the worst" Americans, reform is an issue that is rarely seen as urgent if seen or discussed at all.

The need for Tamms was hard to justify, especially when it drained the state's limited funds. It cost around $23 million per year to operate it, which when it housed 250 inmates came to about $92,000 per inmate per year.[596] A 2008 study found Tamms not only wasn't cost-effective, but Jody L. Sundt one of the co-authors noted that it was "primarily a symbol, a gesture of overwhelming control."[597] Even Cook County Sheriff Tom Dart says long-term solitary confinement "doesn't really work".[598]

Of course, little about our criminal justice system is cost-effective any more. *Newsweek* reported that:

> The cost of our prison addiction is staggering. In recent years, America's total criminal-justice tab - state, local, and federal - has ballooned to more than $200 billion a year, draining government resources at the

worst possible moment. Meanwhile, millions of men - fathers, brothers, wage earners - have been consigned to a vicious cycle of absence, stigmatization, and recidivism.[599]

Yet we continue to spend astronomical amounts of money on mass incarceration, supermaxes, etc. even though these policies are counterproductive and wasteful. We do so only because our irrational fear and hatred have us passing these laws to benefit the few who play on the emotions of the many. This is the result when policies are created based on emotion rather than rational thought.

9

REFUSING RE-ENTRY

The old saw that once one serves their sentence, he or she has repaid their debt to society is officially dead and buried. In today's hyper-vengeful, "tough-on-crime"-infested America, a person who commits a crime is forever branded and never acknowledged as having sufficiently repaid society. Once the stamp of "criminal" has been applied, a person is seen as an outcast, undeserving of a second chance or forgiveness, a pariah for life, always seen as suspect. In an interview with *The Nation* magazine, Michelle Alexander, the author of the book *The New Jim Crow: Mass Incarceration in the Age of Colorblindness,* notes how people "return home from prison and face legal discrimination in virtually all areas of social and economic and political life. They are legally discriminated against in employment, barred from public housing and denied other public benefits."[600]

That's assuming of course that one can actually get out of prison once their sentence has been served. In many states anyone deemed sexually dangerous can fall under civil commitment laws, which means that after they finish serving their criminal sentence they can then be civilly committed to prison in a reversal of the theory of "innocent until proven guilty". The courts have concluded that the government doesn't need to prove that you're sexually dangerous beyond a reasonable doubt, because that standard of proof has "no applicability in the civil commitment process."[601] Now the committed person must prove to a judge that they are no longer sexually dangerous before they will be released. Therefore they languish in prison for years or decades past the time they were sentenced to serve for committing the crime. Often the judge who makes the decision is elected and terrified of being labeled "soft- on-crime" by giving a sex offender their freedom, and therefore won't approve release until he or she believes it is politically safe to do so.

In 2007, *The Nation* noted how rapidly these civil commitment laws spread:

> Around 1990 a handful of states rewrote their mental health laws to reel in sex offenders - most of whom were not mentally ill by any definition - as their prison terms expired. In the mid-90s, especially after the Supreme Court upheld Kansas' Sexually Violent Predator Act, a dozen others followed suit. The panic flared again in 2006 and '07: New Hampshire and New York enacted commitment laws, and a change in Virginia's law quickly tripled its detainee population. Congress approved the civil commitment of sex offenders in

federal prisons, including the growing percentage who land there on pornography charges.[602]

California expanded their civil commitment law in 2007 "to make virtually every sex offender in the prison system eligible for a lifetime of detention". [603] At the California State Hospital where hundreds of them are held, the Mental Health Department "never recommended [the] release", of any of the 200 men who finally convinced the courts to let them out. [604] The Mental Health Department is seemingly a poor judge of who constitutes an actual threat, because when 93 of the releases were tracked for six years - twice as long as the time span used in most recidivism studies - only 6 had been arrested again for sex crimes.[605] That's a far cry from the average recidivism rate for people who leave California prisons in general, which is over 60%, and seems to compellingly dispute the state's claim that they're all "sexually violent predators" and can't be released.

Other sex offenders are being denied parole because they can't find housing that complies with the various ordinances that restrict where sex offenders may live.[606] Depending on the state, county, etc. sex offenders may be barred from living in most of the residences in their home towns depending on how many schools, parks, and play-grounds there are.

What's that you say, there's no love lost for sex offenders, especially those who are sexually dangerous? Your fear is palpable, but in the case of truly sexually dangerous people it is somewhat understandable. Yet, what about children? Do they evoke the same fear? Can you say that there is no love lost if they are held past their outdates?

In Illinois nearly 10% of juvenile prisoners (104 kids in 2009) were in prison after they should have been paroled simply because "officials found homes of families or friends to be unacceptable, or because families refuse to take them back" or "because officials cannot find an appropriate placement in a transitional living program or other kind of facility."[607] We're not talking days or weeks after their expected parole dates either, but rather months and years. As *The Chicago Tribune* noted, two of them had been held for nearly three years after they should have been paroled.[608] What kind of message does it send to those kids that not a single person or organization is willing to give them a second chance? Do you think this will make them more or less likely to want to become an upstanding member of society? If you're told you aren't welcome somewhere, you can't help but to feel you aren't a member. What's more outrageous though, is that society is simultaneously telling these kids that it rejects them while having the audacity to expect them to basically reform themselves, desire societal membership, and successfully reenter society when eventually released.

Once someone finally does make it out to the streets, he or she will join the five million others who are on probation or parole in the U.S., [609] and the over ten million others with criminal records, to experience firsthand the smorgasbord of discrimination allotted to anyone considered a "criminal".

Disenfranchisement

People with a criminal record in the U. S. are rejected by society in a plethora of ways. Just as they were politically muted while in prison, many will find that they are still denied their "right" to vote upon release. More than five million people have permanently lost the right to vote due to having been convicted of a felony.[610] America is the only democracy that permits the forfeiture of the right to vote for committing a crime.[611] This has resulted in nearly a quarter of black men in 10 states not being able to vote.[612]

In Florida alone over a million people were disenfranchised during the 2000 presidential elections.[613] It is widely believed that those extra votes would have put Al Gore safely into the presidency.[614] In 2004 alone, 6 million Americans were denied a vote due to having once committed a crime.[615] Governor Charlie Christ "restored the voting rights of 154,000 former prisoners who had been convicted of nonviolent crimes" according to *Rolling Stone* magazine, but then in March Of 2011, "then Governor Rick Scott overturned [this]..., instantly disenfranchising 97,491 ex-felons and prohibiting another 1.1 million prisoners from being allowed to vote after serving their time."[616]

In two-thirds of states being on felony probation or parole means you can't vote. In 11 states being convicted of a felony means you lose the right to vote forever.[617] The United Nations' Human Rights Committee in 2006 called for the return of voting rights for people released from prison in the U.S.[618] Voting disenfranchisement according to The Sentencing Project in Washington, has "a quantifiable impact on public safety. Voting is a clear indication of a person's commitment to democratic ideals and is an important expressive activity that demonstrates one's membership in society. To deny that right is incongruous with the principles of reentry and sends a counterintuitive message to people who have been released from prison".[619] The message is that they are still not members of society.

Although many people choose not to exercise their right to vote for whatever reason, when someone tells you that you can't vote in America because of your past it causes a deep psychological scar in many. As the three following quotes from interviewees for another report by The Sentencing Project show, its ostracizing effect is clear:

> A I: "It invokes a sense of kind of like your country turning its back on you. You feel like you're not a citizen of the country. So voting is not a right, but a privilege that can be revoked."

> Miles: "Voting is the American way. Once it's taken, you become a third-class citizen, and can't

participate in what this country's all about and
what wars were fought for."

Julius: "Just the word bothers me, disenfranchisement.
It's like, 'As a matter of fact, you're nobody, you
don't count. We don't respect your opinion'."[620]

So why do we take away people's right to vote in the first place?
The above-mentioned report concluded that: "[t]here is no compelling
state interest for continuing to deprive people with a felony conviction
of the right to vote."[621] It is purely punitive and a result of America's
view of "criminals" as less than human, not citizens, and not deserving
of basic rights and freedoms.

Government Assistance

In addition to losing the right to vote, anyone convicted of a drug
offense is banned from receiving both food stamps and welfare thanks
to President Clinton's welfare reform.[622] This translates into more than
half of all women released from prison being denied public benefits.[623]
Also thanks to Clinton's passage of the Higher Education Reform Act
they are also denied access to Pell Grants, [624] which denies those with
drug convictions financial assistance for college.

Employment Discrimination

Without welfare, college grants, and other social benefits like public housing, employment becomes even more imperative for people with a drug conviction than for those without, but finding employment with any type of conviction on your record is highly unlikely in America. One study found that white men were half as likely to be called back for a second interview if they had a criminal record, and black men were two-thirds less likely to be called back again if they had a criminal record. Adding insult to injury, blacks without a criminal record were only as likely to be called back as a white with a criminal record.[625] These unflattering facts about American society have resulted in a 60% unemployment rate for people released from prison after one year.[626] Other estimates put the "unemployment rate among former prisoners [at] 80%."[627]

Too often the only jobs that are grudgingly made available to people with a criminal record are those which nearly no other American will take. Ineligible for many social benefits, people with a criminal record often have little choice but to take the worst and lowest paying jobs society has to offer, or return to a life of crime. It is widely known that Americans will not work agricultural jobs like picking fruits and vegetables. Evidence of that can easily be discerned from the fact that the vast majority of farm workers are immigrants, the majority of whom arrive illegally. As anti-immigrant and racist feelings are increasingly inflamed and codified into legislation, and as immigrants flee or are deported, many crops are left rotting in the fields due to farmers' inability to find Americans willing to pick them.

In the last two years alone a million people have been deported.[628] Georgia has recently joined several other states in passing anti-immigration legislation which has resulted in immigrants fleeing the state and leaving farmers short of workers by the thousands.[629] The governor in Georgia, Nathan Deal, suggested filling those unwanted jobs with people on probation.[630] The farmers though, seem unable to overcome long-ingrained prejudices against, and irrational fears of, anyone who has committed a crime, and don't seem too enthusiastic about the idea no matter how many crops rot in the fields. As Barbara Lawson, who co-owns a farm in the state remarked to *The Wall Street Journal,* farmers "would be scared to death to let ex-convicts work on their farms."[631]

Not only does this show how troublesome it is for "criminals" to gain employment in even unpopular jobs, but it shows the irrational fear that is pervasive in American society. After all, we're talking about probationers - people who committed crimes that were so minor that they didn't require prison time - and still you see people are "scared to death"[632] of them without even knowing them personally or what crime they committed.

In an attempt to address such widespread employment discrimination against anyone with a criminal record, half of a dozen states and two dozen cities have passed "Ban the Box" legislation.[633] This prohibits employers from asking about a person's criminal background until given an interview. This prevents employers from arbitrarily trashing any application where someone would have checked off the "yes" box after questions like: "Have you ever been convicted of a felony?" It is unclear though whether this will translate into more interviews, let alone jobs. After all, nowadays one only has to hit a few keys on the computer to pull up someone's criminal history, as the employer would have all the applicant's personal identifying information right there on the application.

Without a sea of change in public opinion the stigma attached to a criminal conviction will most likely continue to keep people unemployed. Such unemployment works to keep "criminals" ostracized from society, alienating them further by repeatedly rejecting them from the workforce. This not only keeps them poverty-stricken, but often results in further criminal activity which usually means an eventual return to prison. Even if they don't commit a crime it may mean returning to jail or prison due to an inability to pay fines, restitution, fees, etc. Payment of which are often a requirement of their probation or parole, or part of their sentence.

Taxing "Criminals"

As states are increasingly strapped for cash (due in part to mass incarceration), they are passing more and more legislation attempting to transfer the growing costs of the criminal justice system onto "criminals".[634] The irony here is twofold. First, as David Udell at the Brennan Center for Justice noted: "you are loading debt onto people who are in the justice system in the first place due to lack of financial resources".[635] Second, the reason the costs of the criminal justice system are so high in the first place is not due to any increase in crime, but rather due to out of control sentencing laws which require longer sentences, and increased monitoring of people who commit a crime. Not to mention collecting the panoply of fines, etc. which require both more resources to collect than the revenue they actually generate, and the added costs of penalizing non-payment with imprisonment. As Hakeem Jeffries, a Brooklyn Assemblyman noted, "no one thinks it's anything but a barrier to successful re-entry into society, because people with low or no income will owe significant amounts of money."[636]

How many different ways are there to load debt onto someone for a crime? Seemingly too many to count. Most states don't keep track of them all or how they relate to one another.[637] There are basically four major categories that they all fall under though.

First, there is what is called restitution. This varies as to what a person owes in reparation or compensation to cover the loss or damage done to the state or someone who was the victim of the crime. Second, there are a multitude of fines that are imposed as punishment depending on the crime committed and state in which it was committed. Restitution and fines each have a legitimate criminal justice purpose - to repay the victim and to punish the offender.

The other two categories have no legitimate criminal justice purpose. They work only to make reentry more difficult and are not about justice but rather about trying in vain to fill in holes in state budgets. They are what the Brennan Center for Justice calls "user fees" and "poverty penalties".

User fees are basically fees imposed for "using" the criminal justice system. Obviously one doesn't voluntarily use it, but rather does so as a consequence of being charged with a crime. There are too many to try and list, but for instance, in North Carolina a DUI conviction can mean a $1,000 fee for an alcohol monitoring system.[638] Crime lab analysis fees can vary depending on the state. In Illinois the fee is $100 [639], while in North Carolina it's $600.[640] Depending on the state you may be forced to pay arrest fees, booking fees, DNA bank fees, and more.[641] Thirteen of the 15 states studied recently charged fees for needing a public defender which can total hundreds or thousands of dollars.[642] One of the worst fees is in Pennsylvania where they charge prisoners a $60 fee to get out of prison and onto parole.[643] Not only is this unconstitutional due to there being no waiver for indigency,[644] but if someone is too poor to pay the $60, the state is stuck expending $100 per day to keep him or her incarcerated.[645]

The final category, poverty penalties, are applied only if you are too poor to immediately pay off all of your restitution, fines, and user fees, and often end up adding up to more than the initial debt. The Brennan Center for Justice found poverty penalties such as "late fees, interest charges, payment plan fees, and collection fees" can be found in 14 out of the 15 states studied.[646] Thirteen of the states studied charge interest or late fees such as the $300 flat fee in California, or the $11 - $21 late fee applied in certain Florida counties every time you're late with a payment. [647] Michigan slaps a 20% late fee after 56 days.[648] Nine of the states studied charge exorbitant collection fees, either by the state itself like in Alabama and Illinois where the fee is 30% of the amount owed [649], or by private collection agencies like in Florida where they tack on a 40% collection fee.[650] In all three of the latter-mentioned states, these percentages would be criminal if charged by a car dealer as an interest rate. For instance, in Alabama it is considered criminal usury to charge more than 8%,[651] while in Illinois the legal limit is 20%.[652] Nine states tack on a fee just for needing a payment plan.[653] The payment plan fee can reach $100 in some states.[654]

With all of these fines, restitution, user fees, and poverty penalties heaped on people who commit a crime, in addition to the inability to find employment, reentering society and escaping the criminal justice system becomes an often insurmountable task. Imagine being released from jail or prison, illiterate or functionally illiterate, with no employable skills, no social benefits available, and hundreds of dollars in fees, fines, etc. that must be paid or else you'll be fined more, or even reincarcerated. If you have no family to support you and can't find adequate employment, you're basically left with two options: commit a crime to pay off the debt and support yourself; or be reincarcerated to begin the whole cycle anew, adding to your debt pile with new booking fees, etc.

Two examples given in the report are illustrative of the financial quagmire these various criminal justice debts place people in. A woman in Pennsylvania "convicted of a drug crime incurred 26 different fees ranging from $2 to $345, ... added together she faces $2,464 in fees alone".[655] That's nearly five times the $500 she was fined for committing the crime, and more than seven times the $325 she was ordered to pay in restitution.[656]

In California, a woman convicted of fraud and drug charges not only had to pay $40,000 in restitution, but also $136.78 per month in probation fees for three years. Yet, since she was unable to pay off her restitution before her 3 years of probation ended, she was placed on administrative probation, incurring another $33 per month in new fees.[657] Making less than $17,000 per year at her job [658] and ineligible for any government social benefits it was a foregone conclusion that she would be unable to pay $44,924.08 in 3 years when she only earned $51,000 in that entire time. Only a society which is extraordinarily callous, and at best indifferent or at worst deliberately antagonistic to her plight, would demand she do the impossible and then further penalize her when she inevitably fails.

Revoked or denied parole, extended probation,[659] or increased debt aren't the only penalties one can incur when they are unable to pay off their criminal justice debt. An increasingly popular penalty is to revoke people's driver's licenses if they can't pay their fines, etc. At least eight of the fifteen states studied "suspend driver's license based on missed payments."[660] Recently *Prison Legal News* reported another county considering similar measures. The Davidson County Clerk's Office in Tennessee proposed revoking "people's driver's license if their court fees and fines are not paid within a year."[661]

So not only do they lose their right to vote, but now they lose their driving privileges as well. Stating the obvious, the Brennan Center for Justice noted that this will not only make it more difficult for people to keep their jobs or find work, but in order to pay off their fines to stay out of jail or prison or get off probation, many will choose to chance continuing to drive to work and may end up rearrested and reincarcerated for driving without a license.[662]

The Brennan report found that all this debt "impedes reentry and rehabilitation."[663] Not only does the fact that one has a criminal record hinder a person's ability to find employment and housing, but so does this debt. "In many states, criminal justice debt wreaks havoc on individual's credit scores and with it their housing and employment prospects."[664]

Employers are increasingly performing credit checks on job applicants.[665] More worrisome than the poor credit is that on the credit reports it often indicates that the outstanding debt is criminal justice debt informing potential employers of an applicant's criminal history.[666] So even if the state or city has passed "Ban the Box" legislation and the employer doesn't do a criminal background check, the employer would still learn of the criminal history by doing a credit check. People with poor credit (especially a credit report which indicated criminal justice debt) will also have a difficult time finding someone to rent them an apartment, or a bank to give them a loan.

In many states the government is so rabid about demonizing "criminals" and getting it's money that it is indifferent not only to the barriers it creates to ones reentry, but even to how it will affect that person's family relationships. Obviously keeping a person unemployed, perpetually in debt or sent back to prison is harmful to one's family relationships, especially if it makes it harder for parents to pay their child support payments.[667] Not to mention, as we've already seen, a failure to pay child support payments can likewise lead to incarceration itself. In many states it also acts as a poll tax. At least 7 of the states studied require repayment of criminal justice debt to regain the "right" to vote.[668] This is yet another way to deny "criminals" their voice, and makes passing new laws against "criminals" that much easier.

While society may harbor the attitude that these user fees and poverty penalties piled on top of fines and restitution are a great idea and "criminals" deserve no better, attempting to place the financial burden of a criminal justice system designed to benefit corporations on the backs of prisoners is a huge mistake. All it actually does is: 1) create a permanent criminal underclass; 2) increases the costs of the criminal justice system which society ultimately ends up paying for; 3) increases recidivism which makes society less safe; 4) encourages more counter-productive laws to be passed; and 5) further ostracizes people discouraging them from reforming. As has already been shown, incarcerating people for failing to pay their debts costs more than if the state just paid the costs of the criminal justice system. After all, that is what one of the main functions of government is, and what we all, "criminals" included, pay taxes for.

Harassment and Banishment

Employment discrimination, disenfranchisement, and the loading of debt are not the only barriers to successful reentry. Nor are they the only signs of societal rejection encountered by people trying to reenter society after having committed a crime. Now we've returned to actually using signs and banishment. Back in the colonial era there were three punishments for criminals that were later seen as exceptionally mean-spirited and incompatible with reentry into society.

The first was branding - the old scarlet letter. This let the community know at a glance that a person was convicted of a crime.[669] Without plastic surgery being available, it was a lifelong sentence.[670]

Another was outright banishment which meant that the person could not remain in, nor return to, their community.[671] Banishment has made a comeback in many states, if in less obvious ways. It is now used to prevent people who are labeled gang members from residing in a neighborhood in which that gang is known to be active. In Illinois this is done by either the state filing a civil suit against the "gang member" under the Streetgang Terrorism Omnibus Prevention Act,[672] or by making it a condition of one's Mandatory Supervised Release.[673] California prohibits "ex-cons from associating with gang members and visiting drug neighborhoods" according to *Playboy* magazine.[674] Julian Mendoza, who is staunchly against such rules explained that "[y]ou're basically telling guys, 'Don't go home and don't associate with your family'. What are they supposed to do never see their brother or cousin again? It's just an easy parole violation. The police can lock you up again anytime they want."[675]

The third punishment was known as "shaming", where one was forced to hang a sign around their neck advertising their crime. Today we have a more pervasive and sinister type of "shaming" - registries on the internet. The public now uses the "click to print" feature on these to print up "Beware" posters that show a person's face and crime, and then plaster his or her neighborhood with them.[678] This is basically another form of banishment - shame, embarrass, and ostracize a person into moving out of the neighborhood.

The original registries started by listing "sex offenders" only. Every state now has a sex offender registry and the Adam Walsh Child Protection And Safety Act was signed into law at the federal level to try to create a uniform national system.[679] The courts have upheld sex offender registries noting that when "sex offenders" "reenter society, they are much more likely than any other type of offender to be arrested for a new rape or sexual assault."[680] Unfortunately the courts are wrong about the recidivism rates of sex offenders. They actually have one of the lowest recidivism rates of any category of offenders.[681]

There is also a widespread and mistaken belief that child victims of sex offenses are abused by strangers. It isn't strangers or reoffenders that people should be scared of. As *The Correctional Forum* noted in 2011:

> Offenses by strangers are the exception not the rule. The U. S. Department of Justice found that 9 out of 10 child victims of sexual abuse knew their abusers and that approximately 40 percent of all abusers are children themselves. Of the 60,000 to 70,000 annual arrests on charges of sexual assault, only about 115 are abductions by strangers. Megan's Law and SORNA (Sex Offender Registration and Notification Act") are based on the

premise that sex offenders should be required to register because they pose a significant risk of reoffending. But since the vast majority of sex crimes are committed by first time offenders, this measure does not protect the public.

Studies show little or no effect of Megan's Law in reducing sexual offenses or re-offenses... [A] study conducted by The Research and Evaluation Unit of New Jersey Department of Corrections and funded by the U. S. Department of Justice...[concluded that] "Despite wide community support for these laws, there is little evidence to date, including this study, to support a claim that Megan's Law is effective in reducing either new first time sex offenses or sexual reoffenses." Similarly, a New York study found "no support for the effectiveness of registration and community notification laws in reducing sexual offending", and that "over 95 percent of all sexual offense arrests were committed by first-time sex offenders, casting doubt on the ability of laws that target repeat offenders to meaningfully reduce sexual offending." A 10-state study found no systematic reduction in sex crime rates after implementation of registration and notification policies.[682]

A bigger problem though is that most people listed on "sex offender" registries have never raped anyone or committed a sexual assault of any kind, and nor are they dangerous. Take Georgia for example, the Georgia Sex Offender Registration Review Board found that out of the more than 17,000 "sex offenders" on their list, only about 100 were actual "predators" and only about 850 were "clearly dangerous."[683]

So who are the people who are listed as "sex offenders"? Nationally there were nearly 700,000 people listed as "sex offenders" as of December 2008.[684] Often times though, many are listed for crimes that have nothing to do with sex, or were instances of consensual sex. Nowadays, in the majority of states in the U. S. (32 of them) streaking (indecent exposure) is sufficient to get one listed as a "sex offender" if caught.[685] Is there any man out there who hasn't at some point in his life urinated in public? An alley, next to a dumpster, on the side of the highway maybe? In at least 13 states you're a "sex offender" if caught.[686] What either of these crimes has to do with sex is beyond me.

Even when a crime does involve sex, more often than not it is consensual, and crimes that one would think would get one listed don't. So while streaking will get you registered in 32 states, getting caught paying for sex will only get you registered in 5 states.[687] Even though, according to *Newsweek,* "sex buyers ... were nearly eight times as likely as nonbuyers to say they would rape a woman if they could get away with it."[688] Horny teenagers on the other hand are constantly being ensnared by "sex offender" registry laws. Twenty-nine states require registration for acts of consensual sex between teenagers,[689] and unscrupulous prosecutors are increasingly charging teenagers with "distributing child pornography" for emailing or texting nude pictures of themselves or their boyfriends/girlfriends to others.

So while the widespread belief is that everyone listed on sex offender registries are sexually dangerous predators, the truth is that hardly any are. Instead society is routinely discriminating against and stigmatizing people based on false assumptions. This is resulting in ruined lives and even deaths.

Instead of making society safer, they are actually accomplishing the opposite. As Lenore Skenazy recommended on *Forbes.com* "shred your sex offender maps" because "they're worse than useless" and are "making our kids less safe."[690] The article gives three reasons. First, by insinuating that there are more sexual predators in the neighborhood than there actually are, kids are being kept inside where they grow fat playing video games. This diminishes the sense of community and looking out for each other[691], not to mention the health risks of less exercise. Second, they waste police resources and time, tracking people who aren't dangerous, meaning police don't have time and resources to keep an eye on people who are truly dangerous.[692] Third, your kids could easily end up listed as a "sex offender".[693] As we've already seen, innocently horny teens or kids who pee in the bushes can both end up as "sex offenders". Being registered as a "sex offender" could also put their lives in danger.

Another reason that these registries have little usefulness from a law enforcement perspective is that, one, the truly dangerous don't bother to register and instead abscond to who knows where, and two, many registries contain highly inaccurate information. The Vermont State Auditor "found critical or significant errors in 79% of the community based Sex Offender Registry (SOR) records audited", according to *Prison Legal News.*[694]

What should terrify anyone who has a family member or loved one who is registered as a "sex offender", is the fact that the registries put people's lives in danger. Most people on them have reported being harassed and a few people have even been murdered.[695] In April of 2006, a vigilante in Maine got the addresses of two people off of the registry and murdered them.[696] In Washington the year before, someone made a hit list from the registry and killed two people on it.[697]

Even if they don't get you killed they can ruin your life and the lives of your family. Such was the case with Wendy Whitaker. When she was 17 she performed oral sex on a boy who she liked who was 2 weeks shy of his 16th birthday.[698] After jail, prison, and boot camp, she then had to register as a sex offender.[699] The registry lists her crime as "sodomy".[700] Now over 30, her and her husband had to move after she was evicted due to a child-care center being located on her street.[701] If all that were not bad enough, the local news highlighted her and her house when doing a feature on local sex offenders, neglecting to mention the details of her "crime".[702] Her husband then lost his county job when they were forced to move.[703]

These registries stigmatize a person for life, often costing people listed on them their homes or jobs, causing their families to be ostracized, and severely affecting their children. After all, who's going to allow their kids to play with the "sex offender's" kids? Do streakers and horny teens really deserve a lifetime of ridicule and persecution? Does anyone? Yet our "sex offender" laws continue to grow harsher and have less and less to do with sex let alone assault. It doesn't stop at being listed either. What's worse is when you're also made to pay for the listing. In Illinois "sex offenders" are required to pay the costs of registration for life.[704] After all, why should society be required to foot the bill to stigmatize someone for life when they can just legislate the tab onto the backs of the ostracized?

Accompanying sex offender registries in most states are numerous discriminatory laws which dictate where "sex offenders" are permitted to live, effectively banishing them from many neighborhoods, towns, or even cities. In Georgia, for instance, "sex offenders" are prohibited from residing within 1,000 feet of any park, school, church, or any place where children congregate like a library, bus stop, or day care center.[705] In Iowa, the exclusion zone extends to 2,000 feet (although they've now restricted the number of "sex offenders" who qualify),[706] and in Miami it is 2,500 feet.[707]

These exclusion zones have effectively pushed people into what are in all actuality leper colonies - colonies of homeless "sex offenders" who aren't allowed to live in any of their prior residences. So for instance, until they became so numerous as to enrage the local populous by their presence, homeless "sex offenders" had built a colony under the Julia Tuttle Causeway bridge in Miami - Dade County.[708] Although they lacked running water they had electricity thanks to a generator.[709] Electricity was more necessary than water due to the fact that in order to avoid being sent back to prison, the GPS monitors that were fastened to their ankles needed to always be charged.[710] In another instance, until they too were evicted, homeless "sex offenders" in suburban Atlanta set up a tent city on state land.

Adding to the problem is that the registries create additional employment discrimination, meaning many "sex offenders" find themselves inexplicably fired from their jobs.[711] Also their job options overall, already limited by having a criminal background, are further limited by laws which prohibit the hiring of sex offenders in various fields. Take Iowa as an example, registered "sex offenders" there are prohibited from working or even visiting places where kids go, such as schools, libraries, fairs, and even public pools.[712] So even if they could find apartments willing to rent to them that aren't in the exclusion zones, they often can't afford to pay the rent without a job and too often aren't eligible for government benefits either.

There can be little dispute that society has collectively refused to allow people convicted of "sex crimes" to reenter society. The truth is that they are humiliated, ostracized, and discriminated against at every turn, with the end result being that they are permanently rejected. This causes some to reoffend that otherwise wouldn't have, and end up returning to prison. Others are returned to prison for failing to dot their i's when registering. As *The Economist* noted in an article about the U. S.'s "unjust sex laws", in Georgia failure to register or provide an accurate address means 10-30 years in prison the first time, and a life sentence the second time.[713] In Illinois, if one provides false information on the registry they are guilty of a Class 3 felony (2-5 years in prison) and will incur an additional mandatory $500 fine.[714] That's in addition to having already had to pay for the cost of registration which is a $20 initial fee and $10 per year for life.[715]

Even worse is the fact that since our politicians are incapable of giving up the crack pipe of fear-mongering and tough-on-crime rhetoric, the sex offender registry fad is morphing to include other types of crimes as well. This is in addition to the previously discussed outlandish stretching of the definition of a "sex crime".

Lenore Skenazy spoke too soon when writing in 2010 about the irony that there are no registries for murderers or armed robbers.[716]

238

There already were. Florida registered repeat murderers since 2003. Indiana started registering "murderers" the same year. Oklahoma began to do so in 2008, and Montana has been registering those convicted of deliberate homicide since 1995.[717] These four, and numerous others, register a variety of violent offenders.[718] Illinois not only registers sex offenders, but also arsonists,[719] and now, after having for years registered anyone who murders someone who is 17 years old, or younger, recently passed legislation on July 22, 2011 to register all "murderers".[720]

In a society that detests anyone even charged with a crime, it's no surprise that legislation continues to sail through the Illinois General Assembly, even when it has no legitimate function other than to satisfy the vengeful desires of a single victim's family.

When Alaska's sex offender registry was challenged in the U. S. Supreme Court, the court upheld the state's right to their registry under the fictitious claim that the "risk of recidivism posed by sex offenders is 'frightening and high'."[721] In Illinois there's not even a claim that this bill would reduce recidivism. Not only do "murderers" not have "frightening and high" recidivism rates, they have incredibly low, if not the lowest recidivism rates of any category.[722] The U. S. Department of Justice's Bureau of Justices Statistics found that only 1.2 percent of "murderers" were rearrested for murder within three years of release.[723] Whether they were actually guilty or not of the crimes they were rearrested for was seemingly not taken into account.

In New York, a study by the Division of Parole found that none of the 440 "murderers" released between 2004 and 2007 were returned to prison for a new crime.[724] Nationwide "murderers" had the lowest rearrest rate.[725] John Caher, a spokesman for the New York State Division of Criminal Justice Services was quoted in *Prison Legal News* as saying that "murderers" "consistently have the lowest recidivism rate of any offenders."[726]

So why have a murderer registry? Because it is yet another piece of legislation that a public which is rabidly anti-crime and which irrationally fears and demonizes "criminals", will blindly support without knowing anything more than a sound bite spouted by a politician using the bill to prove his tough-on-crime bona fides.

How did the legislation come about? Not out of need, that's for sure. Rather, from a mother's hatred of her daughter's killer. The new law is called Andrea's Law after Andrea Will who was murdered in 1998.[727] (Nowadays it seems every registry law is named after a victim of some crime. Everyone wants a registry named after their child or loved one who was a victim - "Megan's Law", "Andrea's Law", "Zacchary's Law", the "Mary Rippy Violent Offenders Registration Law", etc.[728]).

This is not a case where, had the registry existed at the time, it would have saved Andrea's life. No, it wouldn't have made one iota of difference. The "murderer" was the victim's boyfriend. He hadn't murdered anyone yet and Andrea already knew where he lived and worked. So she not only had the information that a registry would have provided but he wouldn't have been registered anyway. Nor was an argument ever made that this registry will save lives or in any way make anyone safer.

Echoing society's current view that serving your time in prison is insufficient to repay your debt to society, and that "criminals" should not have any rights, nor be allowed to reenter society, the victim's mother, upset that the guy only had to serve 12 years[729] of a 24-year sentence stated: "Should you just be able to walk away? I don't feel it should stop at the prison gate. I don't feel it should stop after a couple of years of probation. Why should he have the same rights and privileges my daughter will never have?"[730]

So why didn't she push for legislation to make the murderers serve their entire sentence? Because Illinois already enacted Truth-In-Sentencing legislation more than a decade ago[731], which requires "murderers" to now serve 100% of their sentence. By trying to get a registry passed and making it retroactive she thought she could increase the punishment of her daughter's killer after he had already served his prison sentence, and one would imagine after he thought he had "repaid his debt to society" according to the law.

The registry requires anyone convicted of murder to register for 10 years. Andrea's killer though will only have to register for the three years that he is on Mandatory Supervised Release because he has moved to Hawaii and out of Illinois'jurisdiction.[732] Instead now 4,300 people[733] will be further stigmatized by having to register due to the laws retroactive nature. It also opens up the possibility that, just as people use the "sex offender" registry to stalk and kill "sex offenders", people can use it to find "murderers" to seek revenge. At the very least they work to further stigmatize people who are already struggling to reenter society after long prison sentences.

Rather than keeping society safer, one can easily envision the murderer registry making society more dangerous. It is significantly more difficult for a person to be restored to useful citizenship when they can't find employment. This registry virtually guarantees that fewer employers will be willing to hire people on it. The bill requires that a person's employer and the employer's phone number be listed as well.[734] Can you think of anything worse for a business than advertising on the internet that you employ "murderers"? How secure do you think that job is when the murder victim's family and friends can look up the employer of the person they hold responsible for their loved one's death and then call to threaten a boycott, or worse yet, show up to harass or kill the employee at work?

Consider the difference between those who commit murder and sex crimes. Gang members make up a much larger percentage of murder victims than sex crime victims. While prior to this registry a fellow gang member of the murder victim would have had a difficult time locating the person responsible for the murder, they will now not only have the person's home address and employer's address, but the person will be unable to change their name to hide from those seeking revenge. The reason being is that changing ones name has now also been criminalized for anyone convicted of murder.[735] How long before gangs utilize this registry as a quick reference to locate and kill the opposition?

It's not just gang member's society needs to worry about either. Now any drunken family member or friend of a murder victim can locate the released "murderer" at the touch of a keyboard or Smartphone and go kill them before they've had time to sober up. Also, with the high rate of false convictions in Illinois (more people were exonerated from death row than executed[736]), not to mention Illinois' propensity for convicting multiple people for a single murder under a theory of accountability[737] (getaway driver, lookout, etc.), means that people who didn't actually kill anyone will also be targeted after having to register.

What's that you say? Who cares what happens to "criminals"? You don't believe anyone who was charged and convicted was really innocent? Okay, then how many innocent bystanders - the "criminals'" employers, friends, family - will be caught in the crossfire? This possibility is not something people on the registry can take lightly. One of those unfortunate enough to have been ensnared by the law's retroactivity was Brian Nelson who was released after serving 28 years. As reported by *The Chicago Tribune* "he lives with his mother and is concerned about how a murderer registry would affect her life."[738] Mr. Nelson noted how a "lot of people, when they get out of prison, have no one to live with but their parents or family".[739] They will all suffer the consequences of this registry as well.

Another person who must now register is Isaac Denson. He told *The Chicago Tribune,* "I have done everything the system asked, [and] now they're going to change the game."[740] He felt that registering would mean that "if all that information is out there, after I have done my time and completed my parole, people will just see me as a murderer, not a citizen, or a running captain, or a father ."[741] These are seemingly things that were given little to no consideration by Illinois politicians in their stampede to pass the bill.

Nor was consideration given to how these "murderers" would react to this registry. They must now increasingly worry about protecting themselves from people seeking revenge since the state is now providing their location to anyone with a grudge. How many released "murderers" will now live in fear of their lives or the safety of their family, feel it necessary to illegally obtain firearms to protect themselves is unclear, but it seems safe to assume that the more realistic it is that one's enemies can find them, the greater the threat, ergo the greater the need to arm themselves for protection.

Only a single legislator in Illinois even cautioned against the registry fad. No one cautioned against any negative ramifications of the registry.

The murderer registry bill originally passed through the Illinois House of Representatives by a vote of 97 to 1 with 4 obstentions.[742] The sole courageous "no" vote belonged to Rep. Monique Davis who warned "It's a slippery slope, ladies and gentlemen. If we keep making registries for different crimes and convictions, where does it stop?"[743] Her colleagues in the Illinois Senate are seemingly fine with such a proposition as they went on to pass the bill unanimously.[744] Governor Quinn signed the bill into law less than two month later.[745]

The expansion of registries is alarming in that the number of people susceptible to future registrations is seemingly limited only by the number of people with a criminal conviction. Especially considering that many new registry laws are retroactive when enacted.

Where does it stop? Should we do preemptive registries? Should we now have all war veterans register as well? Half of them would seem to fit the faux theory used to register "murderers" - i.e. that those who kill once have the propensity to kill again (which recidivism statistics don't actually support). I recall seeing a news report on ABC which said 50% of servicemen in the current wars have killed an enemy combatant. Not to mention a large portion of them have PTSD which makes them more prone to violence, as the high rates of spousal abuse of returning servicemen attest to. Recently one veteran going through a nasty custody battle went on a shooting rampage killing eight people in a hair salon in California. Unlike gang bangers these people are all highly trained with weapons and have ready access to them.

I notice there's no drunk driver registry in Illinois. Could it be because too many politicians drive drunk? The number of drunk drivers who reoffend is much higher than "murderers", and they actually do kill many more people per year than "murderers" do. How long before we start registering them too?

Just as the "sex offender" registries have been disingenuously used to publicly shame people who were not actually guilty of crimes involving sexual assault; and the "murderer" registry was established for no legitimate public safety concern, but rather to discriminate against and ostracize people upon release from prison; another "registry" is being used to shame people just for being released early in Illinois. It's called a "photo gallery" and is yet another example of a registry with no legitimate criminal justice purpose. Instead it was created purely for political theater.

During the 2010 Illinois gubernatorial primaries Governor Quinn was taking a lot of criticism for his decision to implement what was termed MGT-Push (Meritorious Good Time - Push) which released about 1,700 inmates early to save Illinois five million dollars per year.[747] Any politician who ceases to put more people in prison though, is painted as being "soft-on- crime", or even worse when he or she lets people out of prison early. Thus Gov. Quinn was forced to backtrack. He then terminated MGT-Push, and even the three-decade-old MGT program was suspended.

The suspension of the regular MGT program meant that thousands of prisoners were unnecessarily kept in prison longer, where they quickly accumulated. In just a year the prison population in Illinois expanded by more than 3,000 inmates.[748] With an average cost per inmate per year of nearly $25,000,[749] this added $75 million in yearly costs to the state. So what began as an attempt to save the state $5 million per year (money which could have been used to save many police officers' and teachers' jobs that were laid off) turned into a $75 million per year expense, and a prison system even more overcrowded and underfunded. Why? Because the media knows fear sells and politicians know bashing prisoners or "criminals" is always a political winner.

Knowing a political gift when he sees one, Republican gubernatorial candidate, Illinois Senator Bill Brady, jumped on the bandwagon to criticize the governor's MGT-Push program. Seemingly not satisfied with all the money already being wasted by Quinn's reversal, Brady filed Senate Bill 3411 which created the "photo gallery".[751] Riding the wave of anti-criminal sentiment, the bill sailed through both houses in the Illinois General Assembly, passing unanimously and signed into law by Gov. Quinn.[752] The inmates never asked to be let out early, they were just well-behaved, but regardless the 1,700 that got released early were now included in the photo gallery, and so will all other people that are released early when MGT is reimplemented in the future.

Why was this photo gallery needed? It wasn't. As has already been seen, there is little rehabilitation taking place in prisons, and these people were only being released on average 37 days early.[753] So how did releasing them a little over a month early make them more dangerous? It didn't. In fact it can be argued that the real threat to society is wasting $75 million per year that could have paid for extra police officers.

So how was this "photo gallery" legislation sold to the public? With "criminal" bashing being the primary American pastime, it wasn't hard. Nevertheless officials still felt the need to deceive. Police officials, states attorneys, and legislators all claimed that the "photo gallery" was necessary so that the state could keep track of offenders when they are released and have a current photo available.[754] There's one huge problem with the claim. State law already requires that whenever the IDOC releases an inmate early due to any good time they must give advanced notice to the State's Attorney where the inmate was arrested.[755] Also current photos of all IDOC inmates are available on the IDOC website, and all inmates released from Illinois prisons are on Mandatory Supervised Release so they are already being kept track of. Yet money and resources are being wasted on a "photo gallery" nonetheless.

Electronic Tracking

Just as companies and corporations are making money by locking people up, now others want to make money by letting them go. It's not actually freedom they're selling but rather a high-tech, 24-hour, big brother, tracking system. One of the largest companies is Bl Incorporated. Their ExacuTrack anklets are currently clinging to tens of thousands of Americans. They're not only tracking every movement of their wearer, but are "enabling Bl to control their movements almost as if they were marionettes", for years or even decades.[756]

According to a September 2010 article in *The Atlantic,* titled "Prison Without Walls", ExacuTrack's "clientele" includes anyone from "sex offenders" to check bouncers.[757] It's only logical that Bl Incorporated and other companies that track "criminals" with these types of electronic devices will support politicians with political donations in exchange for passing laws to expand the number of people who are tracked as part of their punishment. How long will it be before people who failed to pay their credit card bill are wearing an anklet that alerts police every time they near a mall, just like the drug addicts' does if he or she loiters near places where illegal drugs are known to be sold?

With prisons packed to overflowing, and insufficient funds to build more, we've now privatized another government function creating a monetary incentive to businesses to encourage needless expansion of electronic monitoring of people if they break the law. As the title of the article alludes to, we now have thousands of individual "prisons without walls" where dozens, hundreds, or even thousands of places in society become off limits, creating an invisible prison maze.

Just as "criminals" are often called animals, and the same drugs are now used to execute both animals and humans, Bl Inc. developed this technology originally for use in tracking Holsteins.[758] Also, with society's attitude towards "criminals" the anklet itself is as stigmatizing as if one were wearing a sign that read "criminal". *The Atlantic* article recounts how one man "had trouble visiting his mother in her retirement home, because she worried about explaining why her son always wore a device on his leg. 'She gets upset, and I can't say that I blame her,' he said dejectedly".[759]

With laws already on the books prohibiting parolees and probationers from associating with gang members, how long will it be before people are prevented from visiting or living with their own family because entire neighborhoods are similarly put off limits by the tracking devices. Or how long will it be before the anklets are programmed to alert police any time two people with criminal backgrounds come into contact, allowing police to increase their harassment of "criminals"? How many more possible jobs will become unavailable to "criminals" because of this technology? What does it matter if a city or state has passed "Ban the Box" legislation if an anklet announces "criminal" to an employer before the application is even filled out?

Some of ExacuTrack's "clientele", probably aware of what awaited them in prison, were upbeat over getting an electronic monitor attached to their leg instead. Others aren't. "Some cursed. Others wept."[760] As technology advances, it won't be long before "criminals" are implanted with these tracking devices. Also if society stays on the path of constantly lengthening sentences it's probable that most of those implants will be for life. After all, all it would take is one shoplifter to commit a murder after having the implant removed and legislation would fly through state governments from coast to coast requiring lifetime monitoring for all "criminals".

AFTERWORD

As we've seen, people who commit a crime are increasingly told that they must do more and more to repay society, but are rarely ever allowed to actually, fully reenter society. Sentences are increasingly longer, fines are increasingly higher, and rehabilitation is increasingly hindered by society. Additionally, and unjustly, the family members and friends of anyone who commits a crime are increasingly punished for their loved one's crime. Not only is the one who broke the law stigmatized, but the stigma is so pervasive that it negatively affects his or her familial relationships to the point where the family also feels stigmatized and exploited by society's hatred of "criminals", which breeds resentment.

Our irrational fear and hatred of "criminals" over the past few decades has completely altered our society. Not only are we incarcerating an ever larger percentage of our population, but within a single generation childhood has completely changed. Kids are being walked out of grammar school in handcuffs for things that kids have always done, and parents irrationally believe that hoards of sexual predators are lurking around every corner waiting to kidnap their kids. Most kids nowadays have no unsupervised time to play. Parents are keeping kids inside where they spend all day eating junk food and playing video games. Not only are they getting fatter, but by not being outside, playing in the dirt, etc., their immune systems don't grow as strong. When I was a kid I could leave at dawn with the rest of the kids in the neighborhood and not return until curfew without anyone worrying. Nowadays there would probably be a dozen parents trying to convince the police to put out "Amber Alerts".

Our collective obsession with crime and punishment has us spending outrageous sums of money on ineffectual sentencing laws and other policies that are actually ensuring that people can't successfully reenter society. Money is being stripped from the few remaining prison rehabilitation programs, community programs, schools and police departments, all of which play a significant role in preventing crime.

That's the sad irony. We are so thoroughly indoctrinated to hate "criminals" that we create counterproductive policies and laws that harm society as a whole by forcing people to remain "criminals" forever, growing a permanent criminal underclass, which makes society less safe.

Our roads can't get repaired; teachers, police officers, and firefighters are all being laid off by the thousands; but we have no problem overincarcerating people that we hate at a cost of $200 billion per year. We expend money to pay for the profits of companies that carry out the policies that channel our hatred, while sitting idly by as we sink lower in nearly every world ranking on education, freedoms, social services, etc. How many teachers' salaries could that profit pay for? How many illiterate prisoners could that profit help to learn to read, enabling them to get an education and turn their lives around?

It doesn't look like we'll find out anytime soon, as more and more companies are making a profit off of mass incarceration and the demonization of "criminals", and politicians are as beholden to them and their lobbyists as ever before.

Our hate-filled "tough-on-crime" rhetoric and policies aren't making society safer; they're doing the exact opposite - wasting money while making us less safe. Also when society continuously expresses its hatred towards anyone who commits a crime, and refuses to allow them to reenter society, it breeds a reciprocal hatred in those people towards society. This not only discourages rehabilitation and abandonment of criminal activity, but also breeds an indifference to causing society harm, perpetuating criminal activity. If society clearly doesn't care about you, why would you care about society?

Not only have we abandoned the goal of rehabilitation, but we've also abandoned beliefs that have been central to American society for centuries - that anyone can change, and that everyone deserves a second chance. If you're a teen who commits a crime and goes to prison (probably functionally illiterate and poorly educated), and society repeatedly tells you that you're evil, irredeemable, etc. denying you the right to vote and fining you into perpetual poverty, all while denying you educational, vocational, or any rehabilitative programs - which is more likely? That you'll become an employed, upstanding member of society upon release, or that you'll be disgruntled with no realistic prospect of obtaining a decent-paying job and therefore revert to crime? I'll bet it's the latter.

Senator Webb was quoted in *Newsweek* saying: "We need smarter ways of dealing with people at apprehension, and even whether you decide to arrest. The types of courts they go into - drug courts as opposed to regular courts. How long you sentence them. How you get them ready to return home".[761] 1 whole-heartedly agree. I also agree with U. S. Supreme Court Justice Antony Kennedy who noted in 2004 that: "Our resources are misspent, our punishments too severe, our sentences too long."[762]

More than anything though, as a nation, we need to stop erroneously thinking of criminality as some permanent, incurable disease; stop thinking of people who commit a crime as evil or inhuman; stop ostracizing every single soul that runs afoul of the law; and stop letting people profit off of the incarceration of our fellow citizens.

Joseph R. Dole

POSTSCRIPT

Since the completion of this manuscript Tamms (Supermax) Correctional Center was closed and Illinois has reimplemented a new meritorious good time program and has closed other facilities in the Illinois Department of Corrections as well. Unfortunately these few good signs are still a drop in the bucket compared to the onslaught of "tough-on-crime" legislation that continues to be passed in Illinois and around the country.

NOTES

1. Pyle, Kevin, and Gilmore, Craig. <u>Prison Town: Paying the Price.</u> The Real Cost of Prisons Project. Northampton, Maine. 2005. <u>www.realcostofprisons.org</u>.

2. Weinstein, Corey, MD. "Prisoner's Human Rights". <u>Prison Legal News.</u> April 2011: p.11.

3. Reutter, David M. "States Scramble to Find Lethal Injection Drugs" <u>Prison Legal News.</u> June 2011: p. 9 - - Thomas, Evan, and Brant, Martha. "Injection of Reflection: There's wide support for a death penalty, but those who carry it out are increasingly uncomfortable". <u>Newsweek.</u> November 19, 2007: p. 40-41. - - Flanders, Chad. "The death penalty's slow death". <u>St Louis Beacon.</u> January 31, 2011.

4. "Louisiana Sheriff Cages Suicidal Prisoners in Space Smaller than Required for Dogs". <u>Prison Legal News.</u> June 2011: p. 19.

5. Ibid, p. 18.

6. Ibid, p. 18.

7. Ibid, p. 18.

8. Lazare, Daniel. "Stars and Bars" <u>The Nation.</u> August 27/September 3, 2007: p. 36.

9.   Wood, Graeme, and Wood, Graeme. "Prison Without Walls" The Atlantic. September 2010. http://www.theatlantic.com/magazine

10.   Ibid.

11.   Cannon, Carl M. "Petty Crime, Outrageous Punishment: Why the three-strikes law doesn't work". Readers Digest. October 2005: p. 157.

12.   "America's falling crime rate: Good news is no news". The Economist. June 4, 2011: p. 36.

13.   Johnston, David Cay. "It's Scary Out There in Reporting Land: Why Crime News is on the Rise and Reporting Analysis is on the Decline." Prison Legal News. April 2011: p. 26.

14.   Ibid.

15.   Cohen, Adam. "Rust to Misjudgement." Time. July 18, 2011: p. 25

16.   "That guilty look. Is it time to end the perp walk?" The Economist. July 9, 2011: p. 48

17.   Ibid.

18.   Ibid.

19.   Weinberg, Steve. "Innocent Until Reported Guilty". Miller-McCune.com. October 2008. http://www.miller-mccune.com/printablearticle/675

20.   "Conventional Wisdom." Newsweek. September 5, 2011: p. 20.

21.   Weinberg, Steve. "Innocent Until Reported Guilty".
       Miller-McCune.com. October 2008.
       http://www.miller-mccune.com/printable article/675

22.   Ibid.

23.   Main, Frank. "Murders up 13% from last year". The Chicago
Sun-Times. n.d.2007: n.p.

24.   Heinzmann, David. "City murder tally up". The Chicago
Tribune. January 2, 2007: p. 1 and 11.

25.   Ibid.

26.   Rozas, Angela. "Chicago's murder rate at its lowest since 1965".
The Chicago Tribune. n.d. 2008: n.p.

27.   Ibid.

28.   VonDrehle, David. "Why Crime Went Away: The murder rate
       is at an all-time low. Will the recession reverse that?" Time.
       February 22, 2010: p. 32.

29.   Romano, Andrew. "Jim Webb's Last Crusade". Newsweek.
       September 19, 2011: p. 53 - - Wilson, James Q. "Hard Times,
       Fewer Crimes". The Wall Street Journal. Saturday/Sunday, May
       28-29, 2011: p. Cl.

30.   Wilson, James Q. "Hard Times, Fewer Crimes". The Wall Street
       Journal. Saturday/Sunday, May 28-29, 2011: p. Cl.

31.   Perez, Evan. "U.S. Logs Big Drop in Crime". <u>The Wall Street Journal.</u> Tuesday. September 2011: p. A3 - - Associated Press. "Drop in Violent Offenses Bigger Than Expected" <u>The Wall Street Journal.</u> September 17-18, 2011: p. A5.

32.   Pinker, Steven. "Violence Vanquished". <u>The Wall Street Journal.</u> Saturday/Sunday, September 24-25, 2011: p. C1-C2.

33.   "Violent crime is up". <u>The Week.</u> October 5, 2007.

34.   Kingsbury, Kathleen. "The Next Crime Wave". <u>Time.</u> December 11, 2006: p. 71-77.

35.   Paulson, Amanda. "U.S. violent crime falls slightly". <u>The Christian Science Monitor,</u> n.d., 2008: n.p.

36.   "Confronting Torture in U. S. Prisons: A Q&A with Solitary Watch". <u>Solitary Watch Newsletter.</u> Summer 2011: p. 3-4.

37.   Whitlock, Jason. "The Black KKK: Thug Life Is Killing Black America. It's Time To Do Something About It". <u>Playboy:</u> 2008: p. 64.

38.   Lexington. "A nation of jailbirds: Far too many Americans are behind bars". <u>The Economist.</u> April 4, 2009: p. 40.

39.   Walmsley, Roy. "Prime Numbers: Prison Planet". <u>Foreign Policy.</u> May/June 2007: p. 31.

40.   Lithwick, Dahlia. "Our Real Prison Problem: Why are we so worried about Gitmo?" <u>Newsweek.</u> June 15, 2009: p. 28.

41.   Walmsley, Roy. "Prime Numbers: Prison Planet". <u>Foreign Policy.</u> May/June 2007: p. 31.

42. Ridgeway, James, and Casella, Jean. "Doctors Prescribe Cure for 'Epidemic of Mass Incarceration'" <u>Mother Jones.</u> June 9, 2011.

http://motherjones.com/mojo/2011/06/doctors-prescribe-cure-epidemic-mass-incarceration

43. Lithwick, Dahlia. "Our Real Prison Problem: Why are we so worried about Gitmo?" <u>Newsweek.</u> June 15, 2009: p. 28.

44. Whitlock, Jason. "The Black KKK: Thug Life Is Killing Black America. It's Time To Do Something About It". <u>Playboy:</u> 2008: p. 122.

45. Fields, Gary, and Emshwiller, John R. "As Criminal Laws Proliferate, More Ensnared". <u>The Wall Street Journal.</u> Saturday/Sunday, July 23-24, 2011: Section 1, p. A10.

46. Ibid.

47. Ibid.

48. Ibid.

49. Ibid.

50. Ibid.

51. Ibid.

52. Fields, Gary, and Emshwiller, John R. "As Federal Crime List Grows, Threshold of Guilt Declines". <u>The Wall Street Journal.</u> Tuesday, September 27, 2011: p. Al.

53.   Fields, Gary, and Emshwiller, John R. "As Criminal Laws
        Proliferate, More Ensnared". The Wall Street Journal.
        Saturday/Sunday, July 23-24, 2011: Section 1, p. A10.

54.   Fields, Gary, and Emshwiller, John R. "Federal Asset Seizures
        Rise, Netting Innocent With Guilty". The Wall Street Journal.
        Monday, August 22, 2011: p Al and A10.

55.   Ridgeway, James, and Casella, Jean. "Doctors Prescribe Cure
        for 'Epidemic of Mass Incarceration'" Mother Jones. June 9,
        2011.

        http://motherjones.com/mojo/2011/06/doctors-prescribe-cure-e
        pidemic-mass-incarceration Citing New England Journal of
        Medicine.http://gatelessgatezen.files.wordpress.com/2011/-06/
        medicine-incarceration-nejm-06Q211.pdf

56.   Tapley, Lance. "Texas Tough: The Rise of America's Prison
        Empire, by Robert Perkinson, Metropolitan Books/Holt, 484 pp
        (October 2010), $20.00 paperback". Book Review in Prison
        Legal News. May 2011: p.19.

57.   Lexington. "A nation of jailbirds" The Economist. April 4,
        2009: p. 40.

58.   James, Doris J., and Glaze, Lauren E. Mental Health Problems
        of Prison and Jail Inmates. U. S. Department of Justice, Bureau
        of Justice Statistics Special Report. September 2006 (NCJ
        213600) www.ojp.usdoj.gov/bjs/abstract/mhppji.htm

59.   Tapley, Lance. "Texas Tough: The Rise of America's Prison
        Empire, by Robert Perkinson, Metropolitan Books/Holt, 484 pp
        (October 2010), $20.00 paperback". Book Review in Prison
        Legal News. May 2011: p.19.

60.   Ibid.

61.   Murphy, Jim. "Welcome Home Young War Vets (Now Pretend You Are Normal)" <u>Fellowship Magazine.</u> Spring 2011: p.6. New York, NY.

62.   Ibid.

63.   Ibid.

64.   Ridgeway, James, and Casella, Jean. "Doctors Prescribe Cure for 'Epidemic of Mass Incarceration'." <u>Mother Jones.</u> June 9, 2011. http://motherjones.com/mojo/2011/06/doctors-prescribe-cure-epidemic-mass-incarceration

65.   Lexington. "A nation of jailbirds" <u>The Economist.</u> April 4, 2009: p. 40.

66.   Ibid.

67.   Mai-Duc, Christine. "FOCUS: WAR ON DRUGS: The war on drugs, four decades later." <u>The Chicago Tribune.</u> Tribune Washington Bureau. June 22, 2011: Section 1, p.22.

68.   Nadelmann, Ethan. "Breaking the Taboo" <u>The Nation.</u> December 27, 2010: p. 11.

69.   James, Doris J., and Glaze, Lauren E. <u>Mental Health Problems of Prison and Jail Inmates.</u> U. S. Department of Justice, Bureau of Justice Statistics Special Report. September 2006 (NCJ 213600) www.ojp.usdoj.gov/bjs/abstract/mhppji.htm

70.   Whitlock, Jason. "The Black KKK: Thug Life Is Killing Black America. It's Time To Do Something About It". Playboy. 2008: p. 63-64, 122-128.

71.   Cose, Ellis. "Sanity and Sentencing" Newsweek. December 24, 2007: p. 53.

72.   Lithwick, Dahlia. "Our Real Prison Problem: Why are we so worried about Gitmo?" Newsweek. June 15, 2009: p. 28.

73.   Lexington. "A nation of jailbirds" The Economist. April 4, 2009: p. 40.

74.   Romano, Andrew. "Jim Webb's Last Crusade", Newsweek. September 19, 2011: p. 52.

75.   Muwakkil, Salim. "Black and Blue Chicago: A recent spate of police shootings of African Americans underscores longstanding mutual distrust." In These Times. October 2011: p. 22.

76.   Lithwick, Dahlia. "Our Real Prison Problem: Why are we so worried about Gitmo?" Newsweek. June 15, 2009: p. 28.

77.   Miller-Mack, Ellen, Willmarth, Susan, and Ahrens, Lois. Prisoners of a Hard Life: Women & Their Children. Real Cost of Prisons Project. 2005. Northampton, Maine.

78.   Stern, Kaia. "Shackles and Sunlight". Fellowship Magazine. Spring 2011: p. 12. New York.

79.   Ibid.

80.   Western, Bruce. "Decriminalizing Poverty". The Nation. December 27, 2010: p. 13.

81.   Lexington. "A nation of jailbirds" The Economist. April 4, 2009: p. 40.

82.   Kennedy, Justice Anthony, American Bar Association, Justice Kennedy Commission. Reports with Recommendations to the ABA House of Delegates. August 2004. American Bar Association. Available online at: http://www.abanet.org/crimjust/Kennedy/JusticeKennedyCom missionReportsFinal.pdf.

83.   Serrano, Richard A. "Less time looms for those jailed for crack." The Chicago Tribune. Tribune Washington Bureau. July 1, 2011.

84.   Cannon, Carl M. "Petty Crime, Outrageous Punishment: Why the three-strikes law doesn't work." Reader's Digest. October 2005: p. 154.

85.   Hodai, Beau. "Meet the old war, same as the new war." In These Times. June 2010: p. 20.

86.   West's Illinois Criminal Law and Procedure, 2004 Edition: p. 769-771 (730 ILCS 5/5-8-1). Minneapolis, MN. West Publishing, (March 2004).

87.   Ibid: p. 384-385 (720 ILCS 5/33B-1)

88.   Illinois Department of Corrections Statistical Presentation 2004. Illinois Department of Corrections. October 7, 2005: p. 11, Table 4.

89.   Ditton, Paula M., and Wilson, Doris James. <u>Truth in Sentencing in State Prisons.</u> U. S. Department of Justice, Bureau of Justice Statistics. Washington D.C. January 1999 (NCJ170032): p. 2.

90.   Ibid.

91.   Ibid., p 18.

92.   <u>Illinois Department of Corrections Statistical Presentation 2003.</u> Illinois Department of Corrections. August 30, 2004: p. 126.

93.   <u>Violent Crime Control and Law Enforcement Act of 1994.</u> United States Department of Justice Fact Sheet. October 24, 1994. Available at: http://www.ncjrs.gov/txtfiles/billfs/txt Last accessed December 14, 2010.

94.   Ibid.

95.   LaVigne, Nancy G. and Mammalian, Cynthia A., with Travis, Jeremy, and Vasher, Christy. <u>A Portrait of Prisoner Reentry in Illinois.</u> Urban Institute, Justice Policy Center. Research Report. April 2003: p. 9.

96.   Olson, David E., Ph.D., Seng, Magnus, Ph.D., Boulger, Jordan, and McClure, Mellissa. <u>The Impact of Illinois' Truth-In-Sentencing Law on Sentence Lengths, Time to Serve and Disciplinary Incidents of Convicted Murderers and Sex Offenders.</u> Loyola University of Chicago, Prepared for the Illinois Criminal Justice Information Authority. June, 2009: p.3.

97.   <u>Illinois Department of Corrections Statistical Presentation 2004.</u> Illinois Department of Corrections. October 7, 2005: p.129.

98.   Olson, David E., Ph D., Seng, Magnus, Ph.D., Boulger, Jordan, and McClure, Mellissa. <u>The Impact of Illinois'</u>

Truth-In-Sentencing Law on Sentence Lengths, Time to Serve and Disciplinary Incidents of Convicted Murderers and Sex Offenders. Loyola University of Chicago, Prepared for the Illinois Criminal Justice Information Authority. June, 2009: p.3.

99.   Sabol, William J., Rosich, Katherine, Kane, Kamala Mallik, Kirk, David, and Dubin, Glenn. The Influences of Truth-In-Sentencing Reforms on Changes in States' Sentencing Practices and Prison Populations. National Institute of Justice, Office of Justice Programs, U. S. Dept, of Justice. July 3, 2002: p. 41, Table 3.3. (NG195161).

100.   Illinois Department of Corrections Statistical Presentation 2004. Illinois Department of Corrections. October 7, 2005: p.61.

101.   Olson, David E., Ph.D., Seng, Magnus, Ph.D., Boulger, Jordan, and McClure, Mellissa. The Impact of Illinois' Truth-In-Sentencing Law on Sentence Lengths, Time to Serve and Disciplinary Incidents of Convicted Murderers and Sex Offenders. Loyola University of Chicago, Prepared for the Illinois Criminal Justice Information Authority. June, 2009: p.20.

102.   Ibid., p. 19.

103.   Ibid., p.3.

104.   Ibid., p. 3.

105.   Ibid., p. 6.

106.   West's Illinois Criminal Law and Procedure, 2004 Edition: p. 676 (730 ILCS 5/3-2-9). Minneapolis, MN. West Publishing, (March 2004).

107. Ibid.

108. Ibid., p. 731 (730 ILCS 5/5-4-l(a)(3)).

109. Rosich, Katherine J., and Kane, Kamala Mallik. Truth-in-Sentencing and State Sentencing Practices. U. S. Dept, of Justice, National Institute of Justice. Washington D.C. NIJ Journal. July 2005: Issue No. 252, p. 20.

110. Report to Congress: Violent Offender Incarceration and Truth-In-Sentencing Incentive Formula Grant Program. U. S. Dept, of Justice. Office of Justice Programs. Bureau of Justice Statistics. Washington. D.C. February 2005: p.5.

111. Ibid., p. 2.

112. Sabol, William J., Rosich, Katherine, Kane, Kamala Mallik, Kirk, David, and Dubin, Glenn. The Influences of Truth-In-Sentencing Reforms on Changes in States' Sentencing Practices and Prison Populations. National Institute of Justice, Office of Justice Programs, U. S. Dept, of Justice. Washington, D.C. July 3, 2002: p. iii (NCJ195161).

113. Ibid., p.3.

114. Ibid., p. 26.

115. Illinois Department of Corrections Statistical Presentation, 2002. Illinois Department of Corrections, July 31, 2003: p. 21.

116. People v. Reedy, 186 III. 2d 1, 237 III. Dec. 74, 708 N.E. 2d 1114 (1999).

117. Illinois Department of Corrections Statistical Presentation, 2002. Illinois Department of Corrections, July 31, 2003: p. 21.

118. Sabol, William J., Rosich, Katherine, Kane, Kamala Mallik, Kirk, David, and Dubin, Glenn. The Influences of Truth-In-Sentencing Reforms on Changes in States' Sentencing Practices and Prison Populations. National Institute of Justice, Office of Justice Programs, U. S. Dept, of Justice. Washington, D.C. July 3, 2002: p. 41, Table 3.3 (NCJ195161).

119. Hewitt, Kelli Samantha. "Aging Inmates, Growing Costs." July 1, 2003. Tennessean.com. http://www.tennessean.com

120. Illinois Department of Corrections' Financial Impact Statement, 2009. Illinois Department of Corrections (2010).

121. McMahon, Patrick. "Aging Inmates Present Prison Crisis". USA Today. August 10, 2003.

122. Ward, Ron. "Elderly Inmates Swell Nation's Prisons". Associated Press. February 27, 2004.

123. Olson, David E., Ph.D., Seng, Magnus, Ph.D., Boulger, Jordan, and McClure, Mellissa. The Impact of Illinois' Truth-In-Sentencing Law on Sentence Lengths, Time to Serve and Disciplinary Incidents of Convicted Murderers and Sex Offenders. Loyola University of Chicago, Prepared for the Illinois Criminal Justice Information Authority. June, 2009: p.34.

124. Ibid., p.4.

125. Illinois Department of Corrections' Statistical Presentation, 2004. Illinois Department of Corrections. October 7, 2005: p. 56.

126.   Sabol, William J., Rosich, Katherine, Kane, Kamala Mallik, Kirk, David, and Dubin, Glenn. The Influences of Truth-In-Sentencing Reforms on Changes in States' Sentencing Practices and Prison Populations. National Institute of Justice, Office of Justice Programs, U. S. Dept, of Justice. Washington, D.C. July 3, 2002: p. 41, Table 3.3 (NG195161).

127.   Illinois Department of Corrections' Statistical Presentation, 2004. Illinois Department of Corrections. October 7, 2005: p. 88.

128.   Dole, Joseph Rodney, II., Preliminary Findings Concerning the Financial Cost of Implementing Illinois' Truth-In-Sentencing Laws (2002-2004). January 11, 2011 : p. 16. http://realcostofprisons.org/materials/dole-preliminary-findings .pdf

129.   Ibid.

130.   LaVigne, Nancy G., and Mammalian, Cynthia A., with Travis, Jeremy, and Vasher, Christy. A Portrait of Prisoner Reentry in Illinois.Urban Institute, Justice Policy Center. Research Report. April 2003: p. 9.

131.   West's Illinois Criminal Law And Procedure, 2004 Edition: p. 668 (730 ILCS 5/1-1-2 (d)). West Publishing. Minneapolis, MN. (March 2004).

132.   One in 31: The Long Reach of American Corrections. Pew Center on the States. The Pew Charitable Trusts. March 2009: p. 19.

133.   Olson, David E., Ph.D., Seng, Magnus, Ph.D., Boulger, Jordan, and McClure, Mellissa. The Impact of Illinois' Truth-In-Sentencing Law on Sentence Lengths, Time to Serve

and Disciplinary Incidents of Convicted Murderers and Sex Offenders. Loyola University of Chicago, Prepared for the Illinois Criminal Justice Information Authority. June, 2009: p.4.

134. Cannon, Carl. M. "Petty Crime, Outrageous Punishment: Why the three-strikes law doesn't work." Reader's Digest. October 2005: p. 155.

135. Lexington. "A nation of jailbirds: Far too many Americans are behind bars." The Economist. April 4, 2009: p. 40.

136. Cannon, Carl. M. "Petty Crime, Outrageous Punishment: Why the three-strikes law doesn't work." Reader's Digest. October 2005: p. 155.

137. Ibid.

138. Ibid., p. 155-156.

139. Ibid., p. 156.

140. Ibid., p. 156.

141. Ibid., p. 156.

142. Ibid., p. 152.

143. Ibid., p. 152-154.

144. Ibid., p. 156.

145. Brodheim, Mike. "California Prisoner's Life Sentence Upheld for Tossing Food Tray at Guard." Prison Legal News. July 2011: p. 27.

146. "California's overcrowded prisons. Gulags in the sun. The consequences of three decades of being 'tough on crime'," The Economist. August 15, 2009: p. 28.

147. Whitlock, Jason. "The Black KKK: Thug Life Is Killing Black America. It's Time To Do Something About It." Playboy. 2008: p. 122.

148. Cannon, Carl. M. "Petty Crime, Outrageous Punishment: why the three-strikes law doesn't work." Reader's Digest. October 2005: p. 155.

149. Doyle, Patrick. "West Memphis Three Finally Freed." Rolling Stone. September 15, 2011: p. 20.

150. Leveritt, Mara. "Freeing the West Memphis Three." Newsweek. September 5, 2011: p. 17.

151. Ibid.

152. Ibid. - - Doyle, Patrick. "West Memphis Three Finally Freed." Rolling Stone. September 15, 2011: p. 20.

153. Leveritt, Mara. "Freeing the West Memphis Three." Newsweek. September 5, 2011: p. 17.

154. Ibid.

155. Ibid., p. 16-18. - - Doyle, Patrick. "West Memphis Three Finally Freed." Rolling Stone September 15, 2011: p. 20.

156. Doyle, Patrick. "West Memphis Three Finally Freed." Rolling Stone. September 15, 2011: p. 20.

157. Levin, Hittel, and Conroy, John. "Area Two: Police Commander Jon Burge Tortured Dozens Of Chicagoans And Got Away With It Until Now." <u>Playboy.</u> 2010: p. 77.

158. Ibid., p. 78.

159. Ibid., p. 116.

160. "False confessions: Silence is golden. People have a strange and worrying tendency to admit to things they have not, in fact, done." <u>The Economist.</u> August 13, 2011: p. 75.

161. Ibid.

162. Ibid.

163. Ibid.

164. Ibid.

165. Ibid.

166. Ibid.

167. Drizin, Steven A. and Leo, Richard A. "The Problem Of False Confessions In the Post-DNA World." <u>82N.C.L.Rev 891.</u> (March 2004).

168. Hussain, Rummana. "Woman says cops bullied her in murder probe." <u>Chicago Suntimes.</u>

169. Hussain, Rummana. "Man says cops coaxed false murder confession."<u>Chicago Suntimes.</u>

170.   Ibid. - - Hussain, Rummana. "Woman says cops bullied her in murder probe." <u>Chicago Suntimes.</u>

171.   Reagan, Brad. "Reasonable Doubt. The Surprisingly Weak Science Behind Courtroom Forensics." <u>Popular Mechanics.</u> August 2009: p. 46.

172.   Ibid., p. 51.

173.   Ibid., p. 51.

174.   "Crime and exoneration: Hidden evidence. DNA is changing the way America fights crime, not its policies towards convicts." <u>The Economist.</u> August 1, 2009: p. 25.

175.   Ibid.

176.   Ibid.

177.   Ibid.

178.   Reagan, Brad. "Reasonable Doubt. The Surprisingly Weak Science Behind Courtroom Forensics." <u>Popular Mechanics.</u> August 2009: p. 48.

179.   Ibid.

180.   Ibid., p. 49.

181.   Ibid., p. 46-48.

182.   Ibid., p. 48.

183. "Police line-ups: Killers and fillers. A controversy over how to handle eyewitnesses." <u>The Economist.</u> February 17, 2007.

184. Weinberg, Steve. "Innocent Until Reported Guilty". <u>Miller-McCune.com.</u> October 2008. http://www.miller-mccune.com/printable_article/675

185. Ibid.

186. Ibid.

187. Clarke, Matt. "Prosecutors Who Commit Misconduct Are Rarely Disciplined." <u>Prison Legal News</u>. August, 2011: p. 12.

188. Ibid.

189. Koppel, Nathan. "Public Defenders Stretched Thin by State Cuts." <u>The Wall Street Journal</u>. Thursday, April 14, 2011: p. A5.

190. Ibid.

191. Mauer, Marc. <u>Lessons Of The "Get Tough" Movement In The United States.</u> The Sentencing Project. October 25, 2004.

192. Hernandez, Danny. "Death penalty costly, ineffective." <u>New Mexico Daily Lobo.</u> January 31, 2011.

http://www.dailylobo.com/index.php/article/2011/01/death_penalty_costly_ineffective

193. "Crime and exoneration: Hidden evidence. DNA is changing the way America fights crime, not its policies towards convicts." The Economist. August 1, 2009: p. 26.

194. Liebman, J.S., Fegan, J., and West, V. "Capital Attrition: Error Rates In Capital Cases, 1973-1995." 78 Texas Law Review 1839-1861 (2000).

195. "A Matter Of Life And Death: The Effect Of Life-Without-Parole Statutes On Capital Punishment." 119 Harvard Law Review 1838. April 2006.

196. Mills, Steve, and Heinzmann. "Burge cases come back to forefront. Investigations, suits dealing with ex-cop force Daley's hand." chicagotribune.com December 9, 2007.

197. Ibid.

198. Reutter, David M. "Provision in Florida Law Prohibits Compensation to Wrongfully Convicted. " Prison Legal News. August 2011: p. 32.

199. Ibid., p. 33.

200. "Hey Policeman! Leave Them Kids Alone." (A book excerpt from Police in the Hallways: Discipline in an Urban High School. Nolan, Kathleen. University of Minnesota), published in In These Times. September 2011: p. 32.

201. Stern, Kaia. "Shackles and Sunlight." Fellowship Magazine. Spring 2011: p. 13. New York.

202. Gilna, Derek. "Juvenile Justice Expert Condemns Rhode Island's Jailing of Students for Minor Offenses". Prison Legal News. May 2011: p. 32-33.

203. Williamson, Elizabeth. "Brain Immaturity Could Explain Teen
      Crash Rate: Risky Behavior Diminishes At Age 25, NIH Study
      Finds." Washingtonpost.com Tuesday, February 1, 2005: p.
      A01.
      http://www.washingtonpost.com/ac2/wp-dyn/A52687-2005Jan
      31?languge=printer

204. Bower, Bruce. "Teen Brains On Trial: The Science Of Neural
      Development Tangles With The Juvenile Death Penalty."
      Science News Online. May 8, 2004: Vol.65, No. 19, p.299
      http://www.sciencenews.org/articles/20040508/bob9.asp .

205. Brief for Respondent in Roper v. Simmons, 543 U.S. 551 (July
      19, 2004) (2004 WL1947812). - - Amicus Curiae (Appellate
      Brief) of the American Psychological Association, and the
      Missouri Psychological Association Supporting Respondent in
      Roper v. Simmons, 543 U. S. 551 (July 19, 2004) (2004
      WL1636447).

206. Amicus Curiae (Appellate Brief) of the American Medical
      Association, American Psychiatric Association, American
      Society For Adolescent Psychiatry, American Academy of
      Psychiatry and the Law, National Association of Social
      Workers, and National Mental Health Association, in Support of
      Respondent in Roper v. Simmons, 543 U. S. 551 (July 16, 2004)
      (2004 WL1633549). - - Amicus Curiae (Appellate Brief) of The
      Coalition For Juvenile Justice in Support of Respondent in
      Roper v. Simmons, 543 U. S. 551 (July 16, 2004) (2004 WL
      1628522).

207. Ibid. - - Amicus Curiae (Appellate Brief) of the American Bar
      Association in Support of Respondent in Roper v. Simmons,
      543 U. S. 551 (July 19, 2004) (2004 WL 1617399).

208. Ibid. - - Amicus Curiae (Appellate Brief) of the Coalition For Juvenile Justice in Support of Respondent in Roper v. Simmons, 543 U. S. 551 (July 16, 2004) (2004 WL 1628522).

208. Brief for Respondent in Roper v. Simmons, 543 U. S. 551 (July 19, 2004) (2004 WL 1947812). - - Donald R. Roper v. Christopher Simmons, 543 U. S. 551, 125 S. Ct. 1183 (No. 03-633) (March 1, 2005) United States Supreme Court.

209. Amicus Curiae (Appellate Brief) of the American Psychological Association, and the Missouri Psychological Association Supporting Respondent in Roper v. Simmons, 543 U. S. 551 (July 19, 2004) (2004 WL 1636447).

210. Amicus Curiae (Appellate Brief) of The Coalition For Juvenile Justice in Support of Respondent in Roper v. Simmons. 543 U.S. 551 (July 16, 2004) (2004 WL 1628522) - - Amici Curiae (Appellate Brief) of The American Medical Association. American Psychiatric Association, American Society For Adolescent Psychiatry, American Academy of Psychiatry and the Law, National Association of Social Workers, Missouri Chapter of the National Association of Social Workers and National Mental Health Association, in Support of Respondent in Roper v. Simmons, 543 U.S. 551 (July 2004) (2004 WL 1633549).

211. Ibid. x 3 ((2004 WL 1636447), (2004 WL 1628522) and (2004 WL 1633549)). - - Brief for Respondent in Roper v. Simmons, 543 U. S. 551 (July 19, 2004) (2004 WL 1947812).

212. (2004 WL 1633549) see note #210.

213. Ibid. - - (2004 WL 1628522) see note #210. - - Donald R. Roper v. Christopher Simmons, 543 U. S.551,125 S Ct. 1183 (No. 03-633) (March 1, 2005) United States Supreme Court.

214.	Ibid. x 2 (No. 03-633) and (2004 WL 1633549)) - - (2004 WL 1636447) see note # 209 - - Williamson, Elizabeth. "Brain Immaturity Could Explain Teen Crash Rate: Risky Behavior Diminishes At Age 25, NIH Study Finds. Washingtonpost.com. Tuesday, February 1, 2005: p. A01. http://www/washingtonpost.com/ac2/wp-dyn/A52687-2005Jan 31?language=printer .

215.	(No. 03-633) See note #208 - - (2004 WL 1633549) see note #205 - - 2004 WL 1636447) see note #204.

216.	(2004 WL 1633549) see note #205 - - (No. 03-633) see note # 208 - - (2004 WL 1617399) see note #206 - (2004 WL 1947812) see note #208 - - Williamson, see note #203.

217.	(2004 WL 1617399) see note #206 - - Drizin, Steven A., and Leo, Richard A. "The Problem Of False Confessions In The Post - DNA World." 82 N.C.L.Rev.891 March 2004.

218.	(No. 03-633) see note #208.

219.	Stern, Kaia. "Shackles and Sunlight." Fellowship Magazine. Spring 2011: p. 13. New York.

220.	Categorically Less Culpable: Children Sentenced To Life Without Possibility Of Parole In Illinois. Illinois Coalition For Fair Sentencing Of Children. February 2008: p. 31. Chicago, IL.

221.	Ibid., p. 33.

222.	Woodford, Whitney. "Youth justice: Reformers want the state to redouble its efforts to help juvenile criminal offenders" Illinois Issues. February 2009: p. 32.

223. "Concluding Observations of the Human Rights Committee on the United States of America." Human Rights Committee. 34 U. N. doc CCPR/C/USA/CO/3/Rev. 1 (Dec 18, 2006).

224. Williams, Patricia J. "Absolutely No Excuse." The Nation. December 7, 2009: p. 9. - - Sherman, Mark. "Life in prison too cruel for juveniles?" Daily Herald. Sunday, November 8, 2009: Section 1, p. 14.

225. Liptak, Adam. "Weighing Life in Prison for Youths Who Didn't Kill." The New York Times. November 8, 2009.

226. Nellis, Ashley, and King, Ryan S. No Exit: The Exploding Use of Life Sentences in America. The Sentencing Project. July 2009: p. 3. Washington D.C.

227. "Left Behind." Playboy June 2008.

228. Liptak, Adam. "Weighing Life in Prison for Youths Who Didn't Kill." The New York Times. November 8, 2009 - - Williams, Patricia J. "Absolutely No Excuse." The Nation. December 2009: p. 9.

229. Nellis, Ashley, and King, Ryan S. No Exit: The Exploding Use of Life Sentences in America. The Sentencing Project. July 2009: p. 3. Washington D.C.

230. Woodford, Whitney. "Youth justice: Reformers want the state to redouble its efforts to help juvenile criminal offenders." Illinois Issues. February 2009: p. 31.

231. Searcey, Dionne. "Eight and on Trial: Young Defendants Throw Criminal Justice System Into Confusion." The Wall Street Journal, n.d. 2009.

232.   Mitchum, Robert. "Compelling crime story: The lead in the air did it." The Chicago Tribune. August 19, 2007: Perspective Section.

233.   Constitution of the State of Illinois. Article 1, Section 11. December 15, 1970.

234.   Oliver, Anthony. "U. S. Supreme Court: Cruel and Unusual Punishment of Juveniles". Graterfriends Newsletter. (Pennsylvania Prison Society) June 2010: p. 3.

235.   Graham v. Florida, 560 U.S.___, 130 S. Ct. 2011 (2010).

236.   Liptak, Adam. "Weighing Life in Prison for Youths Who Didn't Kill." The New York Times. November 8, 2009.

237.   Graham v. Florida, 560 U. S.___, 130 S. Ct. 2011 (2010).

238.   Williams, Patricia J. "Absolutely No Excuse". The Nation. December 7, 2009: p. 9.

239.   Mauer, Marc, King, Ryan S., and Young, Malcolm C. The Meaning of "Life": Long Prison Sentences in Context. The Sentencing Project. May 2004.

240.   Moore, Solomon. "Study Finds Record Number of Inmates Serving Life Terms." The New York Times. July 23, 2009.

241.   Ibid.

242.   Ibid.

243. Mauer, Marc. "Comparative International Rates Of Incarceration: An Examination Of Causes And Trends." The Sentencing Project. June 20, 2003.

244. "1992 National Adult Literacy Survey." U. S. Department of Education, National Center for Education Statistics (1992) Washington D.C. http://www.ed.gov/NCES/nadlits/overview.html.

245. Haigler, K. O., Harlow, C., O'Connor, P., and Campbell, A. Literacy Behind Prison Walls: Profile of the Prison Population from the National Adult Literacy Survey. (1994) (NCES Publication No. 94-102). U. S. Department of Education, National Center for Education Statistics. Washington, D.C.

246. Maguire, K, and Pastore, A.L. Sourcebook of Criminal Justice Statistics 1995 (1996) (NCJ 158900) p. 567. U. S. Department of Justice, Bureau of Justice Statistics. Washington, D.C.

247. Mumola, Christopher J. Incarcerated Parents and Their Children. Bureau of Justice Statistics Special Report. August 2000: p. 9 (NG 182335).

248. James, Doris J., and Glaze, Lauren E. Mental Health Problems of Prison and Jail Inmates. Bureau of Justice Statistics Special Report. September 2006 (NCJ 213600).

249. Stangler, Cole. "Been Caught Feedin'." In These Times. August 2011: p. 10.

250. Ibid.

251. Schectman, Joel. "The Return Of Debtors' Prisons In Louisiana." Newsweek. October 4, 2010: p. 6.

252.   Ibid.

253.   Silver-Greenberg. "Welcome to Debtor's Prison, 2011 Edition." The Wall Street Journal. Thursday, March 17, 2011: p. C1-C2.

254.   Clarke, Matt. "Jailing for Debt on the Rise." Prison Legal News. May 2011: p. 26.

255.   Clarke, Matt. "Practice of Jailing Parents Who Owe Child Support Raises Questions; Concerns." Prison Legal News. May 2011: p. 22.

256.   Reutter, David M. "Georgia: Child Support Contempt Findings Create Debtor's Prisons" Prison Legal News. July 2011: p. 40-41.

257.   Ibid., p. 41.

258.   Ibid., p. 41.

259.   Simpson, Cam. "More Immigration Detainee Deaths Disclosed." The Wall Street Journal Tuesday, August 18, 2009: p. A3.

260.   Cockburn, Alexander. "The Bogus Crime Wave." The Nation. February 22, 2010: p. 9.

261.   Ibid.

262.   Ibid.

263.   Ibid.

264.   McWhirter, Cameron. "Ex-Cons Floated as Laborers." <u>The Wall Street Journal.</u> Thursday, June 16, 2011: p. A2.

265.   Jordan, Miriam. "Farmers Press GOP on Hiring." <u>The Wall Street Journal.</u> September 7, 2011: p. A3.

266.   McWhirter, Cameron. "Ex-Cons Floated as Laborers." <u>The Wall Street Journal.</u> Thursday, June 16, 2011: p. A2.

267.   Jordan, Miriam. "Alabama Immigrant Law Irks Business." <u>The Wall Street Journal.</u> Wednesday, August 24, 2011: p. A5.

268.   Ibid.

269.   Ibid.

270.   Ibid.

271.   Ibid.

272.   Perez de Alejo, Carlos. "Detention Watch Network Releases Report On Private Prison Involvement In Immigration Detention." Press Release. <u>Detention Watch Network.</u> May 11, 2011.

273.   Taibbi, Matt. "Jailhouse Nation." <u>Rolling Stone.</u> August 24, 2006: p. 38.

274.   Ibid., p. 38 and 40.

275.   Hodai, Beau. "Corporate Con Game: How the private prison industry helped shape Arizona's anti-immigrant law." <u>In These Times.</u> July 2010: p. 16-20.

276.   Ibid.

277.   Ibid., p. 16-17.

278.   Hodai, Beau. "Meet the old war, same as the new war." In These Times. July 2010: p. 20.

279.   Ibid.

280.   Ibid.

281.   Handley, Joel. "Divesting From Private Prisons." In These Times. August 2011: p. 8-9.

282.   Bales, William, Berk, Richard, and Gaes, Gerald. Public Safety, Public Spending: Forecasting America's Prison Population 2007-2011. p. 1. JFA Institute. The Pew Charitable Trusts. Washington, D.C. www.pewpublicsafety.org.

283.   Simpson, Cam. "More Immigration Detainee Deaths Disclosed." The Wall Street Journal Tuesday, August 18, 2009: p. A3.

284.   Bales, William, Berk, Richard, and Gaes, Gerald. Public Safety, Public Spending: Forecasting America's Prison Population 2007-2011. p. 1. JFA Institute. The Pew Charitable Trusts. Washington, D.C. www.pewpublicsafety.org.

285.   Jones, Lorenzo. "U.S. Prisons: Too Big to Fail?" WIN Magazine. Fall 2009: p. 19.

286.   Ibid.

287. Abu-Jamal, Mumia. "From Bases to Bars: The Military & Prison Industrial Complexes Go 'Boom'." <u>WIN Magazine.</u> Fall 2009: p.12-14.

288. Ibid., p. 14.

289. Ibid., p. 13.

290. Holloway, Lynette. "The Root: Inmate Health Care Another Kind of Prison." <u>www.npr.org</u>. (Partner Content from: The Root) June 8, 2011.

291. Reutter, David. "Merger Creates Largest Private Prison Medical Provider in U.S." <u>Prison Legal News.</u> August 2011: p. 20.

292. Ibid.

293. Ibid.

294. Ibid.

295. Ibid.

296. Allen, Terry J. "Death by Privatization: For-profit prison healthcare system implicated in death of inmate." <u>In These Times.</u> January 2010: p. 13-15.

297. Ibid., p. 13.

298. Ibid., p. 13.

299. Ibid., p. 13.

300. Ibid., p. 13-14.

301. Ibid., p. 14.

302. Ibid., p. 14.

303. Ibid., p. 14-15.

304. Ibid., p. 15.

305. Ibid., p. 15.

306. Holloway, Lynette. "The Root: Inmate Health Care Another Kind of Prison." www.npr.org. (Partner Content from: The Root) June 8, 2011.

307. "$1.2 Million Awarded Against PHS After Florida Jail Prisoner Paralyzed." Prison Legal News. August 2011: p. 24-25.

308. Ibid., p. 24.

309. "Locking in the best price: Private prisons are now widely accepted, but it's hard to get the terms right." The Economist. January 7, 2007: p. 60-61.

310. Chen, Stephanie. "Larger Inmate Population Is Boon to Private Prisons. " The Wall Street Journal. Wednesday, November 19, 2008: p. A4.

311. Denning, Liam. "Prison Companies Are a Conviction Buy." The Wall Street Journal. Monday, May 2, 2011: p. C1O.

312. Chen, Stephanie. "Larger Inmate Population Is Boon to Private Prisons. " The Wall Street Journal. Wednesday, November 19, 2008: p. A4.

313. Denning, Liam. "Prison Companies Are a Conviction Buy." The Wall Street Journal. Monday, May 2, 2011: p. C1O.

314. Ibid.

315. Chen, Stephanie. "Larger Inmate Population Is Boon to Private Prisons. " The Wall Street Journal. Wednesday, November 19, 2008: p. A4.

316. Ibid.

317. Jones, Ashby. "Prison for Ex-Judge in Corruption Case." The Wall Street Journal. Friday, August 12, 2011: p. A3.

318. "Bad Judges: The Lowest of the Low: Another blow against elected judges." The Economist. February 28, 2009: p. 34.

319. Ibid.

320. Jones, Ashby. "Prison for Ex-Judge in Corruption Case." The Wall Street Journal. Friday, August 12, 2011: p. A3.

321. Ibid.

322. "Former Judge Sentenced to 17 ½ Years in Prison" Associated Press. The Wall Street Journal. Saturday/Sunday, September 24-25, 2011: p. A5.

323. "Confronting Torture in U. S. Prisons: A Q&A with Solitary Watch." Solitary Watch Newsletter. Summer 2011: p. 4.

324. Romano, Andrew. "Jim Webb's Last Crusade." <u>Newsweek.</u> September 19, 2011: p. 52.

325. Ibid.

326. "Changes In Voting Districts With Prisons." <u>Coalition For Prisoners' Rights Newsletter.</u> September 2010: Vol. 35-b, No. 9, p.l.

327. "Prisons, Redistricting and the Census." Editorial. <u>The New York Times.</u> February 11, 2010.

328. Ibid. - - Wagner, Peter. "Senator Schneiderman, the Prison Policy Initiative and Other Elected Officials and Advocates Call on Census to Count Prisoners in Their Home Communities." <u>www.prisonersofthecensus.org</u> October 18, 2007.

329. Ibid.

330. "Ex-prisons chief pleads guilty in payoff scheme." <u>The Chicago Tribune.</u> December 16, - - Lightly, Todd, and Long, Ray. "Ex-prisons chief, lobbyists indicted." <u>The Chicago Tribune.</u> Friday, July 20, 2007: Metro, Section 2, p. 10. - - Gibson, Ray, and Casillas, Ofeila. "Prison adviser indicted: He's charged with kicking back payoffs." <u>The Chicago Tribune.</u> Sunday, October 7, 2007: Metro, Section 4, p. 3.

331. Ibid. - - Lightly, Todd, and Long, Ray. "Ex-prisons chief, lobbyists indicted." <u>The Chicago Tribune.</u> Friday, July 20, 2007: Metro, Section 2, p. 10.

332. Gibson, Ray, and Casillas, Ofeila. "Prison adviser indicted: He's charged with kicking back payoffs." <u>The Chicago Tribune.</u> Sunday, October 1, 2007: Metro, Section 4, p. 3.

333. Lightly, Todd, and Long, Ray. "Ex-prisons chief, lobbyists indicted." The Chicago Tribune. Friday, July 20, 2007: Metro, Section 2, p. 10.

334. Making a Killing: How Prison Corporations Are Profiting From Campaign Contributions and Putting Taxpayers at Risk. American Federation of State, County, and Municipal Employees. 2011.

335. Ibid.

336. "California's prison guards' union - Fading are the peacemakers. One of California's most powerful political forces may have peaked." The Economist. February 27, 2010: p. 38.

337. Ibid.

338. Ibid.

339. Ibid.

340. Ibid.

341. Vara, Vauhini, and White, Bobby. "Prison Ruling Rattles California Budget." The Wall Street Journal. Wednesday, May 25, 2011: p. A4.

342. Whitlock, Jason. "The Black KKK: Thug Life Is Killing Black America. It's Time To Do Something About It." Playboy. 2008: p. 63-64, 122-128.

343. Ibid., p. 122.

344. Ibid., p. 122.

345.   Ibid., p. 122.

346.   Ibid., p. 122.

347.   Ibid, p. 124.

348.   "California's overcrowded prisons. Gulags in the Sun. The consequences of three decades of being 'tough on crime'." The Economist. August 15, 2009: p. 28.

349.   The Constitution Of The United States. Amendment XIII. (1865).

350.   Egelko, Bob. "Calif. Judges reject suit seeking to raise inmate wages. Court: Prisoners do not have a legal entitlement to payment for their work." The San Francisco Chronicle. April 12, 2010.

351.   Ibid.

352.   Handley, Joel. "Divesting From Private Prisons." In These Times. August 2011: p. 8.

353.   Jones, Lorenzo. "U. S. Prisons: Too Big to Fail?" WIN Magazine. Fall 2009: p. 20.

354.   "New York Prisoners Man Call Centers." Prison Legal News. August 2011: p. 39.

355.   Whitlock, Jason. "The Black KKK: Thug Life Is Killing Black America. It's Time To Do Something About It." Playboy. 2008: p. 124.

356. Patton, Leslie. "Demand rises for Illinois-made products." Feb. 18, 2009. Retrieved 3/7/09. http://news.medill.northwestern.edu/chicago/news.aspx?id=116755

357. Ibid.

358. Ibid.

359. Ibid.

360. Stein, Nicholas. "Business Behind Bars." Fortune Magazine. September 15, 2003: p. 161-166.

361. Ibid., p. 163.

362. Ibid., p. 163.

363. Ibid., p. 161

364. Whitlock, Jason. "The Black KKK: Thug Life Is Killing Black America. It's Time To Do Something About It." Playboy. 2008: p. 122.

365. JPay, Inc. http://www.jpay.com

366. Dole, Joseph. "Illinois Prisoners Bilked Out of Millions Through DOC Commissary Charges." Prison Legal News. March 2010: p. 24-25.

367. Hamden, Michael. "Outrageous phone rates devastate families of prisoners." www.examiner.com September 1, 2009.

368. Ibid.

369. "Nationwide Research Finds Excessive Prison Phone Rates Exploit Prisoners' Families." Prison Legal News. Press Release, April 12, 2011.

370. Ibid.

371. Ibid.

372. Ibid.

373. "15-Minute Interstate Phone Calls From State Prisons." Citizens United For Rehabilitation Of Errants Newsletter. Summer 2008.

374. "Nationwide Research Finds Excessive Prison Phone Rates Exploit Prisoners' Families." Prison Legal News. Press Release, April 12, 2011.

375. "15-Minute Interstate Phone Calls From State Prisons." Citizens United For Rehabilitation Of Errants Newsletter. Summer 2008.

376. "Nationwide Research Finds Excessive Prison Phone Rates Exploit Prisoners' Families." Prison Legal News. Press Release, April 12, 2011.

377. "Texas Prison Phones and Emails Generate Less Revenue Than Expected." Prison Legal News. August 2011: p. 42-43.

378. Shapiro, Nina. "Prisons Charge Inmates Criminal Rates to Use the Phone, Newspaper Charges." The Daily Weekly. Wednesday, April 13, 2011.

379. "Nationwide Research Finds Excessive Prison Phone Rates Exploit Prisoners' Families." Prison Legal News. Press Release, April 12, 2011.

380. Hamden, Michael. "Outrageous phone rates devastate families of prisoners." www.examiner.com September 1, 2009.

381. Ibid.

382. Ibid.

383. Jones, Lorenzo. "U. S. Prisons: Too Big to Fail?" WIN Magazine. Fall 2009: p. 19.

384. Watson, Joe. "Arizona DOC Makes Visitors Pay for Prison Maintenance, Repairs ." Prison Legal News. May 2012: p. 38.

385. Western, Bruce. "Decriminalizing Poverty." The Nation. December 27, 2010: p. 13.

386. Ibid.

387. Mumola, Christopher J. Incarcerated Parents and Their Children. Bureau of Justice Statistics Special Report. August 2000. (NCJ 182335).

388. Stern, Kaia. "Shackles and Sunlight." Fellowship Magazine. Spring 2011: p. 12. New York.

389. Families Left Behind: The Hidden Costs of Incarceration and Reentry. Justice Policy Center. Urban Institute. Washington, D.C.

390. Ibid.

391. Mumola, Christopher J. Incarcerated Parents and Their Children. Bureau of Justice Statistics Special Report. August 2000. (NG 182335).

392. Lazare, Daniel. "Stars and Bars" (Essay) <u>The Nation.</u> August 27/September 3, 2007: p.29.

393. Miller-Mack, Ellen, Willmarth, Susan, and Ahrens, Lois. <u>Prisoners of a Hard Life: Women & Their Children.</u> Real Cost of Prisons Project. (2005). Northampton, MA.

394. <u>Inmate Journal.</u> July/August 2006.

395. Lexington. "A nation of jailbirds: Far too many Americans are behind bars." <u>The Economist.</u> April 4, 2009: p. 40.

396. Groeninger, Alissa. "Helping jailed dads escape parent trap: Prison initiative aims to break cycle of incarceration." <u>The Chicago Tribune.</u> Thursday, July 14, 2011: Section 1, p. 12.

397. Clarke, Matt. "Report finds Prior Incarceration Hinders Upward Economic Mobility." <u>Prison Legal News.</u> August 2011: p. 26.

398. Mumola, Christopher J. <u>Incarcerated Parents and Their Children.</u> Bureau of Justice Statistics Special Report. August 2000 (NG 182335): p. 4.

399. Ibid., p. 2.

400. Ibid., p. 4.

401. Miller-Mack, Ellen, Willmarth, Susan, and Ahrens, Lois. <u>Prisoners of a Hard Life: Women & Their Children.</u> Real Cost of Prisons Project. (2005). Northampton, Maine.

402. Kamel, Rachel, and Kerness, Bonnie. <u>The Prison Inside the Prison: Control Units. Supermax Prisons, and Devices of</u>

Torture. American Friends Services Committee. 2003: p. 8. Philadelphia.

403. Romano, Andrew. "Jim Webb's Last Crusade." Newsweek. September 19, 2011: p. 50.

404. "Briefing: America's Toughest Sheriff." The Week Magazine. March 5, 2010: p. 11. - - Lazare, Daniel. "Stars and Bars" (Essay) The Nation. August 27/September 3, 2007: p. 34.

405. Mastony, Colleen. "Childbirth in chains." The Chicago Tribune. July 18, 2010: Section 1, p. 1 and 10.

406. Lazare, Daniel. "Stars and Bars" (Essay) The Nation. August 27/September 3, 2007: p. 36.

407. Ibid., p. 34.

408. Ibid., p. 34-36.

409. Ibid., p. 34.

410. Ibid., p. 36.

411. Stern, Kaia. "Shackles and Sunlight." Fellowship Magazine. Spring 2011: p. 13. New York.

412. Perkinson, Robert. "The Prison Dilemma". The Nation. July 6, 2009: p. 35. (A review of the book Cruel and Unusual by Anne-Marie Cusac).

413. Stevens, Dennis J., and Ward, Charles S. "College Education And Recidivism: Educating Criminals Meritorious". Journal of

Correctional Education. September 1997: Vol. 48, Issue 3, p. 106-111.

414.   Gilligan, James. "Reflections From A Life Behind Bars: Build Colleges Not Prisons." The Chronicle Of Higher Education. October 16, 1998. www.chronicle.com

415.   "Policy Brief: Restoration of Pell Grant Eligibility." The Education from the Inside Out Coalition, n. d. www.EIOcoalition.org

416.   Helliker, Kevin. "In Prison, College Courses Are Few." The Wall Street Journal. Wednesday, May 4, 2011: p. A4.

417.   The Second Chance Act of 2005: Community Safety Recidivism Prevention - HR1704. United States Congress.

418.   Manor, Robert. Monitoring Tour of Menard Correctional Center. The John Howard Association. April 6, 2010.

419.   Manor, Robert. Cuts in Prison Education Put Illinois at Risk. The John Howard Association. (2010)

420.   Ibid.

421.   Dodge, Susan. "Budget Ax Hits Prison Education." Chicago Sun-Times. December 12, 2001.

422.   Failing Grade: The Decline In Educational Opportunities for Illinois Inmates. The American Federation of State, County, and Municipal Employees. Campaign For Responsible Priorities. AFSCME, Council 31. (2006).

423. Maki, John. "Director Tony Godinez and the Challenges Facing the Illinois Department of Corrections." The John Howard Association. May 4, 2011.

424. Illinois Constitution of 1970. Article 1, Section 11

425. West's Illinois Criminal Law And Procedure. 2004 Edition: p. 668 (730 ILCS 5/1-1-2) Minneapolis, MN. West Publishing. March 2004.

426. Mosso, G.E. "The Truth About Prison Education." Prison Connections. Winter 1997: Vol. 1, No. 3.

427. Stevens, Dennis J. and Ward, Charles S. "College Education And Recidivism: Educating Criminals Meritorious." Journal of Correctional Education. September 1997: Vol. 48, Issue 3, p. 106-111.

428. "Gently does it. Excessively harsh conditions seem to make criminals more likely to reoffend. Are private prisons the answer?" The Economist. July 28, 2007. p. 27-28.

429. Serwer, Adam. "Books Behind Bars: What are wardens thinking when they censor magazines and books?" April 7, 2011. http://prospect.org - - Sheridan, Matthew J. "Letter to the Editor" Miller-McCune.com Magazine March-April 2009: p. 7. - - Haigler, K.O., Harlow, C., O'Connor, P., and Campbell, A. Literacy behind prison walls: Profile of the prison population from the national adult literacy survey. U. S. Department of Education, National Center for Education Statistics. NCES Publication No. 94-102 (1994) Washington, D. C.

430. The Jailhouse Lawyer's Handbook. Center for Constitutional Rights and the National Lawyers Guild. 5th Edition, 2010: p. 15. New York.

431.   Ibid., p. 15.

432.   Ibid., p. 16.

433.   Ibid., p. 16.

434.   Ibid., p. 16.

435.   Toone, Robert E., edited by Manville, Dan. <u>Protecting Your Health & Safety: A Litigation Guide For Inmates.</u> Second Edition. Southern Poverty Law Center 2009: p.13.

436.   <u>The Jailhouse Lawyer's Handbook.</u> Center for Constitutional Rights, and the National Lawyers Guild. 5th Edition, 2010: p. 16.

437.   Ibid., p. 16.

438.   Dexheimer, Eric. "Authors decry being locked out of lockup: Prisoners can't read acclaimed books that mention banned topics." Thursday, May 13, 2010. <u>www.statesman.com</u>

439.   Rodriguez, Luis J. "Behind the Prison Riot ." <u>The Progressive.</u> October 2009: p. 14.

440.   Ibid.

441.   "California's overcrowded prisons. Gulags in the sun. The consequences of three decades of being 'tough on crime' ."<u>The Economist.</u> August 15, 2009: p. 28.

442.   Bravin, Jess, and White, Bobby. "Top Court Sets Stage For Felons To Go Free." <u>The Wall Street Journal.</u> Tuesday, May 24, 2011: p. A1-A2.

443.   Prison Legal News, April 2011: p. 43.

444.   Reutter, David M. "Seventh Circuit Upholds Indiana DOC's Ban on Pen-Pal Ads." Prison Legal News. May 2012: p. 24.

445.   Serwer, Adam. "Books Behind Bars: What are wardens thinking when they censor magazines and books?" April 7, 2011. http://prospect.org

446.   Ibid.

447.   Ibid.

448.   Dexheimer, Eric. "Authors decry being locked out of lockup: Prisoners can't read acclaimed books that mention banned topics." Thursday, May 13, 2010. www.statesman.com

449.   Ibid.

450.   Ibid.

451.   Ibid.

452.   Serwer, Adam. "Books Behind Bars: What are wardens thinking when they censor magazines and books?" April 7, 2011. http://prospect.org

453.   Ibid.

454.   Potter, Dena. "Publishers sue Va prisons for banning law guide." July 21, 2010. Richmond, Virginia www.dailypress.com

455.   Ibid.

456.   The Jailhouse Lawyer's Handbook. Center for Constitutional Rights, and the National Lawyers Guild. 5th Edition, 2010. New York.

457. Lazare, Daniel. "Stars and Bars" The Nation. August 27/September 3, 2007: p. 36.

458. "Briefing; 'America's toughest sheriff'." The Week Magazine. March 5, 2010. p. 11.

459. Subways, Suzy. "Fasting for Human Rights in Secure Housing Units of California." Prison Health News. Summer 2011: Issue II, p. 4-5. Philadelphia, PA.

460. Smith, Gerry. "Taste, nutrition - and a tough crowd: Prisons must toe fine dietary line." The Chicago Tribune. Sunday, December 23, 2007: Metro, Section 4: p. 1 and 4.

461. Ibid., p. 4.

462. Ibid., p. 4.

463. Ibid., p. 4.

464. "Good Food = Good Behavior." Graterfriends Newsletter. The Pennsylvania Prison Society. April 2008.

465. Reutter, David M. "California Prisoners Still Forced to Drink Arsenic-Laced Water." Prison Legal News. August 2011: p. 26-27.

466. Ibid., p. 26.

467. Ibid., p. 27.

468. "Briefing; 'America's toughest sheriff.'" The Week Magazine. March 5, 2010. p. 11.

469.   Ibid.

470.   Korecki, Natasha, and Herman, Eric. "Cook County Fail?" The Chicago Sun-Times. Friday, July 18, 2008: Metro, p. 10-11.

471.   Ibid., p. 10.

472.   "Prisoner Abuse: How Different Are U.S. Prisons?" Human Rights Watch. Peacework Magazine. June 2004: p. 8.

473.   Ward, Paula. "Guard charged with abusing 20 inmates at SCI Pittsburgh." Pittsburg Post- Gazette. Tuesday, September 27, 2011.

474.   Ibid.

475.   Ibid.

476.   "Hawaii State Auditor Blasts Private Prison Contracting: State Renews Contract Anyway." Prison Legal News. August 2011: p. 38-39.

477.   Reutter, David. M. "Los Angeles Jail Guards Beat Prisoner in Front of ACLU Monitor." Prison Legal News. August 2011: p. 45.

478.   Ibid.

479.   "Fifth Circuit Upholds $355,000 Award Against Dallas County in Jail MRSA Case." Prison Legal News. August 2011: p. 40.

480.   Ibid.

481. Clark, Matt. "Inadequate Medical Care in Texas Jails Kills Hundreds of Prisoners." <u>Prison Legal News.</u> May 2011: p. 16.

482. Reutter, David. M. "$450,000 Settlement in Alabama Jail Prisoner's Death." <u>Prison Legal News.</u> August 2011: p. 49.

483. Ibid.

484. Korecki, Natasha, and Herman, Eric. "Cook County Fail?" <u>The Chicago Sun-Times.</u> Friday, July 18, 2008: Metro, p. 10-11.

485. Simpson, Cam. "More Immigration Detainee Deaths Disclosed." <u>The Wall Street Journal.</u> Tuesday, August 18, 2009: p. A3.

486. Ibid.

487. Ibid.

488. "Texas Prison Phones and Emails Generate Less Revenue Than Expected." <u>Prison Legal News.</u> August 2011: p. 42-43.

489. "Room service not included. Should prisoners pay for being in prison?" <u>The Economist.</u> August 1, 2009: p. 26.

490. Ibid. - - Sachdev, Ameet. "Illinois seeks to repossess prisoner's saved wages." <u>The Chicago Tribune.</u> March 15, 2011: p. 17 and 19. - - <u>West's Illinois Criminal Law And Procedure, 2004 Edition:</u> p. 698-699 (730 ILCS 5/3-7-5) Minneapolis, MN. West Publishing. (March 2004).

491. <u>West's Illinois Criminal Law And Procedure, 2004 Edition:</u> p. 697 (730 ILCS 5/3-7-2a) Minneapolis, MN. West Publishing. (March 2004). - - Dole, Joseph R. "Illinois Prisoners Bilked Out

of Millions Through DOC Commissary Surcharges." <u>Prison Legal News.</u> March 2010: p. 24.

492.   Ibid.

493.   <u>West's Illinois Criminal Law And Procedure, 2004 Edition:</u> p. 711 (730 ILCS 5/3-12-2); and p. 698-699 (730 ILCS 5/3-7-6). Minneapolis, MN. West Publishing. (March 2004).

494.   Sachdev, Ameet. "Illinois seeks to repossess prisoner's saved wages." <u>The Chicago Tribune.</u> March 15, 2011: p. 17 and 19.

495.   Ibid.

496.   Ibid.

497.   IDOC v. Hawkins, 2011 WL 2410392, June 16, 2011. West Law.

498.   Ridgeway, James, and Casella, Jean. "Cruel and Unusual: Solitary Confinement in U. S. Prisons." <u>Solitary Watch Newsletter.</u> Spring 2011: p. 1.

499.   Eisenman, Stephen F., and Reynolds, Laurie Jo. "Guantánamo Bay In Illinois? Downstate Supermax Holds 250 in Long-Term Isolation." <u>Capitol City Courier.</u> February 2009.

500.   Ibid.

501.   Lelyveld, Joseph. "What 9/11 Wrought" <u>Smithsonian.</u> September 2011: p. 62.

502.   West's Illinois Criminal Law And Procedure, 2004 Edition: p. 673 (730 ILCS 5/3-2-2(l)(s)). Minneapolis, MN. West Publishing. March 2004.

503.   Jaegar, Bethany. "IDOC reforms Tamms 'supermax' prison." Illinois Issues. November 2009: p. 10.

504.   Ibid.

505.   Kerness, Bonnie. "Control Units: Illegal Torture Not Just For Guantánamo." WIN Magazine. Fall 2009. p. 21.

506.   Ibid.

507.   Magnani, Laura. Buried Alive:Long-Term Isolation in Calfornia's Youth and Adult Prisons. American Friends Service Committee - Oakland. May 2008.

508.   Kerness, Bonnie. "Control Units: Illegal Torture Not Just For Guantánamo." WIN Magazine. Fall 2009. p. 21.

509.   Magnani, Laura. Buried Alive:Long-Term Isolation in Calfornia's Youth and Adult Prisons. American Friends Service Committee - Oakland. May 2008.

510.   Kerness, Bonnie. " Control Units: Illegal Torture Not Just For Guantánamo." WIN Magazine. Fall 2009. p. 21.

511.   Eisenman, Stephen F., and Reynolds, Laurie Jo. "Guantánamo Bay In Illinois? Downstate Supermax Holds 250 in Long-Term Isolation." Capitol City Courier. February 2009.

512.   Kamel, Rachel, and Kerness, Bonnie. The Prison Inside the Prison: Control Units, Supermax Prisons, and Devices of

Torture. American Friends Service Committee - Philadelphia. 2003: p. 2. - - Kerness, Bonnie. "Control Units: Illegal Torture Not Just For Guantánamo" WIN Magazine. Fall 2009: p. 21. - - Magnani, Laura. Buried Alive: Long-Term Isolation in California's Youth and Adult Prisons. American Friends Service Committee - Oakland. May 2008: p. 3.

513. Ibid. p. 4. - - Kamel, Rachel, and Kerness, Bonnie. The Prison Inside the Prison: Control Units, Supermax Prisons, and Devices of Torture. American Friends Service Committee - Philadelphia. 2003: p. 2. - - Kerness, Bonnie. " Control Units: Illegal Torture Not Just For Guantánamo" WIN Magazine. Fall 2009: p. 21.

514. Ibid.

515. "Solitary Confinement" Coalition For Prisoners' Rights Newsletter. July 2010: Vol. 35-b, No. 7, p. 1. http://www.realcostofprisons.org/coalition.html.

516. "Solitary Watch Project." Coalition For Prisoners' Rights Newsletter. Feb. 2010: Vol. 35-b, No. 2, p. 1. http://www.realcostofprisons.org/coalition.html.

517. Magnani, Laura. Buried Alive: Long-Term Isolation in Calfornia's Youth and Adult Prisons. American Friends Service Committee - Oakland. May 2008: p. 6.

518. Kamel, Rachel, and Kerness, Bonnie. The Prison Inside the Prison: Control Units. Supermax Prisons, and Devices of Torture. American Friends Service Committee - Philadelphia. 2003: p. 4.

519. Jaegar, Bethany. "IDOC reforms Tamms 'supermax' prison." Illinois Issues. November 2009: p. 10.

520. Pawlaczyk, George, and Hundsdorfer, Beth. "Is it worth it? State spends $92,000 per year per inmate to run Tamms prison." Belleville News-Democrat. Thursday, December 31, 2009. http://www.belleville.com

521. Magnani, Laura. Buried Alive:Long-Term Isolation in Calfornia's Youth and Adult Prisons. American Friends Service Committee - Oakland. May 2008: p. 7.

522. Ibid., p. 8.

523. Ibid., p. 7.

524. Ibid., p. 7.

525. Dowker, Fay, and Good, Glenn. "The Proliferation of Control Unit Prisons in the United States." Journal of Prisoners on Prisons. Vol. 4, No. 2,1993: p. 97.

526. Eisenman, Stephen F., and Reynolds, Laurie Jo. "Guantánamo Bay In Illinois? Downstate Supermax Holds 250 in Long-Term Isolation." Capitol City Courier. February 2009.

527. Kerness, Bonnie. "Control Units: Illegal Torture Not Just For Guantánamo." WIN Magazine. Fall 2009. p. 21.

528. "Confronting Torture in U. S. prisons: A Q & A with Solitary Watch. Solitary Watch Newsletter. Summer 2011: p. 3-4.

529. Powlaczyk, George, and Hundsdorfer, Beth. "Is it worth it? State spends $92,000 per year per inmate to run Tamms prison." Belleville News-Democrat. Thursday, December 31, 2009. http://www.bellville.com

530. Ibid.

531. Kerness, Bonnie. " Control Units: Illegal Torture Not Just For Guantánamo." WIN Magazine. Fall 2009: p. 22.

532. Pawlaczyk, George, and Hundsdorfer, Beth. "Tamms torture? Some say a decade of solitary confinement has made inmate insane. Inmate has spent 12 years at Tamms." Belleville New-Democrat. Sunday, January 10, 2010. http://belleville.com

533. Magnani, Laura. Buried Alive: Long-Term Isolation in Calfornia's Youth and Adult Prisons. American Friends Service Committee - Oakland. May 2008: p. 8.

534. Kamel, Rachel, and Kerness, Bonnie. The Prison Inside the Prison: Control Units, Supermax Prisons, and Devices of Torture. American Friends Service Committee - Philadelphia. 2003: p. 6.

535. Magnani, Laura. Buried Alive:Long-Term Isolation in Calfornia's Youth and Adult Prisons. American Friends Service Committee - Oakland. May 2008: p. 8.

536. Lelyveld, Joseph. "What 9/11 Wrought." Smithsonian. September 2011: p. 62-63.

537. Horowitz, Morton J. The Warren Court And Pursuit Of Justice.

538. Eisenman, Stephen F., and Reynolds, Laurie Jo. "Guantánamo Bay In Illinois? Downstate Supermax Holds 250 in Long-Term Isolation." Capitol City Courier. February 2009.

539. Ibid.

540. Snyder, Jean Maclean. "Statement to the Illinois House Prison Management and Reform Legislation Committee." April 27, 2001. Thompson Center, Chicago, IL.

541. Lampert, Nicolas. "Illinois Torture Publicized with Ecological Art: Chicago and Milwaukee Artists Boosts Tamms Year Ten Message with Mud Stencils." June 7, 2009. Last accessed January 25, 2010. http://www.justseeds.org/blog/2009/06/illinois_torture_publici zed_wi.html

542. Jaegar, Bethany. "IDOC reforms Tamms 'supermax' prison." Illinois Issues. November 2009: p. 10.

543. Eisenman, Stephen F., and Reynolds, Laurie Jo. "Guantánamo Bay In Illinois? Downstate Supermax Holds 250 In Long-Term Isolation." Capitol City Courier. February 2009.

544. Burnett, Sara."Supermax inmate suing to lessen solitary confinement." The Denver Post. April 29, 2011. http://www.denverpost.com/fdcp?=unique=1304465148223

545. Ridgeway, James, and Casella, Jean. "Cruel and Unusual: Solitary Confinement in U. S. Prisons." Solitary Watch Newsletter. Spring 2011: p. 4.

546. Ibid.

547. Kamel, Rachel, and Kerness, Bonnie. The Prison Inside the Prison: Control Units, Supermax Prisons, and Devices of Torture. American Friends Service Committee - Philadelphia. 2003: p. 2.

548. Ibid.

549. Dowker, Fay, and Good, Glenn. "The Proliferation of Control Unit Prisons in the United States." Journal of Prisoners on Prisons. Vol. 4, No. 2, 1993: p. 107.

550. Westefer v. Snyder, Case No. 3:00 - cv - 00162 - GPM (7/20/10) (Document 540) United States District Court for the Southern District of Illinois.

551. Magnani, Laura. Buried Alive:Long-Term Isolation in Calfornia's Youth and Adult Prisons. American Friends Service Committee - Oakland. May 2008: p. 4.

552. Ridgeway, James, and Casella, Jean. "Cruel and Unusual: Solitary Confinement in U. S. Prisons." Solitary Watch Newsletter. Spring 2011: p. 4.

553. Dowker, Fay, and Good, Glenn. "The Proliferation of Control Unit Prisons in the United States." Journal of Prisoners on Prisons. Vol. 4, No. 2, 1993: p. 97; citing Wilson, N. K. "Hard-Core Prisoners Controlled in Nation's High-Tech Prisons" Chicago Daily Law Bulletin. April 25, 1991: p. 2.

554. Snyder, Jean Maclean. "Statement to the Illinois House Prison Management and Reform Legislation Committee." Thompson Center, Chicago, IL. April 27, 2001.

555. Frey, Warden Shelton. "Warden's Bulletin No. 05-06." Tamms Correctional Center. Illinois Department of Corrections. January 12, 2005.

556. Subways, Suzy. "Fasting for Human Rights in Secure Housing Units of California." Prison Health News. Issue II. Summer 2011: p. 5. Philadelphia, PA.

557. Ibid., p. 4.

558.   Welborn, Warden George C. "Warden's Bulletin No. 99-88."
       Tamms Correctional Center. Illinois Department of Corrections.
       June 30, 1999.

559.   Magnani, Laura. Buried Alive:Long-Term Isolation in
       Calfornia's Youth and Adult Prisons. American Friends Service
       Committee - Oakland. May 2008: p. 4. - - Kerness, Bonnie.
       "Control Units: Illegal Torture Not Just for Guantánamo." WIN
       Magazine. Fall 2009:p. 21.

560.   Eisenman, Stephen F., and Reynolds, Laurie Jo. "Guantánamo
       Bay In Illinois? Downstate Supermax Holds 250 In Long-Term
       Isolation." Capitol City Courier. February 2009.

561.   Kupers, Terry A., and Moltz, David. "Solitary confinement
       poses a danger to everyone." Bangor Daily News. Feb. 26, 2010.
       http://www.bangordailynews.com/detail/137718.html?print=1

562.   Eisenman, Stephen F., and Reynolds, Laurie Jo. "Guantánamo
       Bay In Illinois? Downstate Supermax Holds 250 In Long-Term
       Isolation." Capitol City Courier. February 2009.

563.   Kupers, Terry A., and Moltz, David. "Solitary confinement
       poses a danger to everyone." Bangor Daily News. Feb. 26, 2010.
       http://www.bangordailynews.com/detail/137718.html?print=1

564.   Magnani, Laura. Buried Alive: Long-Term Isolation in
       Calfornia's Youth and Adult Prisons. American Friends Service
       Committee - Oakland. May 2008: p. 10.

565.   "Confronting Torture in U. S. Prisons: A Q&A with Solitary
       Watch". Solitary Watch Newsletter. Summer 2011: p. 3.

566.   Eberhardt, Sally, and Theoharis, Jeanne. "Stateside Gitmos."
       The Nation. February 7, 2011: p. 9.

567.   Eisenman, Stephen F., and Reynolds, Laurie Jo. "Guantánamo Bay In Illinois? Downstate Supermax Holds 250 In Long-Term Isolation." Capitol City Courier. February 2009.

568.   Kerness, Bonnie. "Control Units: Illegal Torture Not Just For Guantánamo." WIN Magazine. Fall 2009: p. 22.

569.   Magnani, Laura. Buried Alive:Long-Term Isolation in Calfornia's Youth and Adult Prisons. American Friends Service Committee - Oakland. May 2008: p. 4.

570.   Lampert, Nicolas. "Illinois Torture Publicized with Ecological Art: Chicago and Milwaukee Artists Boosts Tamms Year Ten Message with Mud Stencils." www.justseeds.org June 7, last accessed January 25, 2010. http://www.justseeds.org/blog/2009/06/illinois_torture_publici zed_wi.html

571.   "Confronting Torture in U. S. Prisons: A Q&A with Solitary Watch". Solitary Watch Newsletter. Summer 2011: p. 3.

572.   Magnani, Laura. Buried Alive:Long-Term Isolation in Calfornia's Youth and Adult Prisons. American Friends Service Committee - Oakland. May 2008: p. 9.

573.   Ibid., p. 12.

574.   Ridgeway, James, and Casella, Jean. "Cruel and Unusual: Solitary Confinement in U. S. Prisons." Solitary Watch Newsletter. Spring 2011: p. 4.

575.   "Confronting Torture in U. S. Prisons: A Q&A with Solitary Watch". Solitary Watch Newsletter. Summer 2011: p. 3.

576. Eberhardt, Sally, and Theoharis, Jeanne. "Stateside Gitmos." The Nation. February 7, 2011: p. 8-9.

577. Clarke, Matt. "U. K. Terrorism Suspects May Challenge Extradition Based on U. S. Prison Conditions." Prison Legal News. April 2004: p. 44.

578. Burnett, Sara. "Supermax inmate suing to lessen solitary confinement." The Denver Post. April 29, 2011. http://www.denverpost.com/fdcp?=unique=1304465148223

579. Kerness, Bonnie. " Control Units: Illegal Torture Not Just For Guantánamo." WIN Magazine. Fall 2009: p. 23.

580. Ridgeway, James, and Casella, Jean. "Cruel and Unusual: Solitary Confinement in U. S. Prisons." Solitary Watch Newsletter. Spring 2011: p. 4.

581. Pawlaczyk, George, and Hundsdorfer, Beth. "Is it worth it? State spends $92,000 per year per inmate to run Tamms prison." Belleville News-Democrat. Thursday. December 31, 2009. http://www.belleville.com

582. Magnani, Laura. Buried Alive:Long-Term Isolation in Calfornia's Youth and Adult Prisons. American Friends Service Committee - Oakland. May 2008: p. 17.

583. Ibid., p. 17.

584. Ibid., p. 1.

585. Lampert, Nicolas. "Illinois Torture Publicized with Ecological Art: Chicago and Milwaukee Artists Boosts Tamms Year Ten Message with Mud Stencils." www.justseeds.org June 7, 2009.

http://www.justseeds.org/blog/2009/06/illinois_torture_publicized_wi.html

586.   Ibid.

587.   Ibid.

588.   Ibid.

589.   Ibid.

590.   Jaegar, Bethany. "IDOC reforms Tamms 'supermax' prison." Illinois Issues. November 2009: p. 10.

591.   Lampert, Nicolas. "Illinois Torture Publicized with Ecological Art: Chicago and Milwaukee Artists Boosts Tamms Year Ten message with Mud Stencils." www.justseeds.org June 7, 2009. http://www.justseeds.org/blog/2009/06/illinois_torture_publicized_wi.html

592.   Ridgeway, James, and Casella, Jean. "Cruel and Unusual: Solitary Confinement in U. S. Prisons." Solitary Watch Newsletter. Spring 2011: p. 4.

593.   Eisenman, Stephen F., and Reynolds, Laurie Jo. "Guantánamo Bay In Illinois? Downstate Supermax Holds 250 In Long-Term Isolation." Capitol City Courier. February 2009.

594.   "Solitary Confinement Changes" Coalition For Prisoners' Rights Newsletter. July 2010: Vol. 35-b, No. 7, p. 1. http://www.realcostofprisons.org/coalition.html

595.   Ibid.

596.   Pawlaczyk, George, and Hundsdorfer, Beth. "Is it worth it? State spends $92,000 per year per inmate to run Tamms prison." Belleville News-Democrat. Thursday, December 31, 2009. http://www.belleville.com

597.   Ibid.

598.   Ibid.

599.   Romano, Andrew. "Jim Webb's Last Crusade". Newsweek. September 19, 2011: p. 52.

600.   Alexander, Michelle being interviewed by Segura, Liliana. "Cruel & Unusual Prisons." The Nation. June 20, 2011: p. 6.

601.   Fourth Circuit Upholds Federal Civil Commitment Statute Against Constitutional Challenge" Prison Legal News. July 2011: p. 31.

602.   Mansnerus, Laura. "Locked Up In Limbo". The Nation. December 31, 2007: p. 9.

603.   Ibid.

604.   Ibid.

605.   Ibid.

606.   Bogue, Mindy. "Allegheny County Ordinance Struck Down: State law supercedes local residency law." Correctional Forum. Spring 2011: p. 1 and 15. Philadelphia, PA.

607.   Mills, Steve. "Sentence served, still in jail; Young offenders are stuck if they have nowhere to go." The Chicago Tribune. Thursday, April 1, 2000: Section 1, p. 1 and 9.

608. Ibid., p. 9.

609. Lazare, Daniel. "Stars and Bars"(Essay). <u>The Nation.</u> August 27/September 3, 2007: p. 29.

610. Vanden Heuvel, Katrina. "Just Democracy." <u>The Nation.</u> July 21/28, 2008.

611. Ibid.

612. Ibid.

613. Lazare, Daniel. "Stars and Bars" (Essay). <u>The Nation.</u> August 27/September 3, 2007: p.32.

614. Ibid., p. 32.

615. Ibid., p. 32.

616. Berman, Ari. "The GOP War on Voting." <u>Rolling Stone.</u> September 15, 2011. p. 52.

617. King, Ryan S. <u>A Decade of Reform: Felony Disenfranchisement Policy in the United States.</u> The Sentencing Project. October 2006: p. 1. Washington, D. C.

618. Ibid., p. 21.

619. Ibid., p. 18-19.

620. Cardinal, Matthew. <u>Triple-Decker Disenfranchisment: First-Person Accounts of Losing The Right to Vote among Poor. Homeless Americans with a Felony Conviction.</u> The Sentencing Project. November 2004: p. 8. Washington, D. C.

621.   Ibid., p. 16.

622.   Jones, Sabrina, Miller-Mack, Ellen, and Ahrens, Lois. <u>Prisoners of the War on Drugs.</u> The Real Cost of Prisons Project. 2005: p. 4. Northampton, MA.

623.   Miller-Mack, Ellen, Willmarth, Susan, and Ahrens, Lois. <u>Prisoners of a Hard Life: Women & Their Children.</u> Real Cost of Prisons Project. 2005: p. 4. Northampton, MA.

624.   Jones, Sabrina, Miller-Mack, Ellen, and Ahrens, Lois. <u>Prisoners of the War on Drugs.</u> The Real Cost of Prisons Project. 2005: p. 4. Northampton, MA.

625.   Lazare, Daniel. "Stars and Bars" (Essay). <u>The Nation.</u> August 27/September 3, 2007: p. 32.

626.   Bannon, Alicia, Nagrecha, Mitali, and Diller, Rebekah. <u>Criminal Justice Debt: A Barrier To Reentry.</u> Brennan Center For Justice. New York University School of Law. 2010: p. 4.

627.   Reutter, David M. "Band-aid Applied to Florida's Homeless Sex Offender Colony Falls Off." <u>Prison Legal News.</u> March 2011: p. 13.

628.   Gray, Stephen. "Immigration: A Phony War on Deportation." <u>Time.</u> June 27, 2011: p. 16.

629.   Ramachandran, Shalini, and McWhirter, Cameron. "Ex-Cons Floated as Laborers." <u>The Wall Street Journal.</u> Thursday, June 16, 2011: p. A2.

630.   Ibid.

631.   Ibid.

632.   Ibid.

633.   Bogue, Mindy. "Philadelphia Bans The Box." Correctional
        Forum. Spring 2011: p. 1 and 16. Philadelphia, PA - -
        "Philadelphia 'Bans The Box'". Graterfriends Newsletter.
        Pennsylvania Prison Society, May 2011.

634.   Bannon, Alicia, Nagrecha, Mitali, and Diller, Rebekah.
        Criminal Justice Debt: A Barrier To Reentry. Brennan Center
        for Justice. New York University School of Law. 2010: p. 1. - -
        Goodman, Emily Jane. "Overcharged: On top of prison time,
        offenders are slapped with fees they can't pay, creating a vicious
        circle." The Nation. September 22, 2008: p. 22.

635.   Ibid.

636.   Ibid.

637.   Bannon, Alicia, Nagrecha, Mitali, and Diller, Rebekah.
        Criminal Justice Debt: A Barrier To Reentry. Brennan Center
        for Justice. New York University School of Law. 2010.

638.   Ibid., p. 10.

639.   West's Illinois Criminal Law And Procedure, 2004 Edition: p.
        782 (730 ILCS 5/5-9-1.4) Minneapolis, MN. West Publishing.
        March 2004.

640.   Bannon, Alicia, Nagrecha, Mitali, and Diller, Rebekah.
        Criminal Justice Debt: A Barrier To Reentry. Brennan Center
        for Justice. New York University School of Law. 2010: p. 7.

641. Goodman, Emily Jane. "Overcharged: On top of prison time, offenders are slapped with fees they can't pay, creating a vicious circle". The Nation. September 22, 2008: p. 22.

642. Bannon, Alicia, Nagrecha, Mitali, and Diller, Rebekah. Criminal Justice Debt: A Barrier To Reentry. Brennan Center for Justice. New York University School of Law. 2010: p. 13.

643. Ibid., p. 20.

644. Ibid., p. 20.

645. Ibid., p. 20.

646. Ibid., p. 17.

647. Ibid., p. 17.

648. Ibid., p. 17.

649. Ibid., p. 17.

650. Ibid., p. 18.

651. Ibid., p. 18.

652. West's Illinois Criminal Law And Procedure, 2004 Edition: p. 400 (720 ILCS 5/39-l(a)) Minneapolis, MN. West Publishing. March 2004.

653. Bannon, Alicia, Nagrecha, Mitali, and Diller, Rebekah. Criminal Justice Debt: A Barrier To Reentry. Brennan Center for Justice. New York University School of Law. 2010: p. 15 and 18.

654. Ibid.

655. Ibid., p. 9.

656. Ibid., p. 9.

657. Ibid., p. 16.

658. Ibid., p. 16.

659. Ibid., p. 25.

660. Ibid., p. 24.

661. "Uncollected Court Debts Piling Up in Tennessee." <u>Prison Legal News.</u> June 2011: p. 14.

662. Bannon, Alicia, Nagrecha, Mitali, and Diller, Rebekah. <u>Criminal Justice Debt: A Barrier To Reentry.</u> Brennan Center for Justice. New York University School of Law. 2010: p. 24.

663. Ibid., p. 27.

664. Ibid., p. 27.

665. Ibid., p. 27.

666. Ibid., p. 27.

667. Ibid., p. 27-28.

668. Ibid., p. 29.

669. Dizikes, Cynthia. "Bill to keep tabs on freed killers goes to Quinn: Murderers would have to register for 10 years." The Chicago Tribune. Thursday, June 30, 2011: Section 1, p. 1 and 6.

670. Ibid.

671. People v. Leroy, 357 Ill. App. 530, 828 N. E. 2d 769, 293 Ill. Dec. 459 (April 12, 2005) (No. 5-03-0333) Illinois Appellate Court, Fifth District.

672. West's Illinois Criminal Law And Procedure, 2004 Edition: p. 857-860 (740 ILCS 147/1 et al.)Minneapolis, MN. West Publishing. March 2004.

673. Ibid., p. 682 (730 ILCS 5/3-3-7(a)(13)and (15)).

674. Whitlock, Jason. "The Black KKK: Thug Life Is Killing Black America. It's Time To Do Something About It." Playboy. 2008: p. 128.

675. Ibid.

676. Kamel, Rachel, and Kerness, Bonnie. The Prison Inside the Prison: Control Units, Supermax Prisons, and Devices of Torture. American Friends Services Committee. 2003: p. 6.

677. Ibid.

678. "America's unjust sex laws: An ever harsher approach is doing more harm than good, but it is being copied around the world." The Economist. August 8, 2009: p. 9.

679. Campoy, Amy. "States Resist Federal Sex-Offender Registry." The Wall Street Journal. Saturday/Sunday, April 9-10, 2011: p. A3.

680. Smith v. Doe, 538 U.S. 84, 123 S. Ct. 1140,155 L Ed. 2d 164 (March 5, 2003) (No. 01- 729) United States Supreme Court.

681. Dizikes, Cynthia. "Bill to keep tabs on freed killers goes to Quinn: Murderers would have to register for 10 years." The Chicago Tribune. Thursday, June 30, 2011: Section 1, p. 6.

682. Bogue, Mindy. "Myths About Sex Offenders Continue to Influence Legislation." Correctional Forum. Summer 2011: p. 15. Philadelphia, PA.

683. Skenazy, Lenore. "Oddly Enough: Shred Your Sex Offender Map." Forbes.com. June 25, 2010.

684. "Unjust and ineffective: America has pioneered the harsh punishment of sex offenders. Does it work?" The Economist. August 8, 2009: p. 22.

685. "America's unjust sex laws: an ever harsher approach is doing more harm than good, but it is being copied around the world." The Economist. August 8, 2009: p. 9. - - Skenazy, Lenore. "Oddly Enough: Shred Your Sex Offender Map." http://Forbes.com June 25, 2010.

686. Ibid.

687. Ibid.

688. Bennets, Leslie. "The John Next Door." Newsweek. July 25, 2011: p. 60-63: 61.

689. "America's unjust sex laws: an ever harsher approach is doing more harm than good, but it is being copied around the world." The Economist. August 8, 2009: p. 9.

690. Skenazy, Lenore. "Oddly Enough: Shred Your Sex Offender map." Forbes.com. June 25, 2010.

691. Ibid.

692. Ibid.

693. Ibid.

694. Prison Legal News.

695. "America's unjust sex laws: An ever harsher approach is doing more harm than good, but it is being copied around the world." The Economist. August 8, 2009: p. 9.

696. "Unjust and ineffective: America has pioneered the harsh punishment of sex offenders. Does it work?" The Economist. August 8, 2009: p. 22.

697. Ibid., p. 22.

698. Ibid., p. 21.

699. Ibid., p. 21.

700. Ibid., p. 21.

701. Ibid., p. 21.

702.   Ibid., p. 21.

703.   Ibid., p. 21.

704.   West's Illinois Criminal Law And Procedure, 2004 Edition: p. 813 (730 ILCS 150/7) Minneapolis, MN. West Publishing. March 2004.

705.   "Georgia Eases Sex Offender Restrictions in Face of Federal Court Challenge." Prison Legal News. March 2011: p. 28. - - "Unjust and ineffective: America has pioneered the harsh punishment of sex offenders. Does it work?" The Economist. August 8, 2009: p. 21.

706.   Ibid., p. 23.

707.   "America's unjust sex laws: An ever harsher approach is doing more harm than good, but it is being copied around the world." The Economist. August 8, 2009: p. 9.

708.   Reutter, David M. "Band-aid Applied to Florida's Homeless Sex Offender Colony Falls Off." Prison Legal News. March 2011: p. 13.

709.   Ibid.

710.   Ibid.

711.   "Unjust and ineffective: America has pioneered the harsh punishment of sex offenders. Does it work?" The Economist. August 8, 2009: p. 23.

712.   Dickson, Caitlin. "Barely a Teenager and Marked for Life: Federal law requiring juvenile sex offenders to register as

predators for life does more harm than good." In These Times. September 2010: p. 22-23.

713. "Unjust and ineffective: America has pioneered the harsh punishment of sex offenders. Does it work?" The Economist. August 8, 2009: p. 23.

714. West's Illinois Criminal Law And Procedure, 2004 Edition: p. 814 (730 ILCS 150/10) Minneapolis, MN. West Publishing. March 2004.

715. Ibid., p. 811 (730 ILCS 150/3).

716. Skenazy, Lenore. "Oddly Enough: Shred Your Sex Offender Map." Forbes.com. June 25, 2010.

717. Dizikes, Cynthia. "Bill to keep tabs on freed killers goes to Quinn: Murderers would have to register for 10 years." The Chicago Tribune. Thursday, June 30, 2011: Section 1, p. 6.

718. Ibid.

719. DiBenedetto, Stephen. "House OKs murderer registry" The Chicago Sun Time. April 6, 2011: p. 2.

720. Illinois House Bill No. 0263 (HB0263). 97th General Assembly. Bill Status and Full Text http://www.ilga.gov/legislation.

721. Smith v. Doe, 538 U.S. 84, 123 S. Ct. 1140,155L. Ed. 2d 164 (March 5, 2003)(No. 01-729) United States Supreme Court.

722. Illinois Department of Corrections Statistical Presentation, 2004: p. 47. Springfield, IL. October 7, 2005.

723.   Dizikes, Cynthia. "Bill to keep tabs on freed killers goes to Quinn: Murderers would have to register for 10 years." The Chicago Tribune. Thursday, June 30, 2011: Section 1, p. 6. - - Brodheim, Mike. "Paroled Killers Barely Re-Offend." Prison Legal News. July 2011: p. 18.

724.   Hill, Michael. "Amid parole controversy released murderers stay out of trouble." Newsday.com. March 23, 2008 last accessed March 24, 2008 http://www.newsday.com/news/local/wire/newyork/ny-bc-ny-paroleviolentfel0323mar23,0,3426432.story

725.   Recidivism of Prisoners Released In 1994. United States Department of Justice, Bureau of Justice Statistics, Special Report. June 2002 (NCJ-193427).

726.   Brodheim, Mike. "Paroled Killers Rarely Re-Offend." Prison Legal News. July 2011: p. 18.

727.   Wilson, Todd. "House OKs bill to register murderers."The Chicago Tribune. April 6, 2011.

728.   Dizikes, Cynthia. "Bill to keep tabs on freed killers goes to Quinn: Murderers would have to register for 10 years." The Chicago Tribune. Thursday, June 30, 2011: Section 1, p. 6.

729.   Ibid.

730.   Wilson, Todd. "House OKs bill to register murderers."The Chicago Tribune. April 6, 2011.

731.   West's Illinois Criminal Law And Procedure, 2004 Edition: p. 692-696 (730 ILCS S/3-6-3) Minneapolis, MN. West Publishing. March 2004.

732. Dizikes, Cynthia. "Bill to keep tabs on freed killers goes to Quinn: Murderers would have to register for 10 years." The Chicago Tribune. Thursday, June 30, 2011: Section 1, p. 6. - - Wilson, Todd. "House OKs bill to register murderers." The Chicago Tribune. April 6, 2011.

733. Dizikes, Cynthia. "Bill to keep tabs on freed killers goes to Quinn: Murderers would have to register for 10 years." The Chicago Tribune. Thursday, June 30, 2011: Section 1, p. 6.

734. Illinois House Bill No. 0263 (HB0263). 97th General Assembly. Bill Status and Full Text http://www.ilga.gov/legislation

735. Ibid.

736. "Our View: Moral, practical reasons to end death penalty." Rockford Register Star. January 28, 2011.

737. West's Illinois Criminal Law And Procedure, 2004 Edition: p. 226 (720 ILCS 5/5-1 and 2) Minneapolis, MN. West Publishing. March 2004.

738. Dizikes, Cynthia. "Bill to keep tabs on freed killers goes to Quinn: Murderers would have to register for 10 years." The Chicago Tribune. Thursday, June 30, 2011: Section 1, p. 1.

739. Ibid. 6.

740. Ibid. 6.

741. Ibid. 6

742. Illinois House Bill No. 0263 (HB0263). 97th General Assembly. Bill Status and Full Text http://www.ilga.gov/legislation

743.   Di Benedetto, Stephen. "House OKs murderer registry." Chicago Sun Times. April 6, 2011: p. 2.

744.   Illinois House Bill No. 0263 (HB0263). 97th General Assembly. Bill Status and Full Text http://www.ilga.gov/legislation

745.   Ibid.

746.   ABC World News. 2011

747.   Garcia, Monique. "Ill. to free 1,000 prisoners to save money." The Chicago Tribune. September 21, 2009. http://www.correctionsone.com/pc_print.asp?vid=1888679

748.   Grimm, Andy. "Inmates surge to record high. Governor's halt to early-release programs after backlash is cited." The Chicago Tribune. Tuesday, November 23, 2010: section 1, p. 4.

749.   Maki, John. "Top Ten Things to Know About Illinois' Prisons." John Howard Association. December 13, 2010. http://www.huffingtonpost.com/john-maki/top-ten-things-to-know-ab b 795889.html?view=print

750.   Garcia, Monique. "Ill. to free 1,000 prisoners to save money." The Chicago Tribune. September 21, 2009. http://www.correctionsone.com/pc_print.asp?vid=1888679

751.   Illinois Senate Bill No. 3411 (SB3411). 96th General Assembly. Bill Status and Full Text. http://www.ilga.gov/legislation

752.   Ibid.

753. O'Connor, John. "Ill. still struggling to identify early released violent inmates." Associated Press. January 25, 2010. http://www.correctionsone.com/pc_print.asp?vid=1995222

754. Lester, Kerry. "Brady: Quinn needs to sign released prisoner photo bill." Daily Herald. July 15, 2010: Section 1, p. 8.

755. West's Illinois Criminal Law And Procedure, 2004 Edition: p. 693(730 ILCS 5/3-6-3(a)(5)). Minneapolis, MN. West Publishing. March 2004.

756. Wood, Graeme, and Wood, Graeme. "Prison Without Walls." The Atlantic. September 2010 Last accessed November21, 2010. http://www.theatlantic.com/magazine

757. Ibid.

758. Ibid.

759. Ibid.

760. Ibid.

761. Romano, Andrew. "Jim Webb's Last Crusade." Newsweek. September 19, 2011: p. 50.

762. "Reports with Recommendations to the ABA House of Delegates." America Bar Association, Justice Kennedy Commission. August 2004.

ABOUT THE AUTHOR

JOSEPH RODNEY DOLE II

Mr. Dole is currently serving a life-without-parole sentence after being wrongfully convicted. He continues to fight that conviction pro se. He has been continuously incarcerated since 1998. He spent nearly a decade of his life in the notorious Tamms Supermax Prison in complete isolation. Tamms was shuttered in 2012 after an intense campaign by human rights groups and the families and friends of prisoners who were confined and tortured there. Mr. Dole's first essay, which won him first place in a prison writing contest, was included in the book "Lockdown Prison Heart"(IUniverse, Inc., 2004).

Since then he has written a number of articles, essays, poems, research papers, and legislative proposals, two of which were catalysts for Illinois legislation (a bill and a resolution). He has won four different PEN America Writing Awards for Prisoners.

He has been published in *Stateville Speaks Newsletter*, *Prison Legal News*, *The Journal of Prisoners on Prisons* (Vol.20,No.2, 2010), *Graterfriends Newsletter*, *The Insider Magazine*, *The Mississippi Review*, *The Public I Newspaper*, as well as numerous places on-line such as www.realcostofprisons.org, PrisonLawBlog.com, and SolitaryWatch.com. Most recently an essay of his was included in the anthology "Too Cruel, Not Unusual Enough" (www. theotherdeathpenalty. org).

Mr. Dole is both a jailhouse journalist and a jailhouse lawyer, as well as a watchdog fighting to ensure that Illinois agencies are in compliance with the Illinois Freedom of Information Act.

He is also a member of the National Lawyer's Guild. Mr. Dole has educated himself by taking dozens of correspondence courses and reading hundreds of books.

You can contact Mr. Dole via snail mail at the following address, and he will respond to all letters he receives:

Joseph Dole K84446
Stateville Correctional Center
P.O.Box 112
Joliet, IL 60434

www.ingramcontent.com/pod-product-compliance
Lightning Source LLC
Chambersburg PA
CBHW062047270326
41931CB00013B/2973